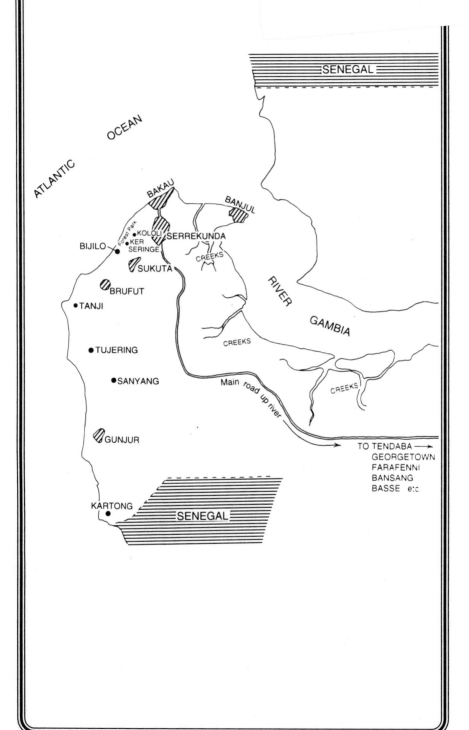

SENEGAL

ATLANTIC

OCEAN

BAKAU

BANJUL

Forest Park

KOLOLI

BIJILO

KER SERINGE

SERREKUNDA

SUKUTA

CREEKS

RIVER

BRUFUT

TANJI

GAMBIA

TUJERING

CREEKS

SANYANG

Main road up river

CREEKS

GUNJUR

TO TENDABA →
GEORGETOWN
FARAFENNI
BANSANG
BASSE etc.

KARTONG

SENEGAL

Together Under the Baobab Tree

Rosemary Long

Eric Dobby Publishing

Published by
Eric Dobby Publishing Ltd
12 Warnford Road, Orpington, Kent BR6 6LW

First published 1994

A catalogue record of this book is available from the British Library.

ISBN 1-85882-021-9

Typeset in 10pt on 11pt Palatino by Kevin O'Connor, Poole
Printed and bound in Spain

Contents

Author's Note i
Prologue 1
Watch out for the Watchman! 5
Awa-dingding Moves in 14
The Wet Economy 24
No More Mrs Nice Guy? 36
Domestic Disturbances 49
Life, Death and Marmalade 61
Unhappy is the Bride 71
Love Conquers All 81
Romance and Rascals 89
The Pharmacist's Tale 99
International Relationships 107
Dumplings and Dressmakers 117
Getting to the Grass Roots 127
The Old Black Magic 137
The Leaning Tower of Bijilo 147
'She Showed Me Her Bottom' 157
A Black Imp on My Shoulder 168
Friends and Neighbours 180
Wild Things 191
Goodbye, Nyet Kunyul, Goodbye Andrea 205

Author's Note

Although the Gambia is my home, and the years I have lived here seem to me like the largest and most significant part of my life, I am, in truth, still pretty much of a newcomer.

It is inevitable, therefore, that some of my assumptions and perceptions will be, in some people's eyes, faulty. What I see as amusing and endearing, they may see as serious and irksome. What I regard as sorrowful and unjust, they may believe to be inevitable and part of their culture, even the will of God.

I can only say that what is in this book is how I feel, how I see what surrounds me and how I react to it all, which is with affection and appreciation tinged from time to time with exasperation. I have tried to be frank and honest all along, but no doubt I have made mistakes, got hold of the wrong end of the stick from time to time, or misinterpreted the situation. My love for the Gambia and my gratitude to its people for welcoming me here remains unaltered.

On matters of geography, history and economics I have relied often on several invaluable sources. Terry Palmer's constantly revised *Discover the Gambia* is one. Etienne Egberg's *A Naturalist's Guide to the Gambia* is another (and I am happy to hear that a Swedish writer is hoping to relaunch a modern version of it). *The Insight Guide to the Gambia and Senegal* has also helped me learn more about my surroundings, and so have a number of old books and colonial records only available on the shelves of the School of Oriental and African Studies in London, whose library is a veritable treasure trove.

Sierra Leonean artist Joe Yamsin advised me on the supernatural. Prime snippets of local news came from the pages of the brave and enterprising *Gambian Daily Observer* newspaper, whose editor Kenneth Best has brought a refreshing wind of change to Gambian journalism.

On matters of spelling of local dialects, place names and people's names, I have used phonetics where I have been in doubt, for there is no inflexibly correct way of spelling words which have come through history by mouth rather than in print.

On only a couple of occasions I have changed the names of the people who frequent my pages, to avoid embarrassment. If any whose names are NOT changed feel embarrassed, then I ask them to forgive me and imagine how I feel, with my whole life exposed on these pages!

Ray has become used, now, to people pointing and saying: "Pssst! That's the chap who married that middle-aged woman from Glasgow!" But he still feels embarrassed, and to him most of all I say thank you for putting up with me.

Prologue

The baobab tree is naked. Its branches, silvery grey, trace elaborate patterns against the evening sky, like the veins on a butterfly's wings.

The leaves have gone, blown in the wind then dropped when the breeze became bored, to lay a crinkly gold carpet under our flip-flopped feet. The fruits remain, suspended like Chinese lanterns. The children will cut them down with cutlasses as long as themselves, crack them open and chew the sherbet-flavoured flesh.

By the time this book is finished, new pale green buds will have exploded from the gaunt grey trellis of bark, unfurled and extended and grown dark and wide to offer us their shade; then they will drop again and the air will distribute them as though they were scurrying birds.

There will have been marriages and births, sickness and, probably, death. We will have laughed and fought and cried and caressed, danced and stamped our feet, said goodbye to old friends and welcomed new ones. I will have learned a little bit more about my funny little adopted country and my moody, proud, stubborn, sweet, exasperating husband. I may even have learned a little about my own complicated self.

I can see myself in a mirror as I write. Beads of sweat on a brown face, bottled blonde hair scraped up in a pony tail. Where are the curls I had in Glasgow? Pinkish patches on my left shoulder where the exploding aerosol splashed me with flames a year earlier. A network of lines at the outer corners of my eyes. A definite sagging under the chin.

But it is, on the whole, a contented face. And into the mirror comes Ray. His long, strong fingers rest on my shoulders and he kisses, absent-mindedly, my moist perspiring neck. "I love you," he says vaguely. "Where did you put the key for the generator shed?" And he goes off to clean a filter or top up the oil. Maybe he'll pull up some cassava. Find me some little cherry tomatoes and venomous peppers. I never asked for orchids!

"You will marry again," said my palm-reading friend in Glasgow a long time ago. "No, no, no," I said. "I'll live with a rich, witty Scottish writer, or lawyer or teacher, maybe. But marriage? Absolutely not!" I would, I daydreamed, meet this rich wit on a plane to New York and we'd share a sophisticated flat in a desultory way, snatching muesli and orange juice and black coffees before he jetted to a conference and I went to interview a famous footballer or a controversial politician. We'd holiday in Greece and Sardinia and have dinner parties for other journalists or lawyers or teachers.

Or I'd meet no-one on a plane but enjoy my solitary independence, with only my cats to complicate my life and no-one to monopolise the duvet, leave rings on the bath or complain about the phone bill. A fully developed woman, busying myself with good works, good times, good books, watching the remorseless passage of the years and waiting for something — but I wasn't sure what — to happen.

And then I met Ray. Not rich, not witty, not literary. I live on the outskirts of a Gambian village with monkeys and lizards and giant hornbills as neighbours. I eat mangoes and monkey-fruit and rice. I didn't just marry again once, I did it twice; once in Ray's own village, once in a Glasgow registry office. All of which shows that no-one should ever make too many plans, life is full of little tricks, and nothing, but nothing, is impossible.

The other day, for instance, the local newspaper carried a report of pollution in the Upper River Division. Was it toxic waste? Pesticides from the fields? No, the popular theory was that it was the body of a dragon, washed upstream and rotting within the murky green, mangrove-fringed depths of the great River Gambia.

"A dragon!" I chortled. "There aren't any dragons!"

"Mariama," sighed Ray patiently. "Don't be so stupid. Of course there are dragons. They are huge creatures that live in the water, as big as whales, and they breathe fire out their mouths when they come on land. The only way to frighten them off is to hold a mirror in front of them, for they are afraid of their own image."

"Have you seen one?" I asked.

"Er, no. But there is one just along the beach from my beach-bar, where that little river enters the sea. I've never seen it. But I know it's there."

Maybe he's right. Maybe there are dragons in the Gambia. Nothing is impossible, after all.

From my window I can see the forest of Bijilo. Black velvet plums with copper-coloured clustering flowers and dark, flat velvety fruits; African rosewood with papery pods; gingerbread plums, whose brown potato-shaped fruits delight the families of monkeys for whom the forest is home; the silk cotton trees which bloom crimson and dispense capsules of white floss used for spinning thread. Oil palms, Guinea peaches, fig trees, ironwood, camel foot, Senegal coral, custard apple, locust bean, Senegal cherry and, of course, the baobab, the tree of the Gambia, giver of shelter, food, drink, fibre and protection from evil.

It is possible the Carthaginians probed this far 1500 years ago, and later the Berbers and the Moors, the Portuguese, the French, the

The great calm winding River Gambia which rises far away in Guinea, at the fishing village of Tendaba, site of Tendaba camp, home of pelicans, crocodiles, bush-pigs and goggle-eyed tourists.

Courlanders (from what is now Latvia), and of course the British, buying and selling, mostly grabbing, gold and grain, salt and ivory, cotton and gum and human flesh (for £17 a head or its value in sugar). Such a small country, some 4000 square miles, nowhere wider than 30 miles but distinguished by its remarkable river, which rises some thousand miles away on the Fula Jallon Plateau of the Guinea Republic. Its population is now over the million mark, swollen by some immigration from Senegal, Guinea and Mali, but mostly by sex. For there is a joyous disregard for family planning and a macho pride in producing six, seven or more babies per wife. The growth rate, an unprecedented 4.1 per cent, has meant a 50% rise in population in the last decade, and almost half the people in the Gambia are babies, children and teenagers.

In the midst of all this youthfulness, I am a venerable figure indeed, but it is to Ray's credit and that of the Gambians in general, that I have never been made to feel old, not even middle-aged. Perhaps it's the rice and fish and mangoes I eat, or just the way Ray makes me feel, but whatever it is it's worth more to me than all the rejuvenation creams, anti-cellulite treatments and cosmetics in Bond Street.

Life is pared down to essentials. For Ray's family, the all-important considerations are having enough money to buy rice, praying that your children will survive through childhood, fasting through Ramadan then slaughtering a sheep and celebrating another year together thanks to the greatness of Allah. My life is not quite theirs. I do not stoop over a wood-fire as his mother does, nor do I bend my back hour after hour in the rice fields the way so many Gambian women do, thin and pliant as the slender sticks of bamboo that cluster beyond the forest.

But I see them laugh together sometimes, sharing a secret female camaraderie and I wonder if they, even in the hardship of their lives, have something precious which no white woman will ever capture. The precursor to this book, *Under the Baobab Tree*, touched lightly on my first year-and-a-half in this unique and beguiling country. But the discovery process goes on. In a country where "of course there are dragons," I have something new to learn every day.

Watch out for
the Watchman!

Had someone put a bad spell on our compound? On a placid, early summer evening, with the sky turning from pearl to purple, the sweet taste of green gunpowder tea on our lips and the gentle sound of palm-leaves clucking together in the breeze, this is what we discussed.

The marabout had said it when the generator was stolen. 'Someone has buried something on your land to bring bad fortune on you.' He hazarded a guess that the 'someone' could be a person with a grudge. 'Perhaps someone you have recently fired?' 'Ahai!' shouted Ray, 'Him!' He named our former watchman, who looked like an amiable scarecrow in flipflops? Surely not, I thought secretly. It was true we had asked him to leave because he slept so long and deeply when he was supposed to be guarding our property. But he wouldn't . . . Ray was less charitable. 'It must be him!' he said, looking fierce.

Had he sneaked in one night — for the dogs were his friends — and dug a hole and planted there a dark and destructive symbol to explain away the times when the tomato seeds dried up and died, the car developed a slow puncture, my typewriter jammed and Ray had a headache? Not to mention thieves making off one black and confusing night with our vital source of pumping and lighting power, the generator? The little group of uncles and brothers on our verandah all nodded and sighed and decided he must have been the culprit.

It was the following day that the marabout carried out his own spell to cancel out the effects of any buried malevolence. He gazed hypnotically at a scrawny unsuspecting chicken, muttering incantations, and the chicken keeled over and its ghost went to that great farmyard in the sky. I was very upset for the obvious methodology here was that as the bird croaked, so too he would suffer, if not death, at least a bad belly-ache, his bad spell rebounding on him . . .

Oh, poor soul. For it was he who had been wished upon us the very day we moved into our house, in the spring of 1990, when it was a mere shell and we camped in one room.

The builders were still banging and plastering and roofing and tiling. Schoolgirls scampered over the unfenced land to fill their water-bottles at the standpipe next to the forest. Cows grazed in front of our door and stretched their necks to reach the new leaves on the baobab tree. He wiped his floppy hands on trousers like a greasy oil-rag and said:: 'Yes, sir. Gotten himmel. Thank you,' and scrounged a cigarette. 'He's your watchman,' said Ray's uncle, the builder, looking apologetic.

During the first year and a half of my life near the village, our new watchman slopped and slept and spat and strewed rubbish in his wake until our ways parted. I would not care to think of him dead or sickening from something, even if he HAD buried a bundle of bones and stones among our cassava plants. I needn't have worried. A few days later we met him working happily on a nearby building site, spitting magnificently, flip-flops whacking the earth as he walked. 'Yes, sir. Gotten himmel!' he smiled broadly and even Ray looked relieved. 'It must have been someone else,' he muttered later. 'Maybe,' I ventured, 'it was no-one. Maybe we just got our generator pinched because someone felt like pinching it . . .' He looked at me with tolerant sympathy. 'Mariama, you don't understand Africa.'

But I tried. I learned. The things that people feared were not so much the snakes, the wild animals (neither of which is actually very common; you're more likely to be bitten by an ant), or even thieves and muggers, but the bad spirits that caused these creatures to harm you. It is some eighty years since the last lion or elephant was seen in the Gambia, but when they were there they did not attack man unless driven to do so by unfriendly spirits. People look cautiously for little knots of animal hide concealing stones or leaves or scraps of paper placed in front of a gateway . . . egg-shells strewn a certain way across your path . . . fresh earth where a juju may have been buried.

Almost everyone has a marabout, even some of the most devout Muslims and some Christians. I am told that some people leave the pretty little services in the tiny Catholic church in Kololi then go home to houses with shrines containing artifacts appeasing other gods far more feared, perhaps, than the one to whom they have just conventionally prayed.

All over West Africa there are Presidents and government ministers who will not travel on a day prescribed as dangerous by their marabout and prosperous businessmen consult them as you might consult a lawyer or an accountant. A man would pay a marabout to track down a thief, help him win a court case, bring luck in a business deal, make a sick child healthy, a poor crop flourish. Before Ray and I travelled on a visit to Britain, his mother was advised to buy a white chicken to ensure good luck for our voyage. Considering the number of marabouts here, I could be cynical and wonder why there are any sick, unlucky or poor people left. But I must not be cynical for I have heard things which beggar explanation and I have met with examples of the marabout's power which cannot be quite explained by Western logic. When my Scottish fortune-telling friend Darlinda reads the tarot cards or my palm, or does my astrological chart, I listen to what she says, so I must not pooh-pooh the African equivalent, I tell myself.

And the stories that surround them are fascinating, whether or not you suspend disbelief. Consider, for example, the power that can be channelled by a marabout if he is given a black cat. The cat must be utterly all-over black, and it must be killed and skinned in a certain manner with certain words being spoken. The skin can then make a kind of amulet which the client will wear on his arm, and as he pushes it up past his elbow he will become... invisible! This is extraordinarily useful, as you can imagine, particularly to drug smugglers passing through customs, adulterers fleeing from suspicious husbands and bank robbers helping themselves to the contents of a vault. It is also, I understand, much sought-after by illegal immigrants so that they can cross borders without being troubled by questions about their passports.

It is interesting to remember that black cats were, in mediaeval Europe, used as witches' familiars, while black cats crossing in front of you in Surbiton or Stockholm are a sign of good fortune. Here, poor moggy has to be dead, which is, presumably, why you never ever see a black cat in the Gambia; any that might be born in a litter or imported by a naive ex-patriate are obviously grabbed as soon as they put their soft little noses out of the door!

But enough of that for the moment—though we are bound to come back to it. Before and during the theft of the generator we had no watchman, something the thieves had apparently sussed out for themselves after 'casing the joint' beforehand. We carried buckets of water ourselves from the well or the standpipe; we watered the bananas and raked up dry leaves, not to mention the harmless relics left by Musa, rusty tomato tins, empty Lucky Strike packets, foetid rags which had been his clothes, empty milk tins and cracked jam jars. We ached in every muscle, but when the dogs barked at night I had to shake Ray awake so that he could trudge round the perimeter of the compound with his cutlass, shining his torch nervously into shadows and yawning through his fear.

The generator thieves had all escaped or found bail, and Ray's dad said sternly: 'This is not safe. You MUST have a watchman.' I sometimes wondered why. The Honda 2.2 was back in its little tin shed and surely the burglars wouldn't return to the same place? But it is the custom for all compounds to have watchmen, so I must bow to the inevitable.

First there was Nabi. Nabi was the very sweet, shy, insecure Guinean who looked after our beach bar the year before. He was pleased yet visibly nervous when we offered him the job. He threw himself into the watering and weeding side of things with gusto. The bananas never looked lusher; he raked and mulched and planted marigold seeds in the beds before our windows hitherto crammed with jagged weeds and stones. He was a veritable Capability Brown.

But Nabi was nervous. News of our robbery had buzzed around Bijilo almost before it happened and the gossip and speculation had resulted in the three hapless felons gaining a reputation something on a par with the Great Train Robbers, only more so. They were, in local discussion under the baobab tree or at the bantaba or village meeting place, no longer misguided youths but giants of evil and viciousness, to be blamed for every theft that had ever occurred in the area, from the purloining of Grandpa's donkey to the driving off of the schoolmistress's husband's cows.

I had my own views on this. When the thieves were caught, redhanded, by the police, with considerable help from Ray and his brother Lamin, who drove them to the compound where the loot was concealed, the next step was to drag them here to the scene of their crime, where a horde of villagers cuffed and slapped them and looked surprised when I begged them to desist. I have not yet accustomed myself to the Gambian custom of instant retribution, though I know it is because, in the view of local citizens, the criminals will be allowed to escape by the police (either through carelessness or because they had been bribed) or will get out on bail. Our lot did, indeed, disappear soon afterwards but that doesn't stop me having a weak stomach for vigilante measures. They looked a pretty wimpish lot to me as they stood, handcuffed, heads bowed, beside the Land Rover dodging blows, but their place in the history of Bijilo was assured and their abasement upon capture did not diminish their mythical notoriety and capacity for wickedness. So Nabi believed, and he was convinced that they would return and wreak vengeance on us all.

If we went out after dark, Nabi would cower down in the back seat of the Land Rover, trembling at every whispering head of grass, every flickering shadow of leaf, every scurrying insect or darting frog. If the dogs barked, he huddled down lower, clutching his jujus, muttering prayers beneath his breath, eyes rolling, teeth chattering. 'Please, please don't leave me here alone,' he gulped. 'I don't want to be slaughtered. I am too young to die.' No matter how much we assured him the thieves would not return and that he must sit up and do his duty, he was still terrified, and it became clear that his job satisfaction was zilch. He must go.

I hissed to Ray: 'Why doesn't he believe the juju on his wrist will protect him?,' and Ray told me to keep quiet. This is the exasperating side of marabout magic. If you can't afford to pay for a REALLY powerful juju or gris-gris, you always have the fear that the other guy's marabout is stronger than yours. So what, I ask Ray, is the point of bothering about it at all? On the other hand, if you have complete unswerving faith in a small, cheap gris-gris, wouldn't that be more effective than a big high-priced one that you weren't absolutely sure of? These questions infuriate Ray, in spite of the fact that he tries to pretend he doesn't believe in 'all that rubbish'. He does, of course. But he is in good company. Many educated and sophisticated German and Swiss and French travellers find their way to the men in the markets who sell special amulets and potions to bring them good luck and safe passage through life. It's quantifying the results that presents problems.

Nabi, anyway, didn't seem to have enough faith in HIS armband. He scurried off. I felt sorry for him. Perhaps it was all my fault anyway. Perhaps if I HAD believed in these things more unquestioningly and sought the protection of a local dispenser of magic, we wouldn't have had all these problems with watchmen and our generator wouldn't have been nicked in the first place! But, whatever the reason, here we were with a gap in our personnel and Ray's dad nagging us every day to find someone. And in the end, he became tired of waiting for us to act and turned up on our verandah towing Mr M in his wake. 'Try him,' he said. 'He's a good, God-fearing man.' We looked at him doubtfully. Mr M had a bad squint and a smile that showed teeth that looked as though they belonged to someone else. He had a fine, deep rich voice and he used it a lot. We all shook hands and sat on the verandah to discuss qualifications, terms and conditions.

'I am a master gardener,' said the rich fruity voice. 'I am a trained security guard,' it added. Many references were made to Allah and His assured blessing on Mr M's humble presence in our midst. Every time we opened our mouths he gushed: 'Thank-you very much, Ma'am. Oh yes, sir, thank you Mr Faal, sir.' It was all too much. Ma'am? Mr Faal, sir? Could we cope with this combination of servility and superb qualifications?

Ray's father was very impressed and intimated that he expected us to do the decent thing and hire this splendid chap there and then, so we did. 'He's a bit overpowering,' I whispered to Ray. 'Yes, I know, but maybe he'll be OK,' he whispered back. We decided to take advantage of the situation to go our for a meal, the first time we'd been able to play hookey for some time.

When we came back, there was Mr M, still on the verandah, ensconced in one of our wicker arm-chairs, surrounded by the paraphernalia of attaya tea-making (the aforementioned green gunpowder tea, whose preparation and swallowing is such a traditional and beloved ceremony in the Gambia). Small enamel tea-pot, little whisky-sized glasses, sugar, Carnation milk, a few herbs and the box for the tea were spread out on my coffee-table, at the other side of which sat a short, smiling girl whom he introduced as 'my good wife, Mariama. Same name as you, Ma'am, eh? Ah, yes, it is very good, thank-you, thank-you.' Without our quite realising what was happening he had arranged for

Mariama to move in with him, into — for want of any other accommodation — one of our little tourist huts, currently empty as this was the off-season. We sat sipping green tea, feeling our lives had been taken over. 'Oh, isn't this nice Ma'am, Sir?' chuckled Mr M hospitably, passing round the glasses, surveying the house and the land around it with a cheerfully proprietorial gaze. 'Oh yes, I know that we are all going to be very happy here.'

In bed, I hissed at Ray. 'He never told us he had a wife. Your father never told us . . . Why is he taking over our verandah? Can't you do something?' Ray was silent for a while. Then he said: 'Maybe he'll be OK when we get to know him,' and shut his eyes while I lay awake, listening to Mr M all around us.

In the mornings, he would, I have to admit, work in the garden, hoeing and raking. If I tried to loosen the earth round a hibiscus or pull a weed from Nabi's marigold bed, Mr M would dash over and grab the fork from my hand. 'Ma'am, ma'am, let your garden-master do it!'

Afternoons, he was back on the verandah, playing host. And evenings. He would hold forth about the greatness of Allah and how faithfully he, Mr M, prayed and abstained from alcohol (looking disapprovingly at our warm Julbrew beers), and about what an honour and privilege it was for a humble person such as himself (though magnificently qualified, he would remind us) to work for such wonderful human-beings as Mr Faal, Sir and Ma'am. How happy, he would add, we are all going to be, living together, hand in hand, shoulder to shoulder, for ever and ever.

I began hiding inside, sweating. The verandah was occupied territory. If I did sneak out while Mr M was still in the garden or the hut, and put on a soothing Vivaldi tape or a bit of Brüch, he would bustle over, tut-tutting and change my tape for a blast of Bunny Wailer. 'You mustn't sit alone, Ma'am. I will chat to you and keep you company.' I wanted to scream.

'I can't stand it!' I screeched (in a whisper) to Ray. 'I need some privacy. I need space.' One of the most joyful, tranquil times of day for me is (was) early evening, sitting (alone) with Ray outside our own door, on our own chairs, in our own space, watching the sun melting into the sea behind the black outline of the forest. Now everything was to be a foursome?

'You talk to him then. I can't,' said Ray, embarrassed. Not that he didn't want to be alone with me (well, I hope so!) but it would have been hard for him to explain to another Gambian how unsociable a tubab can be. Gambians are by nature gregarious, from the time they are born, in a roomful of women, through childhood, in a cluster of brothers and sisters, cousins and neighbours, into adulthood, sharing the home with a huge extended family, smoking and debating at the bantaba, blethering under the baobab.

They are as sociable as the flocks of yellow village weaver birds which cover the branches of the tree outside our bedroom like golden blossoms and chatter, chatter, chatter all the time. 'Bumsters' (the name given to young men who 'follow' tourists on the beach) genuinely don't understand that white people enjoy, sometimes, walking alone or with a partner, or that shared silences can be romantic, or that privacy is precious. So when they say, smilingly, 'Hullo, how are you? What's your name? Can I talk with you?' they get very hurt and offended if their quarry either ignores them or says: 'Please leave us alone.' They think we're rude. We think they're a nuisance. Which of us is right?

I didn't care. I wanted to be alone. I gritted my teeth, smiling viciously, and advanced on Mr M, talking fast before he could get an unctuous word in. 'Now Mr M, I want you to be comfortable, so why don't you and Mariama take these two nice basket chairs to the hut and relax over there while Mr Faal and I discuss a little business?' After all, people PAY to occupy these cute little huts and sit outside them in the sunshine, I might have added, but didn't. 'Yes, Ma'am, thank-you very much,' said Mr M and wandered off. It was the word 'business' that clinched it. Gambians respect business, however ephemeral. A guy with a tray full of empty plastic bottles to sell will put down his profession on his application for a passport as 'businessman'. A person going to Banjul in a bush-taxi to buy a carton of cigarettes to resell to tourists will tell you he's going 'on business'. And no-one will sneer.

But if the days were a trial, the nights were a cabaret. That first night, after we went to bed, we heard Mr M's 'trained security guard' technique.

'Clack! Clack! Clack!' went his cutlass as he whacked it with a length of steel rod, a fearsome noise calculated to terrify would-be burglars, or so he assumed. 'Ahem! Ahem! Ahem!' went his throat, as he coughed enormously, to remind would-be thieves that he, Mr M, was vigilant and tough, ready to carve and cough them into submission.

We twitched the curtain aside and knelt on the bed, peering through the louvred glasses and the mosquito netting, at Mr M on patrol. His torch darted back and forward, overhead (in case of aerial attack?) and downwards (tunnelling felons?). At ten metre intervals along the inside of the wall, he would stop, peer fiercely into the darkness beyond and shout: 'Who is there? Go away! Anyone coming here he is going to be dead!' He shouted this in English, then in Wollof, which was our language, then in Jola, which was his. Mandinka, Serahuli or Fula burglars would just have to make a guess at it.

We exploded into fits of giggles and this made Stanley and Maradonna begin barking, which in turn made Mr M cough and clack with renewed vigour. The dogs also have a habit of barking at low-flying bats, scuttling beetles, bobbing rabbits and even the crackle of the wind through a rotten branch, so the clacking and coughing went on at intervals all through the night.

We were no longer giggling when we wakened in the morning at seven to find, at the gate, a messenger from Ray's Uncle Assan. Blearily, grumpily, we asked him what he wanted. 'I want Mr M,' he said menacingly. Mr M loped over smiling ingratiatingly. 'Morning, Sir. Morning Ma'am. I have guarded your place very seriously. No thieves have entered.' He looked as though he might salute.

When he saw the messenger, his face crumpled, and he drew the man discreetly to one side and mumbled earnestly as the newcomer shouted and shook his fist.

'What's a matter?' mumbled Ray, still half-asleep. 'Eh, sorry, Suh! Sorry, Mr Faal-suh! Assan wants to see me. A matter of business. Please to excuse me.' And he rushed off down the lane towards the village, the other man following and looking tough. Later we heard what had happened. Uncle Assan, the village clerk and general Mr Fixit for anyone who wants to do any kind of business in the village had commissioned Mr M some weeks ago to dig a well for some tubabs (white folk) with dreams of building a house on a stretch of open land beyond the mosque and the bantaba. He had even, at the tubabs' expense, given Mr M an advance of 300 dalasis.

Mr M had dug down one desultory metre, spent the advance and then come to work for us, forbearing to mention this prior commitment. It was Ray's mum who told us about the interview between the village clerk and the erstwhile well-digger. 'Assan shouted at him as if he was a dog,' she gloated. Mr M shuffled and whimpered and hung his head. 'I will call the gendarmes!' Assan roared, 'unless you finish this well SOON!'

Mr M returned to us and called upon the ineffable goodness of Allah to inspire us to lend him 300 dalasis. We replied, quite truthfully, that we didn't have that number of bututs, never mind dalasis, since we hadn't had any tourists in for months. Anyway, we added, relishing it, it was his own fault for welshing on a contract.

'But what am I to do?' he asked, striding up and down, beating his breast and raising his eyes and his voice to the empty sky. We were inspired. We suggested that as a special favour we would allow him to leave his duties with us in the afternoons and early evenings, provided Mariama would keep an eye open for any visitors arriving at the gate. He could go and dig the well until it was completed. That way, we reasoned gleefully, he might be so exhausted by nightfall that he wouldn't have the energy to clack and cough, and we might get some sleep.

You must not think I was alone in having these trying experiences with watchmen, or that I was a snooty white woman exploiting a poor

Gambian. Gambians also have watchmen, and they too could spend hours telling you of their problems.

A writer in the local paper recently spluttered into print about her frustrations with regard to the species. 'If I ask him to brush the yard, he says he has just washed his hair and doesn't want to get dusty. If I have guests the night man says: When are they going? I am waiting to get some sleep.' Once I removed his shoes and hat while he was asleep on duty and he said, when I shook him, 'No, no I was just resting my eyes' . . . and so on.

It is true, they are not paid much. But then again, much of their time is spent sitting gazing into space, when all that is required of them is to open gates for visitors and make sure no-one scrambles over the wall and makes off with a car battery or a radio (or a generator). They are often frail old men, whom you feel guilty about, wondering how they would cope with a posse of armed robbers. Fortunately posses of armed robbers are virtually unknown.

Without watchmen, the Gambia would be a duller place. They provide a topic of conversation and an occasional giggle, and they probably laugh at us as much as we laugh at them. I have a secret vision of groups of them meeting together to drink attaya and discuss their employers. 'Mine is such a fool,' one will say, 'he asks me to rake up leaves even though he knows very well more leaves will fall within a day.' 'Ah, yes,' another will chip in, 'mine too. He is so lazy, he won't even carry his own briefcase from the car. And he pretends he doesn't understand what I say to him.' And they will all sigh and shake their heads at the burden of having bosses like us.

Awa-dingding Moves In

To sleep, perchance to dream... How I longed to manage some shut-eye, without barking dogs, coughing and clacking watchmen, itchy mosquito bites or a mind so full of plans, memories and speculations that I couldn't settle, no matter how peacefully Ray slumbered.

I would lie on my back, on my side, on my stomach, writing a novel in my head, composing menus, planning the dresses I would have made by the tailor one day, when we could afford it. I would rise and pad about, or make a cup of coffee (not calculated to encourage sleep) or even type some pages, write some letters, in the flickering candlelight, which invariably encouraged a little cloud of winged creatures, chucking themselves at the light like lemmings spotting a cliff-edge.

I knew every inch of my small house in the dark, could wend my way past the bed-end, into the loo, or past the straw baskets of unused blankets, battered hats, unplayed Scrabble sets and appalling paperback romances, towards the gas-ring, fumbling for a lighter, knowing that if I made too much light Mr M would evolve out of the darkness shouting: 'Who is there! Go your way! Bastard!' and the dogs would begin to howl in support of his efforts.

I never slept well in comfy old Glasgow, surrounded by thick walls, night-store heating units, reassuring traffic noises and the occasional Glasgow drunk lurching five floors below my window shouting 'Gaun yersel, ya bastard!' so how could I sleep here, where there were secret rustlings and unexplained creaks and bumps, birds making silly nocturnal sounds and village dogs getting up impromptu concerts to herald the five o'clock prayers? Many years ago I interviewed Barbara Moore, the eccentric vegetarian long-distance walker, and she told me it was perfectly possible for people to exist healthily on four or five hours a night's sleep. Margaret Thatcher did it, after all. So why couldn't I?

When I was married before and living in a Clyde Coast resort eighty-four miles by road from the Glasgow Evening Times office, I rose at 5.10 am, and the habit of waking then had stayed with me; later, I'd lived in Glasgow city centre and accustomed my body clock to dozing

Afternoon in a quiet corner of Serrekunda — not easy to find a quiet corner in a bustling town of 100,000 inhabitants. 'Serans' (oranges) are green but sweet.

off then and snatching another hour-and-a-half before I jumped out of bed, fed the cats, changed their litter, had a bath, listened to the news and scampered round the corner to the office. In the Gambia, where it was necessary, or at least polite, to rise before any resident tourists, throw bleach down the toilets and chop up bread for breakfast, this system was appropriate enough. A quarter-to-seven rise was exactly right for West Africa, for that was when the darkness of night-time was sloughed off like Batman's cape and dawn broke in a pleasant silvery glow that made getting up a delight. The only problem was these broken hours, tossings and turnings and nocturnal meanderings beforehand. Ironically (and happily) our guests always seemed to sleep like babies.

But I had to deal with exigencies that must surely never have disturbed the Iron Lady's complacent dreams. One night, I was floating on the brink of near-sleep when I felt something tickling my leg. I flashed a torch and looked indignantly towards my horizontal husband, but he was snoring, on his stomach, black and sinewy, his wide bony shoulders creating a triangle with his skinny waist. I wish I had a pencil, I thought, I would sketch him like that.

But I was still being tickled. I eased the sheet very gently back and shone the torch onto my sun-browned thigh and there was a cattle-tick crawling lazily over my skin, seeking a suitable tender spot on which to start sucking out a late supper. Such a glamorous life one leads in the tropics. I squeezed it cruelly between my finger-tips and set fire to it in the ash-tray. It came as no big surprise. There is an unending procession of these blood-sucking insect parasites here, though no more, I suppose than in the sheep-rearing county of Argyll in Scotland where once I lived.

Stanley and Maradonna, our two lolloping curly-tailed mutts, orange furred and typically Gambian, required to be 'gone over' every few days, inch by inch, with tweezers and burning cigarettes. There is a horrible satisfaction in watching the bloated body of a tick going pop. I recalled that once the Scottish Society for the Prevention of Cruelty to Animals took someone to court for grilling still-live prawns. What would they say to my night-long immolations?

Our Dutch lodgers, Helma and Roel, had found one tick clamped fondly on the soft golden bottom of their son Ian, aged three. He then had to wear pants, which annoyed him a lot, since he had preferred streaking through the bush and the tall grasses nude, his white-blond head bobbing like a tuft of fluff from the silk-cotton tree.

By now, though, he would be obliged to wear proper clothes all over, and even shoes and socks. For, just after the theft of the generator, and before the arrival on the scene of mawkish, menacing, molar-displaying Mr M, it had been time, after five months, for the Rauenfelder family to go home to the Hague. They had only meant, after all, to stay with us for a few nights, or weeks, but they had become very dear to us and we wept to see them go.

Roel had tried with notable lack of success, to sell his Land Rover — a red British ex-Army ambulance, to be specific — for all of the five months. He had a number of offers, but never any cash on the table. They had long since run out of money and paid us in kind: the jack from the vehicle, Dutch music tapes, pots and pans, even a cassette player. A friend had telexed them some guilders and, since Helma was by then hugely pregnant, they had grudgingly accepted that their year in Africa (Algeria, Mali, Benin, Togo, Guinea Bissau, Senegal, not to mention our back yard) was well and truly over.

'Sell the Land Rover for me if you can, Ray,' Roel had said, almost in tears. 'One day I'll come back from Holland for the money and we'll have a Julbrew together.' For his consumption of the local beer had been fabulous.

Tall and rangy with brilliant blue eyes and an outrageous sense of humour, he would miss sprawling in a sagging deck-chair in tattered shorts reading my old paper-backs while Helma cooked and washed and sewed. 'You're a male chauvinist pig,' I would yell at him, laughing. 'He is, isn't he?' Helma would agree. 'I am, aren't I?' he would smile lazily.

For the last few days, though, he managed to raise himself into a vertical position and cracked open crates which had laid ignored for months, sorting and discarding, packing his African drums with Helma's little bags of cooking herbs, spices, dyes and local perfumes, all calculated to cause suspicious looks among customs officials in Frankfurt before they boarded a train to Holland. Helma, with the calm gentle eyes and Madonna smile, a Great Earth Mother, began shedding the skins of their African experience, spreading odd items in the sun. 'Here are some tea-towels, Mariama. And have some prickly-heat powder, all these Dutch children's books, this tin-opener, these pans . . .' She looked sad and confused and apprehensive about how Ian would settle in the city. His strident yelps of 'f*** off!', directed at dogs, flies, monkeys and some local kids who touched his fair hair, would not go down well at his new nursery school.

Helma had been a Dutch art student, a happy hippie, travelling the Afghan trail to India, wandering in the Philippines, living in squats. We had little in common but motherhood and a shared life in Africa, but we liked each other and laughed together a lot, and life without her and rascally Roel would be diminished. To cheer us all up, we went for a meal none of us could afford at the Swiss restaurant in Kairaba Avenue, leaving Ray's brother Modou to keep an eye on the compound. And that's when we found Awa-dingding.

We were sipping Irish coffees — the first I'd tasted for several years, such extravagance! — and Ian was slobbering over an ice-cream given to him by Madeleine, the owner of the establishment, when Ray disappeared under the table. We all made jeering remarks about his modest beer intake, when he reappeared holding something tiny and trembling in his outstretched hand. He frowned in disgust and held it as far away from his body as he could. 'I felt something touching my feet and it was this thing,' he said dourly.

'This thing' was a kitten as small as a mouse, its eyes still glued shut, its pink flesh barely dusted by the floss of future tortoiseshell fur, disgustingly matted and crawling with fleas and lice. It was not a pretty sight. But I have always been a sucker for cats. Leaving my three well-fed, indolent Scottish cats behind in Glasgow had caused me agonies of guilt. None of them had ever looked quite like this. It kicked and scratched like a trapped insect. 'Oh, the poor wee mite,' I gabbled. 'We must take it home. We can't leave it here.'

Madeleine, overhearing, nodded her head enthusiastically. 'Yes, please take it,' she urged. She and Arthur have lived in the Gambia for many years. She runs the restaurant; he hires Citroen 2CVs to visitors. We feel we have something in common. But I looked at her with suspicious disapproval. 'Is it yours?' I asked accusingly. 'No, no. It's a stray, perhaps from some litter in the bush.' Her dog, it seemed, kept bringing it to them, like a gun-dog with its quarry, and plonking it down under the tables. 'I can't keep it. I have too many cats already. Arthur would go crazy.' This was true. Large languorous cats sprawled here and there in the shadows; she was almost as much of a cat-lover as I was. 'Don't worry. We'll have it,' I said, while Ray sighed deeply and ordered a restorative beer.

We drove home. Ray refused to touch it any more, so Roel was deputised to hold the kitten, swearing in Dutch. It was past midnight. 'Are you coming to bed,' my husband enquired sleepily. 'No,no, I have to see to the cat,' I explained. 'Oh, for God's sake! Leave it till morning,' snapped the non-cat lover. But how could I? It jerked its head upwards on a fragile neck like a newly-hatched chick.

It was blind but not dumb. It squeaked and opened and shut its gummy triangular mouth in a fiercely demanding manner. It was a minute cluster of fine bones inside filthy skin, no flesh at all. I found the eye-dropper I'd last used to feed a baby rabbit the year before, mixed some tinned milk with warm water and began aiming into the creature's throat. It scrabbled and sucked so hard it almost swallowed the dropper, its spindly claws clutching desperately at my fingers, shuddering with the emotion of satisfied hunger. I was sure it must be just a few days old and had perhaps almost never had milk, for surely its mother must have abandoned it or, more likely, been drowned by some intolerant compound-owner.

Next morning, while Ray tutted and humphed, I scrubbed the sticky body with soapy water and Dettol, calculated either to kill it or render it passably clean. It squirmed and croaked and I wondered if I was being too ruthless but at least it had begun to look like a baby cat and it continued to gulp watery milk with an astounding savagery and in enormous quantities for such a minuscule moggy. Until then, with one exception which I will describe in a moment, our only resident cat had been Penny, given to us as a kitten by an English couple and, like them, clean, quiet and nicely-behaved. Not at all like this new little monster.

'What should we call it?' I asked Ray, who by this time was resigned to its presence, if not ecstatic. 'Oh, well, I suppose we should call it Awa-dingding,' he grunted. 'Awa-what?' I asked, uncomprehending, but there was a complex and unusually sentimental reason for his suggestion. For we HAD had a kitten before, a very beautiful, pert, adorable female with snow-white breast and stripey silver coat, and we had called it Caroline after our English friend who worked for a charity down the coast. Ray, quite out of character, had developed a downright soppy regard for this little kitten. Tragically, it was horribly mutilated when it found its way into the engine of our Land Rover. Its hindquarters were squashed out of all recognition, while it still gazed up at us miaowing pitifully, and we wrapped it tenderly in a blanket and took it to the ITC (International Trypanotolerance Centre) where a sympathetic Glasgow vet had it put out of its misery, leaving us sobbing our hearts out.

I screamed irrationally at the driver who had unwittingly slaughtered the kitten, but it wasn't really his fault. Life in Africa is a tough game of survival for cats, perhaps harder for the sweet, pretty ones than for the tough ugly ones like our new acquisition.

Anyway, Awa was the name given to Caroline by the village women with whom she worked. And 'dingding' is Mandinka for 'baby' or 'young'. So our cat was Little Awa or Awa the Younger. It thrived. Born in the gutter it grew up with gutter manners, a graceless awkward body, blotchy orange, black and grey coat, a sly narrow face and an insatiable craving for food which never left it, presumably because of its disadvantaged start in life. It is not a lovable cat but I care for it deeply and Ray, well, Ray tholes it.

Caroline was less than enchanted at the tribute to her implicit in the naming of our pet. 'If it had been beautiful, I wouldn't have minded,' she pouted, 'but look at it! Such a gawky thing!' She herself is extremely beautiful and, dare I suggest it, a tiny touch vain. On this occasion she was also very annoyed, but not at the name of the cat. She had, she had persuaded herself, been bitten by a 'tumbo-fly'. I don't quite know what tumbo-flies are, except that they are said to lay eggs in dank clothing which has, for instance, been left hanging on the washing-line too long. Locals say the way to avoid them is to iron clothes with a hot iron, otherwise flies which hatch out in your clothing will burrow into your skin. Personally I never iron anything. The local iron is a kind of flat-iron filled with hot charcoal which I am far too lazy to try, and an electric iron, I'm glad to say, uses such a lot of power that it makes the lights dip alarmingly, so Ray has forbidden its use. But Caroline's clothes were always band-box smart, carefully washed and pressed by the two wives of her landlord.

It couldn't be a tumbo-fly, we felt. And it wasn't. It turned out to be an undramatic but very painful boil. We all, those of us who live here, get twitchy about things that might happen to us — though our apprehension usually far outweighs our actual experience of tropical ailments. They make gruesome reading, though.

I didn't worry about the big bogeys like cholera, typhoid, hepatitis and malaria (until I actually caught malaria, but that was much later) as they are mostly perfectly preventable and I was far more likely to be troubled by boils, flu or sunburn. But bilharzia bothered me, unlikely as I was to be affected by it. It just *sounded* so yukky! I quote Terry Palmer's advice to Gambian travellers: 'Bilharzia is carried by schistomes, creatures which live in the rivers and ponds. The female is 25mm long with the 12mm-long male permanently clasped around her. Her eggs, free-floating in the rivers, hook on to human skin and work through the body into the liver. One strain passes out through the bladder, another through the rectum, both causing loss of blood.' Ugh! Remind me never to go paddling in the creeks!

Caroline, her boil buzzing uncomfortably, nevertheless came for our final farewell meal on the verandah for Helma and Roel. She had some lively conversations with Helma, about elephants: cloth ones which Helma had designed using scraps of batik for the women of Caroline's adopted village to copy on their hand sewing-machines which had been gifted to them by other friends of ours in the UK. Sadly, the cute little jumbos never materialised but the women did make baby clothes and table-cloths and we all enjoyed the challenge of helping Helma design a marketable elephant without too many difficult angles and corners. Maybe one day we'll revive the idea.

Tearful goodbyes then, with Roel stoically swallowing Julbrew until he finally boarded the plane. We felt flat, lonely, wistful as we waved them off, and Ray said: 'Let's got to Casamance!' What a good idea!

The first time I'd gone to southern Senegal, with travel-writer Terry and a batch of other people, I hadn't really enjoyed it. We had hurtled onwards to the Cap Skirring area, at that time peppered with hotels of the Club Med variety, and the journey back was cold and bumpy and punctuated by grim-looking soldiers in camouflage gear jumping out of the bush holding rifles under our noses. The rebel activity which was to blemish the image of the region for the next couple of years (and temporarily close down those big commercial hotels) was just beginning.

Very simply, the rebels wanted autonomy for a part of Senegal separated from the Dakar capital by many miles (the whole of the Gambia lay, like 'the ham in a sandwich' as one writer had described it, between the capital and the Casamance region, which was the lush rice-producing food-bowl of the country). Often, the separatist struggle disintegrated into silly but savage tribal feuds between Jolas and Mandinkas, traditionally mistrustful of one another, and it played havoc with the tourist trade in an area already very underdeveloped and even primitive in comparison with the Gambia. The locals would come to Banjul and Serrekunda by bush taxi for the thrill of going into supermarkets and buying wine and salt and curry powder, not to mention cement and paint, all of which were either unobtainable or very expensive in the tiny villages with no electric power, running water, tourist pubs or (apart from those at Cap Skirring and Ziguanchor far in the south) large hotels. It was exactly this unspoiled rural charm that gave it its appeal for us and for back-packing French, German and Dutch visitors who shied away from the more organised package tourism practised in the Gambian coastal areas.

We set off in our little yellow Citroen, roof open, feeling like truants, escaping from the toilet-cleaning, banana-watering, shopping and socialising routing of our life in Bijilo. We passed the colony of baboons, in the chalky quarry across the road from a dense forest. Large lugubrious grandfathers sprawled among young macho males, mothers with drooping teats and clinging babies, sitting on the rocks or convening under the trees, or loping boldly across the road in front of us.

We spent one night at our dream hotel, the Kalissai, where, because of the rebel threat (much more talked about than real) we were the only guests, strolling in the luxuriant gardens, lying on the elegant beach beds with acres of empty beach stretching to either side.

We basked in the sybaritic luxury of hot showers, air-conditioning, thick pastel towels and crisp cotton sheets, sipping appallingly expensive Flag beers on the exquisite terrace and eating fabulous fish soup in the restaurant at night with Michel, the owner's son. We would be even more broke than usual for months to make up for this splurge, but it was worth it.

The second night we spent at Situkoto Campement, run by a Kafountine cooperative of villagers, managed by Ray's friend Diack (pronounced Jack), known as Diackson (as in Michael Jackson!). The 'workers' and the few tourists in residence all swung dreamily in hammocks or played gentle games of draughts or backgammon. Occasionally, when pressed, someone would pump up some water from the well so that we could have a shower or flush the communal toilet. It was all blissfully laid-back. Breakfast was yeasty village bread and local honey, and there was nothing to do except lie on the sand, swim in the clear blue sea or stroll a couple of miles to the intriguing remains of a wrecked Chinese trawler; or sit in rickety basket-chairs, reading and smelling the fish being grilled in garlic and tomato for supper. Next day we walked through the trees to visit Mama Karamba.

Her real name is Nicole. She is half-gypsy, half-French, a little sparrow of a woman with round saucer eyes of brilliant blue and a voice as sweet as the honey we'd had for breakfast. Her husband is a drawling, eloquent Englishman with an old school accent. There is a rumour that he was disowned from a vaguely aristocratic family when he ran off with Nicole, who is, I think, his third wife. It may not be true, but it's a good story. He looks rather like a pastoral Patrick Lichfield and is constantly creating new schemes to get rich, none of which ever seem to happen. Like us, they hover on the brink of penury; like us they allow the sun and the insidious charm of West Africa to dull their desire for hard cash.

Nicole with the cornflower eyes had all the cooking skills of a French peasant, and could create gourmet meals from the simplest ingredients.

She had none of my material advantages (if you could call a two-ring gas cooker and a sink without running taps advantages!) as her cooking was done in an open kitchen over a wood fire and her ingredients were virtually all plucked from nature for, as I have pointed out, there were no supermarkets in this area, no handy little drums of Schwartz oregano or ground ginger or coriander. Instead she used local herbs and fish and instinctive flair.

They lived in a round hut with a grass roof and a mattress on the floor. Clothes hung on twigs suspended from the domed ceiling. Outside, we sat at a huge battered table under a spreading canopy of tree-branches, where we could see the sea beyond a little grass hut with palliasses used for overnight guests, and, through the trees, a lush meadow with grazing cows that looked for all the world like a field in Normandy. Nicole's cat rubbed against our legs while she fried chunky slices of shark in garlic and herbs and mixed a big salad of local lettuce and tomatoes.

We were reluctant to leave, but we promised we'd see them again (we did, but in slightly different circumstances, as you will discover later). I hoped, as we drove home, that neither commerce nor politics would ever change Casamance too much. It has been likened, in its many water-logged rice-paddy areas, to the French Camargue, and its lagoons harbour some spectacular bird and animal life, while its people are known to be more relaxed and agreeable that their northern brothers near Dakar, where there are elegant shoe boutiques, traffic lights, jazz clubs, factories and bustling crowds, none of which are known here in the somnolent south. The Casamance region of Senegal alone is far bigger than the Gambia. Our Francophone neighbour, all in all, occupies nearly 200,000 square kilometres around our borders, making it over seventeen times larger than us. Its population, however, is just seven times ours, for the Gambia is densely peopled compared with most African countries.

It says a lot for President Sir Dawda Jawara that in spite of this imbalance of space and citizens, he has firmly resisted any attempts to assimilate the Gambia into Senegal, proudly affirming the Gambia's sovereignty without creating any rift with his brother-president Abdou Diouf. The actual borders of the Gambia were cynically drawn by the British during the carve-up of West Africa by the colonial powers in the 19th century (it was claimed they were drawn with compass and ruler at the distance a gun-boat could fire from the centre of the river) and many Gambians have Wollof or Mandinka relatives in Senegal, but that doesn't stop them being fiercely proud of their independence.

For me, Casamance had the charm of, say a remote Scottish island or a tiny English hamlet. Wonderful for unwinding, but I wouldn't want to live there all the time. On the way home, as well as musing on the future of that Senegalese slice of green and golden land, I was also musing on my Gambian advantages. As if reading my thoughts, Ray stopped at a supermarket and came out clutching a bottle of Californian chablis. Try finding that in Kafountine village.

The Wet Economy

The weeks rolled by sluggishly. In Scotland I knew when it was Sunday because I wasn't at work and most of the shops were closed and I had Sunday newspaper sections and colour supplements to plod through. I knew when it was Monday because it was the start of the week and I had a controversial column to create in a hurry and a row of sub-editors waiting expectantly, grumbling if I couldn't explode instantly on to my high-tech screen with punchy opinions that would give them a good headline.

Here I had days that ran into other days with no special seven-day graph to delineate them in my mind. Not that things didn't happen. Things happened, OK, but not in any logical sequence. The market in Serrekunda was as busy on Sunday as any other day. Mechanics and electricians and plumbers could be found any day of the week . . . or rather, were as elusive and infuriatingly hard to pin down on a Monday as on a Thursday or a Sunday. The women went on planting their rice; the men sowed their peanuts, no matter what name was on the day. I would say vaguely to Ray: 'What day is it?' and he would gaze back at me blankly. 'Em, maybe Tuesday? Or is it Wednesday?'

The arrivals and departures of tourists gave us flight days to punctuate our weeks, but now there were no tourists. Now we were poised on the brink of the rainy season. The sky was cunningly azure at noon, then sneaked some purple or slate grey on to its palette and before you knew it sharp little white waves were flicking up the sea that had been smoothly turquoise and the horizon had turned navy-blue and big dollops of water were dropping from the sky. Thunder which had been mumbling to itself like a sleepy lion all day would edge nearer, now a clumsy prehistoric beast, snorting and bellowing and spitting fire, white sheets of lightning which showed up every twig, every stone, every shuddering leaf in dazzling clarity. The air would be full of sound, yet seem strangely still, suspended, then the drops of water would link hands and become waterfalls. Ray would cut a spreading fan-shaped branch from a palm-tree and we would use it as an umbrella, but I didn't mind getting wet. I wanted to throw off my clothes and stand in the cool, refreshing cascade of solid water, my face turned heavenwards. This would have scandalised the neighbours, of course, so I never did. Not yet anyway.

But in the months of May, June and even July, these days were rare. Mostly the sun lounged in the sky as though it was a blue hammock, grinning down at us with a smile as hot as an open oven. On the beach we would plunge into the sea and find it as warm as a jaccuzzi, thick and soft as though someone had stirred bath oil into it. A year later, the Gambia was to make a vigorous effort to develop all-year-round tourism. For it was ridiculous that these balmy, blue-canopied days should be wasted on the likes of us. We, who had to work, be it typing a few thousand words a day (as I try to do) or weeding and hoeing (as I nagged Ray to do) or doing any of the everyday jobs that Gambians have to do regardless of the season . . . we may moan about the humidity and pine for a sharp breeze. But for tourists, able to plunge into a pool at will, turn on the fan, sip an ice-cold beer, the summer was asking to be exploited. Even the rainstorms when they came, mainly in August and September, are spectacular, awe-inspiring, and are of short enough duration not to ruin anyone's holiday.

For us, however, even with the typing and the hoeing and the afternoon hours swimming or fishing on the beach, time hung as heavy as the sky. Back from the beach, there was rice to clean, cassava to prepare, peanut sauce to stir. But after we'd eaten, the night loomed long and warm and eventless ahead of us. We sat in the candlelight, for without tourists' money we couldn't afford to run the generator nightly. Four hours of petrol cost about £2.20, which would work out at nearly £70 a month if engine oil was included. Way beyond the resources of a Gambian household. The candlelight was romantic, and silent, unlike the generator, but also irresistible to flying ants with gauze wings which on certain nights would fill the room and die, leaving piles of silvery remains to be swept up. The winds that cleared the path of oncoming storms were blessedly cool and discouraged insects but they also blew out the candles or made the flames flicker wildly so that reading or writing was impossible.

'Wanna play Crazy Eight?' I would mutter morosely and Ray, whose capacity for sleep still amazes me, would blink and pull himself out of a dream and into a sitting position, removing his head from my lap where it had felt heavy as lead and caused pins and needles in my right knee.

The cards would be sticky and greasy, adhering to our fingers then blowing off in the wind. Arguments would break out when hearts and spades became confused in the shadows. We would listen to radio, then at nine o'clock on would come the news in Jola and Serahuli, incomprehensible to both of us. Ray would fall asleep again. If I went to bed, I wakened at 1 am, thinking it was morning, then realising how many empty hours stretched before me. Bad enough to be an insomniac in winter, with seven or eight hours to toss and pace and ponder through. But in summer, the nights were endless.

The fact that the Gambia is so near the Equator (which passes through Gabon, Congo, Zaire, Uganda and Kenya not much more than a thousand miles or so south) means that nights and days change very little all year round. Our longest days are in midsummer, when we can do without lights till 8pm. In winter it is 7pm when the sun suddenly drops like a discarded orange peel into the dark basin of the ocean and the nights are often moonless and black as pitch. It has advantages; none of those awful 4pm lighting-up times that made Glasgow so grim and disconcerting in midwinter. But neither were there the splendid Scottish evenings when you could read a book at 10 pm. Most Gambians wake with the sun and sleep with the stars. But most Gambians have a far larger capacity for sleep than I have. Secretaries will sleep over their typewriters when there is no work for them to do; shopkeepers will lie on top of bags of rice and snore; dockworkers will sprawl on a sack or on a wheelbarrow or in the shade of a lorry and snooze till someone calls them.

And so it was, to fill some of these clammy evenings, that I first became a Gambian cinema addict. Ray claimed that he had never ventured inside a cinema until I dragged him into one in Glasgow in 1990 when we first visited my mum. He said Gambian cinemas were dens of thieves and pickpockets. I don't think this was necessarily true, but when the Asimarie picture-house opened, new and much-publicised and surely respectable, we decided to try it. No advertisements were carried in local papers to tell us what films were showing, mainly because the programmes changed every night, so each visit was a surprise.

Enormous garish posters outside whetted our appetites, even if they were in French or German or Arabic, with lurid pictures of devils and swordsmen and Bruce Lee. The building, near to the police station in Serrekunda, was spacious if basic, with capacious stalls and steep narrow concrete stairs up to a tip-tilted balcony. The roof was made of corrugated iron, but so was the roof of the State House and of our bungalow. No brocade curtains or carpets but a couple of fans occasionally twirled above us to move the humid air around. We sat in the expensive upstairs seats (about 70 pence) because Ray was sure all the riff-raff and potential criminals would be downstairs. Such a snob he had become! Bruce Lee was immensely popular, or anyone who looked vaguely like him and clobbered enough villains with cracking kicks and barking blows of the heel of his hand. The noise level was ear-splitting. The hoi polloi downstairs hooted in pleasure with each punch and stab, and occasionally someone would jump into the aisle and do a little shadow-boxing and kicking of his own until restrained by a bouncer. Car chases and gun battles were deliriously applauded. There was very little sex. In some films, sex scenes of probably very low-key titillation had obviously been cut out, particularly if the film had come via a Muslim country. On the other hand, we once saw a Hong Kong kung-fu production which included some appalling but hilarious near-porno-graphic footage, to which the audience, including me, didn't quite know how to respond. It was a relief when the girls got their knickers back on again and everyone started shooting and kicking.

It lasted a long time. The programme would start before nine and go on till after one in the morning, usually with three full-length films to give patrons real value for money. Ironically, it was about half-way through that I, the great insomniac, would find myself being shaken awake by Ray. 'Mariama. You're missing a good bit!' And Bruce Lee would be twirling and flattening fifteen men in ten seconds. The international flavour of film-watching in the Gambia is intriguing. On one memorable night we watched a Chinese film dubbed in bad American English with sub-titles in both Arabic and French. This could be an effective way of teaching languages except that the soundtrack was often so bad it was impossible to make out the words, and anyway, no one was interested in the subtleties of dialogue. It was the fights they came for.

We saw Indian films and Japanese films and once, oddly, a British thriller with lots of stiff upper lips and not enough blood and batterings to satisfy the audience. Crackling American voices were invariably dubbed over scowling samurais and sultry princes, often bearing no relation to the action of the mouth-movements. Sometimes the whole screen flickered and went blank and everyone would roar and hiss. Quite often a message would appear hugely across the picture saying: 'This video is for demonstration purposes only.' On home videos, as we were later to discover, this is also a problem. Pirated videos are the norm rather than the exception and customers here were, for instance, able to see a wobbly copy of *Home Alone 2* which flickered from colour to black-and-white from minute to minute, long before the official video was available in the UK.

To keep me awake during the third or fourth hour of wham-bam entertainment, Ray would usher me outside on to an upstairs balcony, a bare concrete affair with a couple of dilapidated chairs. It was possible to view as much action from there as from inside as the balcony overlooked the courtyard where crowds were still queuing, joking, fighting, trying to persuade some benefactor to buy them a ticket and yelling greetings to their friends on the street. Night-time Serrekunda throbbed with life, cars crawling and honking over every inch of unmade road, elbowing pedestrians out of the way, most of whom were selling kebabs, cigarettes, mentholatum, black mints, joss-sticks, air-mail envelopes, melons or boiled eggs.

In the cinema yard, an enterprising Lebanese supermarket firm had opened an ice-cream shop. In the auditorium, the heat grew intense as hundreds of bodies sweated with excitement and mosquitoes drifted through, looking among all the crowds for my ankles, their favourite feast. I scratched a lot. But it was fun. Once, when the building had been closed for repairs for several weeks, hundreds of addicts suffering from withdrawal symptoms crammed in the courtyard for the re-opening. Everyone pushed and shoved trying to get to the front of the queue and several violent altercations broke out. The staff hopped up and down bellowing commands for people to wait their turn but no-one took any notice. Ray sneakily told the manager that since I was a tubab, I could not be expected to survive such claustrophobic pressures and managed to haul me inside and upstairs ahead of the hordes, none of whom seemed to resent this racial privilege.

The atmosphere was a bit like the Oscars in Hollywood, without the live stars. People dressed up, either in stiffly-starched voluminous African robes, the women showing off their gilt and silver, or in outrageous European garb, baggy jeans, boots, Batman tee-shirts, high-domed imitation leather 'Rasta' caps, felt snap-brims. We would arrive home, wending our way through sticky puddles and black trenches carved by trucks and buses, dogs sleeping as though dead in the middle of the road, night revellers walking five miles or more to their villages, and reach the compound at 2 am, where Mr M would eye us disapprovingly, no doubt speculating on what wicked pursuits we had been following at such an ungodly hour. Once, feeling guilty, we gave him money to take Mariama to a matinee and they came back gasping with amazement at the things they had seen.

There were a few other highlights to brighten the languid monotony of the summer season. Brendan, our Irish friend, a planning officer deployed by an Irish aid organisation in the Gambian planning department, invited us to his birthday party. He was recovering from a severe bout of Hepatitis A and he needed cheering up. His house, a long low apartment at the far side of Bakau, was one of a group described, postally, as Low Priced Government Housing. It didn't have the same ring to it as Chez Nous or Dunroamin but it had woven Gambian cloth hung on the bare cream government-issue walls and thick clumps of trees and shrubs nodding outside the steel-barred windows. As usual the guests were a motley cosmopolitan crew, a German holidaymaker, an American human rights worker, an Irish priest, an Irish archivist, an English VSO nurse, a Welsh doctor, a Gambian doctor, a Gambian bricklayer, and us.

Irish songs alternated with reggae music and people sat on the floor sipping Coke and Guinness and wine. At nine o'clock Brendan announced grandly: 'I'm going to fetch the caterers.' He went off in his little jeep and came back with more Gambians heaving enormous chipped enamel bowls of benachin (Wollof rice and fish), cooked by the builder's wife, who had either not been invited or had been too shy to come. It saddened me somewhat that wives here were so often left at home to their own devices (cooking, washing, growing vegetables, brushing out the compound, feeding their babies) while the men went out to enjoy themselves. On the other hand, this is not a Gambian phenomenon. I have seen it in Glasgow many times, and it happens all over the world! Sometimes it even happens to me.

It's true the women could be seen fluttering along the road of an afternoon, dressed like butterflies in riotous coloured cottons and organzas, to attend a naming christening, chattering merrily and eyeing up the other dresses. And there were young girls out on the streets at night but unfortunately most of them were plying a certain trade rather than merely enjoying the evening air. Women, at least near the coast and in the towns, were not oppressed the way they might be in other Muslim countries, and there was a high level of promiscuity, but nevertheless, married men certainly led a more socially-active life than their wives, if only because the wives had so many children to look after. One reason was that some of the men, Muslims in name, liked the chance to slug back a few beers or stouts, and they were convinced their wives would report them to the elders or to the Imam if they saw them drinking alcohol. Lots of Gambian men drink, and most smoke. But I have seldom seen a Gambian woman drink wine or beer, and I have hardly every seen one smoking, unless she is a sophisticated rich girl just back from overseas studies.

Continuing the international theme we'd enjoyed at Brendan's, we had a lunch-party on our verandah. Tom and Joan were there for we had grown uncommonly fond of the Ayrshire doctor and his Lanarkshire nurse. Tom was the consultant paediatrician at the Banjul hospital, where he struggled to cope with the emotional strain of knowing that babies would die under his eyes every day, and that basic equipment — as basic as dressings, sheets and syringes — would always be in desperately short supply. The principal causes of infant deaths were dehydration resulting from diarrhoea, malaria and malnutrition, and the death-rate was something like fifteen times higher than in the worst housing-schemes in the worst cities in Britain. All the same Tom and his dedicated and gifted Gambian colleague Dr Aiyo Palmer managed to launch a new intensive care unit helped by funding from Sweden and elsewhere. And I was happy that a feature I wrote about his work in the Scottish Sunday Mail newspaper inspired readers to send thousands of pounds to help with improving the survival chances of Gambian babies (a fund which continues to operate through Dr Palmer even after Tom returned to Scotland).

Tom was a short, spare figure who looked about half his actual age, so that large Gambian grannies would say to him, 'We're waiting for the doctor, boy,' unable to believe that this skinny youth (he was actually 37 then!) was a vastly experienced paediatrician specialising in tropical medicine. Joan, his wife, a sonsy, supremely reassuring woman who used to mother me in spite of the fact that I was a dozen years older than she, voluntarily ran sessions in the wards showing the new mothers how to care for their babies, with particular emphasis on weaning procedures. For many of the babies brought in suffering seriously from malnutrition were bloated and puffy, unlike the stick-like victims of famine in, say, Somalia. What they had was kwashiorkor, so called from a Ghanaian word meaning lack of nourishment when removed from the mother's breast. They were fed all right, but not with the protein they needed. Joan would urge them to mix groundnut paste with the weaning 'pap' and our American artist friend Andrea made bright posters showing the local foods available.

Much as we admired their medical skills, it was the Mackays' humour and kindness and down-to-earth refusal to get sucked into the conventional ex-pat scene that endeared them to us, and I still think fondly of Tom grabbing Ray by the elbow and saying, 'Right man, let's you and me go and do a wee bit fishing, eh, pal?' Another Scot at our lunch-party was Rory the irrepressible architect, who first introduced us to Tom and Joan and there was an Indian executive from the charity that Caroline worked for, Caroline herself, Ray's mum, Mr M and Mariama, and Farid and Iman, with their friend Aman. Farid was a coloured South African, tall and rather patrician-looking, with olive skin, a hooked nose and a beard. He read and wrote Arabic fluently and was a teacher of the Koran as well as a self-taught motor engineer. His wife Iman was a jolly Englishwoman who had converted to Islam with gusto when she met him. They had come to the Gambia from England seeking a Muslim paradise but had in fact found a slapdash, tolerant, hit-or-miss kind of attitude to the religion they adhered to so staunchly. Iman wore white or pastel cotton swather around her head, neck, arms and ankles and she always brought her prayer-mat when she came for coffee.

They both waited on tenterhooks for the day that they and Aman (a Soweto exile with a young son) would be restored to South Africa. Farid had been expelled from that troubled Republic more than a dozen years before for, as he put it 'blowing things up' and secreting ANC people out of the country concealed in his van. Now amnesty had been declared and he visited the UNDP offices almost every day seeking word about passage home to Johannesburg to see his family. He had told Iman about his homeland and perhaps hindsight had illuminated the good memories and obscured the bad ones, for the South Africa she spoke of to me seemed to bear little relationship to the one of which I read in magazines and newspapers.

Rosie from Germany wasn't at the lunch, but she could have told them how, often, going back can be a distressing shock to the system. Her husband was a Namibian and they had stayed, with a group of other Namibians, in Bijilo's little guest house (a spartan two-roomed building in a plot of mangoes in the centre of the village) several years before, which was how Ray had grown to know them. Now she was back on holiday with some friends and we asked her what had happened in the meantime.

'Things have not been good,' she told us pensively as we sat on the beach together watching ospreys dropping like stones to catch fish and slender pirogues bouncing over the burnished surface of the sea. 'Namibia became 'free' so we went home, as had been my husband's dream for so long. But it was not a good experience. The south is where the game reserves and rich countryside are and perhaps that is how the world sees Namibia. But most of the blacks are congregated in the poor north of the country. There are Afrikaaner stockades still, surrounded by barbed wire, patrolled by dobermann pinschers, with signs that say: 'Intruders will be shot'.

The whites had despised Rosie because she had married a black and refused to speak to her. The blacks were distantly courteous but hostile and suspicious. 'Now they don't trust foreigners, anyone with a white skin. I understand their feelings but I was very lonely and unhappy. My husband couldn't find a job because the Namibians regarded anyone who had left the country and gone abroad as traitors to their people, so they won't employ them.'

They went again to Germany but the husband was bitter, still pining for his roots even though he knew those roots were damaged irreparably, and I suspected, though Rosie didn't say so, that it had put a great strain on their marriage. All marriages are hard work. Mixed marriages demand extra understanding and tolerance and if political and territorial obstacles are stirred into the mixture, it must take a very strong love indeed to survive.

The Indian charity boss was called Jag. He took us one evening for a meal at a new Indian restaurant in the tourist belt. The manageress was wearing a kind of Indian Rana outfit, very exotic with flashing eyes in a dusky golden face. Then she said, in a vivacious Welsh accent: 'Hullo, I haven't seen you for ages, neighbours!' I realised it was Maria, who works days with the ITC cattle station offices, and is building a bungalow near to ours. She is from Cape Verde, hence the golden skin, but was reared in Wales. Hitherto I'd only seen her in a skirt and blouse, shouting instructions at her builders!

We drove home through the mud, to the sound of millions of frogs in chorus. I say frogs, but I think they may be West African toads, though both creatures are common here and there are also tree frogs, tiny and colourful with adhesive fingers and toes, though I have yet to spot one of these. Anyway, the frogs, as I and the Gambians choose to call them, occupy every inch of muddy, stagnant water in the summer and sing in ecstasy, louder and louder as night progresses. The 2CV barely disturbed them as it coped nobly with the glaucous, olivaceous rivers of gunge through which we had to pass. These puddles unnerved me. My intellect told me they couldn't be more than six or eight inches deep, but they were so dense and menacing my gut told me we would drive into the centre and be swallowed up into some bottomless hole. So far this hasn't happened, though I have many times had to wade into the unknown liquid to help push stranded cars and I have always wondered vaguely what might be in there, what might catch my ankles with suckers and tentacles . . . quite irrational, but I can't help it.

I don't know of any other car, apart from four-wheel drive, that could have conquered our route home — though many tried it, and became more moored in the mud like hippopotami . . . One evening we came back from the beach to find a large Mercedes squatting on its haunches up to its waist in viscous water right outside our gate. Two stout ladies in opulent African dress were standing in the blazing late afternoon pre-sunset glare, perspiring and looking disgusted. The driver waded about in the mud, sighing and shouting: 'If it wasn't for you foolish women we wouldn't be here. It's because of you we got stuck. You're the ones who wanted to visit friends nearby. It's all your fault.' The women cast a withering glance towards him and turned their well-upholstered backs. I would have invited them inside but they were afraid of our dogs. I didn't blame them as Stanley was bouncing like a rubber ball so that anyone who looked over the wall came face to face with his bared teeth. This is a trick he learned as he grew and he can jump walls far higher than ours, a veritable Zebedee.

I gave the ladies a bench to sit on outside in the lane and made them some coffee. The car sank deeper and deeper. I towed it with the Land Rover but the rope broke. The women watched implacably, lips curled. I tried again and this time, with another rope and some fierce acceleration the car clambered out of its mud-bath like a fat lady at a health spa. It was full to its armrests with stinking black water, and, predictably, it refused to start. The women rolled their eyes heavenward.

The man baled out the noxious fluids with a plastic cup. We discovered that he was a successful Gambian entrepreneur who had lived in Sweden for many years. He wasn't used to this kind of thing. Later he was to stand as a candidate in the general elections and we cheered him on since we felt we were linked by a muddy finger of fate, but he lost. Probably he went to Sweden again, where life was less exasperating. Meanwhile, we drove him to Serrekunda and drove round and round in circles till we were able to track down his auto-electrician, who happened to be at a wedding. There were drummers and griots, blaring disco music and people twirling and laughing in the streets around the marital compound.

The man reacted with commendable good nature. Can you imagine hauling a British electrician out of a wedding late on a Saturday evening? He pushed through the clapping giggling children and lavishly-wrapped young women and came back to Bijilo with us. The women were still sitting primly on the bench, in the dark, sighing, and refusing to greet the businessman-politician with more than a shrug. But I had Stanley held in a hammer-lock by the watchman and invited them all into the house while the electrician stripped down the starter motor and dried it out, a task which took several hours. The ladies thawed out and their brother relaxed and we all chatted and laughed at the ways of the Gambia. 'These people, you can do nothing for them,' complained the businessman. 'I fixed up big contracts in Sweden, at good prices, which would have been good for this country, but I couldn't get anything to happen here unless I bribed an official. So I said: forget it, and went back to Sweden.' Much later, they all left and drove off cautiously into the night.

During the summer months, I was often tempted to erect a sign saying 'Rescue Service', and charging D25 every time we dug, pushed, shovelled or towed a car out of the slime. The money would have been useful. With no tourists, we had no income. People assume if you are white you must automatically be rich. Everyone who needs shoes, a frock for a wedding, a bag of rice, school fees, comes to us for help and a string of begging letters is brought to our door between Ramadan and October. The people seldom write themselves, even if they can write. It seems the procedure is to ask someone else to do it; perhaps it lends more authority or pathos. The letters are always elaborately phrased, full of flowery greetings and felicitations. If we can help we help, but sometimes we have to say no. I always feel they don't believe us when we say we are as hard up as they. White people CAN'T be poor. In fact, at that time I was desperately making soups and vegetable stews from anything I could find in the garden, the tomatoes that clustered around the bananas, the wicked peppers that grew in front of the window, the few aubergines left from last year, some stringy cassava. I made flat slabs of bread in the frying pan, after carefully sieving the weevils from the local flour, which is much cheaper than the imported packets in the big shops. We cut down on coffee, buying awful chicory stuff which was undrinkable anyway.

We stopped going to the cinema and went back to Crazy Eight by candle-light. We put petrol in the car a gallon at a time and used it for essential journeys only. Otherwise Ray pedalled the bike, sweating freely, along the muddy paths in baking sun or torrential rain, picking up letters from the post or bread and tomato paste from the local shops.

The essential items of shopping for me, like any Gambian house-wife, were onions, garlic, tomato paste and oil. These, with chilli pepper and rice formed the basis of benachin (the Wollof rice cooked with all of these and livened by scraps of fish), suppa (okra stew), and domada (peanut stew). I tried to widen the menu with tomato sauce and pasta or meatballs made with a minimum of meat. I hardly ate garlic in Scotland; now my breath reeked of it. In the village, variations in meals were few. Rice wasn't the authentic traditional food, but it had become so and continues to be so, despite all efforts by GAFNA, the Gambian Food and Nutrition Association, a most praiseworthy body, to encourage people to grow and use sorghum and millet and other more natural crops. Bongo fish is used day in day out with the various sauces I have mentioned, all basically made of the same things, with okra or peanut paste additions. Potatoes are too expensive for village Gambians to use. Meat only appears when a cow is killed in the village for a special occasion. I suppose the goats and sheep I see wandering about must be killed and eaten but I never see the meat except at festivals. People keep chickens but I seldom see them eaten; mostly they sell them, to white people like me, or hotels or cafes.

Sometimes, if we catch a fish I can't cope with — a giant ray, for example — we give it to Ray's mum and she uses the flesh to make fish balls, redolent with hot pepper and spices. She always sends some round to us as a thank-you for the gift.

If I had an oven, I whined to Ray at this particular period in our lives, I could make bread puddings to use up the dry bread, potato and vegetable pies, quiches and all kinds of economical items. How can I extemporise with two little gas-rings? 'Mariama,' he replied bleakly, 'my mother has cooked for nine of us all my life on a wood fire. Stop nagging.' An oven, he maintained, would be a frivolous extravagance. Then one day he came rushing in looking like someone who'd lost a butut and found a dalasi. 'Mariama, good news! My friend has seen this Er-Quatre' (as Renault Fours are known here). 'It is a taxi and the man who owns it needs money in a hurry to go to Europe.' So what? I was singularly unimpressed. People here don't necessarily price items they are selling according to their market value. Often, it's all to do with how urgently they need money, whether it's to build a house, impress a girl or go to another country. Sometimes you can get good bargains that way. But a Renault taxi? Surely a frivolous extravagance?

'Mariama, think! We can have Lamin driving it for us as a local taxi in Serrekunda. He will work all day and late at night and make thousands of dalasis every week during the rainy season, so now we will have an income. Soon it will pay for itself and we will have a profit.' I felt there must be flaws in this argument, but it so happened I had 'flu at the time. My eyes and nose and throat were hot and stinging, my body felt like a heap of old wet rope, and the last thing I wanted to think about was the taxi business. 'Do what you want; just leave me in peace,' I growled and curled up on the bed sweating on the sheets, hoping the aspirin I'd swallowed would stop me from dying.

Later, restored to normal working order, I walked round to the friend's house to see our potential nice little earner. It lay in bits in the yard, surrounded by inquisitive goats. I have never seen such a forlorn, battered apology for a vehicle. It looked more like an abandoned sardine tin, but scruffier. And I had been, remember, the wife of a Scottish motor mechanic for over twenty years. I had seen some old bangers in my time, but never one as distressed as this. It required, he informed us tranquilly, a new cylinder head gasket, a new drive-shaft, new ball-joints, new everything. Then it would go to a welder who would try to stick bits of it together before it finally disintegrated in shock at having all these internal surgical procedures.

When all that was done, we would have to renew its taxi licence in our names, and insure it. But that didn't happen until it had broken down under us several times, or refused to start at all, or had to be braked suddenly when one clanking component or another had fallen off on the road like a severed limb. This? This was a bargain? I snarled at Ray. It had by now cost us two-and-a-half times its original price (a price which in my opinion indicated that the desperate Gambian had needed the money for a first class ticket on the QE2 or perhaps Concorde, to get to Europe). New things went wrong with it every hour. Ray shrugged and went into a huddle with his friend, who looked over at me sympathetically and whispered something to his nephew. 'What did he say?' I scowled suspiciously. 'He said he understands why you are upset. He knows that in Britain, when anything goes wrong with a car, you just trade it in and buy a new one.' Ray looked pleased that he had solved the puzzle of my unreasonable attitude, and then perplexed when I proceeded to blow a gasket right in front of him. 'Tell him that I have tramped through more British scrap yards than he has had hot rice dinners, looking for parts for secondhand cars. Tell him that I have never owned a new car in my life and have, indeed, owned and driven several cars much older than this ..... this ... thing. Tell him I had a twenty-year-old Morris Minor, an ancient Ford Prefect, an almost obsolete Hillman Imp and an antediluvian Fiat, but I have never, never seen one in a condition like this!' I kicked the back wheel of 'this' and the rear number-plate fell off.

Never mind, many of the cars in the streets of Serrekunda looked every bit as awful as our 'new' taxi, and they seemed to get around all right and ply their trade quite successfully. Perhaps it would really make some money for us. Perhaps. . .

No More Mrs Nice Guy?

At last came the momentous day when Lamin, eldest of Ray's younger brothers, drove the little Renault Four to Serrekunda to launch us into our career as taxi-owners. I myself had only tried to drive it once, in the garden, and found that the gears creaked in a configuration unknown to me and, all in all, I'd have been happier and more comfortable with a donkey and cart. I have, in fact, often suggested to Ray that we should acquire a donkey and cart, but he is appalled at the idea. It would, I think, lower our status in a country where everyone aspires to have a car, even a ruined Renault Four.

There are tourist taxis, which charge what seem to me extortionate prices to take visitors wherever they want to go and which require a special licence from the Ministry of Tourism. There are big blue public service buses, which charged at that time one dalasi to go to Banjul, and there are bush-taxis, usually mini-buses, some extremely smart Swedish and German models, some ancient heaps of rust, spruced up by pieces of flowery linoleum on the floors or bunches of plastic flowers at the windows. Others are pick-up vehicles with canvas awnings over the back, where up to a dozen people squeeze in on wooden benches, their bones shaking all the way to the southern fishing enclaves. 'Local taxis' is the name given to cars which pick up locals and charge five dalasis for a short journey, more by negotiation for a longer trip. They can range from opulent Volvos and Peugeots to battered boxes like ours. Nearly all have the plastic flowers, or holy pictures, rear sun-blinds with images of Marilyn Monroe, Bob Marley or the Ayatollah Khomeineh. There are some messages on the sides, like 'Let Them Say', which I didn't understand but approved of anyway. All are treasured by their owners, even if they have no door handles and they have to stop every half-mile to top up the radiator.

Lamin was out on the road until the small hours of the morning, returned to sleep a few hours in his cupboard-sized room in his dad's house, then went back to work next day. Breathlessly we waited for him to come and pour dalasis into our laps.

'He must be doing well. He's away so long, business must be good,' said Ray, confidently. Ray is always confident. If I say: 'Do you think we'll get some rain to cool the plants?' he'll say 'Oh, yes, it will rain.' If I say; 'Do you think we'll get many bookings from tourists this year?' he'll say, 'Yes, yes, I'm sure we will.' I should know by now what he means is that he hopes so. No Gambian likes to predict bad news. They'd rather say something that was palpably untrue but nevertheless cheerful and reassuring than something accurate but unpleasant.

Lamin arrived at last. 'How much did you make?' we ventured, wondering if we might treat ourselves to a real restaurant meal, or at least buy some whitewash for the huts, some plants for the garden. 'I made nothing,' he said, dead-pan. 'Nothing ?' we gasped then, as full realisation hit us, we both shouted together: 'What do you mean, you made NOTHING?' 'Actually,' he answered tightly, 'I made 36 dalasis. But then the front axle broke and I had to have it welded, which cost D45. Now you owe me nine dalasis.'

Ray, seeing his optimistic dream fall apart, had to be restrained from leaping on Lamin's throat and searching him for undeclared coins, while I, who never liked the horrible car anyway, had to be dissuaded from putting a match to it there and then. Later, Farid, the exiled South African, who had a workshop in Kanefing, agreed to allow it to sit in his yard with a placard saying FOR SALE in its window. We would wait until some customer caught sight of it and said: 'What a dear little car! What character! What potential!' We would wait a long time. I was very depressed, and every time the wee car was mentioned I huffed and puffed like a Gambian dragon and Ray remembered he had some trees to prune at the other side of the compound.

I was also boiling mad at a certain young man, another relative of the Faals, who works at the time-share resort along the beach, a pleasant, ingenuous youth, but he'd tried my patience too far. Months before he had come to us all wide-eyed innocence and sorrowful mouth, begging us to 'borrow' him our plane and saw because he wanted to start up his own carpentry business.

'Borrow' is Gambian for 'lend', which can also be translated as 'give'. Gambian English is an art form. 'Insist', for example, is usually uttered to mean 'refuse'. ('That donkey insists to carry that load'). Ray, whose English, though started at school, has mostly been acquired phonetically, refers to the car's 'windscream' and 'brake flu'. I knew that if we 'borrowed' Bob our tools we'd never see them again, but since we seldom used them I agreed to give them to him to keep, provided he first used them to make two tables for us, with wood supplied by us and to a design carefully drawn by me.

Weeks went by and only after we had nagged and shouted and threatened to take back our tools, did a table arrive. It was completely different from the one I had drawn, with a plywood top instead of the

white-wood planking I'd envisaged, and splay legs like a 1950s' 'con-
temporary' coffee-table, the kind you always trip over. 'Ah, but plywood is very good. Much better than wood.' I sighed and said thank
you. At least it was a table. In vain we waited for its twin to arrive. To
confuse us even more, we went to the compound where the enterprising
would-be carpenter lived, and found that he was working at a quite
different occupation and had absolutely no intentions of opening his
own carpentry shop. 'Eh, well, really it's my brother who is doing it, this
man here,' he said, pointing to a morose chap who was putting the
finishing touches to an elegant set of bed-ends, varnished and polished
but looking as though they might well have started life as pieces of wood
from our shed, the ones that should have made the tables.

The brother, of course, wasn't a real brother, but some distant
relative from Senegal who had come to live in the village. He refused to
speak to us at all, so it was to him that I expleted and stamped my feet.
One day he turned up carrying a small, skimpy gnarled object flaking
with old paint, which looked as though it might have been used to
display sea-snail or cabbages in the market in its youth. 'You see, I said
I would bring you a second table,' he said, smiling and looking smug. 'I
always keep my promises.'

I exploded. 'Get that blankety-blank monstrosity out of here right
now. I am calling the police, the gendarmes, the army. You are a crook,
a thief, a con-man. You are a disgrace to the village. I am no longer going
to tolerate your tricks . . .' and so on.

Ray wasn't there, thank goodness. He gets embarrassed when I let
fly like that. But the only alternative is to shout and scream at him in my
frustration and it's hard to make him understand that he is only a
channel for my wrath. He has a vague notion that tubabs should behave
always with dignity, but I see Gambian women yelling at tradesmen
when they've got a grievance, and once in a while I just want to do what
comes naturally in circumstances such as these. So I did, and he fled. It
goes without saying that my threats were empty ones. I would never call
a policeman, and I had almost resigned myself to the fact that our
plywood, splay-legged table would never have a twin, which, for
aesthetic reasons, was probably just as well. But venting my feelings
made me feel better!

The `carpenter' chap is still a friend. Ray has told me, seriously,
'The way to true friendship is to have one very good argument with a
person. After that, you are real friends.' And it's true. After I had a battle
royal with the girl in Gamtel over a message that hadn't been sent
properly or one that had arrived for us without our being informed, both
of us retired almost in tears, and next time, greeted each other with
awkward smiles. Since then, we have been the greatest of friends.

I was, perhaps, even more irritable and rude than the occasion
deserved because he caught me in the midst of spring cleaning — or

rather summer cleaning — the kitchen cupboard. It was a shameful jumble of old boxes of jam-jars and bottles, a sack of onions, obsolete car-batteries, bags of bay-leaves, rusty tools and empty suitcases. I wondered vaguely if there might be a snake skulking silently beneath it all. I wondered also about the small red lizards which Helma had called salamanders when they darted from her crates as they packed to go to Holland. A salamander is supposed to live in fire, so I don't think the nomenclature was right, even in a country with dragons, but I knew that when our little brother Eliman saw them he backed away, claiming that it was such a lizard which had bitten his grandfather in the leg, causing it to swell enormously (the leg, not the lizard) and the grandfather subsequently to die painfully.

I had serious reservations about the validity of this diagnosis, but burrowed nervously into the clutter of the cupboards feeling like an explorer entering dense jungle. There was one small lizard but it looked like a gecko and whizzed up the wall too fast for me to ask it to state its identity. No snakes, no mice, no frogs, not even spiders. But, much worse. As I began lifting our old cardboard cartons and bags I found their bottoms disintegrating in clouds of termite paste. The paste is made as these white ants travel through or towards wood, paper, fabric, any natural fibre they can eat, and it comprises sand or clay and their saliva, forming very hard tunnels or, out in the bush, the huge mounds often looking like turreted fairy castles, which tourists photograph in delight. They aren't actually ants at all, but look like white maggots on legs and I loathe them. I longed for a nice hissing snake, or a toothy rat or enormous spiders, for they fill me with far less loathing. As I lifted out a large suitcase I saw that the whole floor was moving with them. More fell down as I chiselled the trails from the walls with a kitchen knife. This was now the beginning of the tourist season, and Ray was far up-river with some holidaymakers. I imagined him sitting on a verandah with a beer, or lolling in a boat pointing out the scenery to relaxed Germans in immaculate shorts, while I scraped and swept with dust and ants in my hair.

I poured Domestos over every crevice and hole where the termites might have tunnelled in, knowing it would only hold them at bay, but knowing also that the other things 'guaranteed' to disperse them (creosote, old engine oil, etc) were equally ineffective. I think when Ray's uncle built this house he built the kitchen area right on top of a termite nest, perhaps even knocking down a termite hill before he began building, without smoking the whole thing clear of its occupants. Now this corner seems to be the international headquarters for every termite from every corner of Africa, or so it seemed to me on days like that one. The rest of the compound, the little tourist huts, the toilets and showers are all fine. Only this vital part of my kitchen is constantly under siege.

Still, the big clean-out made me feel very virtuous, and in a way I was glad Ray was up-river, because he would have said (as men do) 'Why don't you leave it till tomorrow?' And he wouldn't have let me throw out the heaps of jars, mounds of paper and boxes, old dusters, broken car components and dead batteries. Gambians never throw ANYTHING out. Watchmen and local kids still sift through my pile of rubbish and slope off with bleach bottles, fish-flavoured plastic bags and empty coffee-tins. I don't mind this, as anything that diminishes the steadily growing mountain of non-degradable refuse is welcome. We used to skulk into the bush with a wheel-barrow and dump it well out of sight, but now we've heard that a man from Banjul is building a compound there, so we can't do that any more. We used to bury it, till I realised that the whole garden could become a thinly-covered layer of rusty tins, burnt plastic and old bottles. I often offer the empty bottles and jars to villagers because I know they can sell them in the market, where they are in great demand for peanut oil, kerosene and palm oil. Oddly enough people are very loath to take the trouble to come and collect them and carry them to town. Perhaps it's easier just to ask for money, I thought dourly, as yet another little note was brought to my doorstep by yet another beaming child who knew he'd get a biscuit or a ball-point pen from me if he looked cute. These notes were written on jotter-paper, graph paper, or, in the following case, on a receipt from the Gambia Cooperative Union:

Dear Sir. This is acknowledge you that, I will be getting married on the 18th November 1991. Your present to this graceful occasion will be highly appreciated with full thanks

You can work that one out for yourself, but the next one, from the Land Rover driver, needs a translation:

Hello Brother and my bus Ray, it's me writing. Do my bus, I got a stranger just now. An I want you to help me in some ten dalasi because if my wife which come just now. To my bus you are the only one who can sulf my this problem because you know how I am in this village. Thanks by your good friend, Do this an greet Mariama for me Thanks.

That meant: 'Hello, Brother, my boss Ray. Due to my (new) boss I have a visitor just now and because I have also taken a new wife, I want you to help me with ten dalasis. You are the only one who can solve this problem, and you know my reputation in the village. Say hullo to Mariama for me. . .'

It was hard to say No, and the letters weren't by any means all begging letters. Some were outlines of documents I was expected to type out neatly and beautifully spelled, on my nice white paper (if I had any). A tubab with a typewriter could surely have nothing better to do than act as scribe for all and sundry. Curriculum vitae, letters to friends in Europe, job applications and references all came my way.

Nabi, for instance, our ex-watchman (the one with the green fingers and yellow belly) sent me a note in Guinea French, written more or less phonetically which took me an hour to fathom. In Nabi's French 'quitter' (to leave) was written 'kite'.

Reading a language you studied at school thirty-five years ago, written as it sounds to a Guinean for whom Wollof is not his native tongue, presented a rich challenge that I couldn't resist. It appeared to be, I decided, a letter to his family whom he hadn't seen for many years, telling them he had fallen on hard times and would like to come home to the bosom of his kinsfolk, like the Prodigal Son. I did my best, using my pompous 1950s past pluperfect and adding a few flowery embellishments of my own. I noticed long afterwards that Nabi was still around, so either he never found a stamp to send the letter, it got lost in transit, or the family felt that having done without him for so long they could continue to manage, especially if he was penniless.

Then young Musa arrived. There are many Musas here. You must bear with me if it becomes confusing. He was soaked to the skin, muddy-footed, dripping, and he said his school reports had been completely destroyed by the heavy rain. Could I type it for him as he wanted to apply for a job? He had helpfully written out for me his own glowing version of the missing paper, indicating that he had passed all manner of subjects with flying colours. I suspected that it would have surprised his former headmistress had she seen it, but I typed it out anyway, with lots of underlinings and capital letters and asterisks to make it look impressive. Whether it was all true was not the point so much as the fact that Musa, a bright and pleasant boy, was so keen to seek out a job instead of lolling under a tree smoking Lucky Strike and drinking green tea as many of his contemporaries did. The imbalance of youth in the population has created enormous youth unemployment. It is a continuing headache for the President and his ministers, and it leads to big influxes of boys from the provinces coming to the towns and the tourist resorts in search of work, or more often, easy pickings. The tourists, unknowingly, contribute to the problem. They might take a liking to a nice, friendly helpful boy and give him, say D50 (less than the cost, for them of, say, two large beers in a hotel). But it is like three good days' wages to the boy. So now he thinks: Why look for a boring back-breaking job digging roads or shovelling cement, when I can earn more money with my smile and my conversation? A whole new social spiral of discontent and acquisitiveness is set in motion.

I was mulling over these things and handing the typed report to the prize pupil, when I heard a violent banging and some hysterical shouting coming from the rear of the compound where the banana trees are slowly thickening and where the generator shed stood in a lonely spot against the back wall. The generator, prised away from the police who had wanted to keep it indefinitely as evidence, even after the miscreants had been bailed or allowed to escape, was safely sitting in a corner of our bathroom. But perhaps the thieves had come back with reinforcements? Surely they wouldn't dare? What on earth was going on? 'Quick! It's there! It's coming! Take care! Here's a big stick! Aaaaiee! Yaaah!' came the noises. I went round to investigate.

Ray was standing on the wall thumping the generator's tin roof with a steel rod. 'It's that snake again,' he roared. At least he tried to; it actually came out like a nervous cackle. Gambians are terrified of snakes, and they regard all of them as dangerous, regardless of the fact that only three or four extremely reclusive species out of the thirty or so that have been identified are poisonous. The sensible thing to do when you see a snake is to give it a wide berth, stay calm, and let it scuttle off.

This is not the Gambian way. The Gambian way is to leap up and down yelling, throwing bricks, whacking at the ground with sticks. No wonder the odd cornered snake strikes back! I suspect this one, which Ray had surprised (or rather, been surprised by) when he opened the generator shed to find a screw-driver in the midst of Mr M's firewood and cassava (on one occasion, it contained melons, which exploded in the intense metal-enhanced heat) was the same one that he and Musa had been tracking many months before while our barbecue guests sat blissfully eating and drinking under the tree. In the meantime it had grown larger and thicker, and in fact, if you listened to Ray and the villagers who had gathered round to 'help' by screeching and throwing things, it was now the size of a South American anaconda.

It was in fact quite large, black with a red collar, probably very cross at being awakened from its comfortable sleep looped round the rafters of the shed. Mariama, Mr M's practical little wife, shrugged at all this brouhaha and went on washing clothes at the well, rubbing and wringing and achieving a whiteness and brightness far superior to that achieved by automatic washing-machines with panels of complicated programme settings. I sat on a wall and lit a cigarette and settled down to watch the action. The old gardener who comes to sell us frangipani and jasmine and eucalyptus said he would stand outside the shed with a stick and clobber the reptile when it emerged, which it was bound to do if Ray banged and rattled the roof. To be sure, it did, looking highly indignant. The old man took one look, yowled in terror, and ran. His long robe flapped like Mariama's washing. He hitched his skirts up over his twig-like brown shanks and made a sound like Awa-dingding when you tread on her tail; 'Yeeeow! This snake is too big! It cannot be killed with a stick. You need to shoot it with a gun.' Mud spattered the air around his scampering feet, and Mr M, overhearing, nodded sagely in agreement. 'Thank you very much sir, you are right, sir, yessir, that is what I have been saying to Mr Faal many times.' Mr M had been pestering Ray to buy a gun ever since he went to the movies and saw a Charles Bronson film. The thought of him blasting off at every quivering shadow was both funny and fearsome. The noise he made coughing and clacking was quite bad enough without gunshots ricocheting round the walls as well.

His 'trained security guard' technique continued to unnerve our nights. 'Aimless ones!' he would bellow into innocent empty spaces in the bush. 'Why don't you go and do honest work like me? You idle thieves. You will lose your lives here!' I dreaded the advent of any honest visitor after dark had fallen because Mr M never waited to see if the barking of the dogs heralded criminals, callers or cows and goats. He hollered at anyone and anything, and would no doubt have shot at anyone and anything, given half a chance.

The snake, fed-up with all the noise, sneaked off through a hole in the wall. The crowd decided it had gone towards the primary school and set off chanting fiercely in that direction. Ray closed the shed and tried to look calm and tough. Mr M muttered about Magnums and AK47s. Afterwards he came to request medicine for Mariama. 'What seems to be the trouble?' I asked in my unofficial capacity as completely ignorant medic for anyone in the village who can't afford to go to the clinic in Sukutu. (This has included Ray's dad's bronchitis, his grandfather's constipation, cuts and bruises and heat rashes. No one heeds my advice; all they want is a pill or a nasty medicine to swallow. I tried suggesting beans and bran and fresh vegetables for grandpa's atrophied bowels, and he looked at me scornfully. 'Just give me medicine like the clinic gives me,' he begged, showing me an old prescription for cascara.)

'It's her body,' answered Mr M obligingly. 'Yes, but which part of her body,' I asked patiently. Diagnosis is not easy. Dr Tom used to talk of this, people arriving and pointing vaguely at the area between chest and groin so that he had to plough his way through various possibilities like a metal-detector seeking a coin in a beach full of sand. Mariama rolled her eyes pityingly at her husband and indicated her back and shoulders. 'Ah' I said. 'I know the trouble. It's because you let her pull up so much water. Why can't you help her?' He didn't like this at all, and took her to the clinic for a second opinion. She came back with a prescription for medication for 'fever and dizziness'. She had been neither feverish nor dizzy but she took the pills anyway and both she and Mr M seemed to feel much better.

Our friend Mr Camara told us about his visit to the dentist. 'He gave me an injection, but he didn't wait for it to freeze my gums, and began immediately pulling out my teeth. 'So I punched him on the face.

He kept pulling and pulling and I resisted and we both fell in a heap on the floor. The tooth came out as we fell.'

My sister-in-law regularly suffers from 'a pain in the belly', which is certainly a manifestation of teenage menstruation, happening for a few days at the same time every month. All the boys in the family perpetuate the myth of the girl's bad stomach. Female ailments are never discussed, and Ray doesn't know where to look when a white guest says casually: 'Mary's not coming swimming today. She's got her period.' As for pregnancy, it was a genuine surprise for Ray to learn, from me, that white women gestated for exactly the same number of months and in exactly the same way as Gambian women. In the very early months of our marriages, when it might just (miraculously) have been possible for me to conceive, I suggested writing to my daughter and asking her to send me out a pregnancy testing kit. 'You could ask your daughter for that? That would never happen here. A mother and daughter would not discuss these things. It would be very embarrassing.' If so, it's a pity. More mother-and-daughter talk might mean fewer early pregnancies, mothers dying in childbirth and venereal disease.

Frequently, Mr M would seek medicine for his 'bad back'. 'Try exercise,' I would snap back, having spent a morning picking up bits of concrete and palm branches which were lying all over the garden. 'Sometimes bending and stretching can work wonders.' He sniffed at me and went to lie down. My own therapy was swimming. I was 44 when I learned to swim in Whitehill Baths in Glasgow and it took many gulping, spluttering weeks before the young and touchingly patient instructor persuaded me that I wouldn't drown if water went over my head. The eight puffing ponderous breast-strokes I'd achieved under his tuition had now, in the salty supportive Atlantic, multiplied many times and Ray had encouraged me to plunge fearlessly under the breakers instead of floundering on them like driftwood. At the time of the autumn rains I had become as brown as cinnamon from afternoons of sun and salt water. But I knew the wide-armed welcoming sea was also a sinister killer. Seven Ghanaian fishermen had drowned when their pirogue capsized in a storm; small children were easily sucked in by coaxing currents. The sea was not to be trusted, not even to produce food. For it was said Chinese or Senegalese trawlers were dragging all the fish from the sea, and our favourite butterfish and ladyfish were harder to find and dearer to buy.

At Sanyang beach, that empty stretch of pale soft sand, we found dozens of catfish washed up on an angry high summer tide. We took them home and gave them to Mr M and Mariama who smoked them on a fire. They are, I believe, delicious when properly smoked, but they look so ugly with their Pekingese faces I've never tried them yet. I enjoy the smoked bongo fish though. We pretend it's smoked trout for it tastes every bit as good, if it wasn't for the bones.

Awa-dingding, now a scraggy, demanding fixture in our lives, insisted on unsmoked bongo fish and refused to eat anything else. This was a nuisance because the bongo fish sellers came to the village only in late afternoon, on fleets of bicycles, panniers wobbling in front or behind loaded with fish. Butterfish and ladyfish were for tourists and ex-pats. This local fish, rich in minerals and vitamins and protein, was much cheaper and every husband worked to give his wife her daily fish money — usually five to ten dalasis a day depending on social and financial standing. The rice was bought monthly, for about D150 (approximately £11), leaving very little for rent and clothes, transport and fish. No wonder the women worked so hard in their plots growing okra and cassava and 'bissap' (a kind of local sorrel) to eke out their cooking. Or they would hitch up their skirts and wade into the mud-flats looking for shells like winkles to substitute for fish. Old ladies would scour the sands at dawn for cuttlefish, large squid-like molluscs with ugly bodies dripping with tentacle-like extensions and thick inky bags which stained the hands for days. Tourists sought the dried-out shells to take home for their budgies.

Finding food, preparing it and cooking it could take many hours of each day, pounding endlessly at substances we would chop or grate or put through a blender, scraping scales from tiny fish, gathering 'ladies' fingers', pulling yams from the earth. Eating was a ceremony that acknowledged the labour and financial sacrifice that had gone into the meal.

The whole family, and any guests who had popped by unexpectedly (for no-one would ever be turned away) would squat round the communal bowl, big as a baby's bath, enamel painted with lurid roses or hibiscus. Handfuls of food would be scooped up with dexterity, everyone being sure to leave enough so that each had a morsel of fish, and the elders received the delicacies like the eyes and the lips.

It is a social occasion that may look primitive to visiting whites, yet it carries with it a conviviality and recognition of the bonds of family which no longer exist in most of the west. There, families seldom even eat together, and often the kids eat junk-food on the run. Here the kids don't have the option of fish fingers or Big Macs. In fact, I have taken Ray's younger brothers and sisters for what I thought was a treat — chips and Coke in a beach bar — only to see them forcing the chips down unwillingly, probably wishing they were rice. I once saw Eliman chewing on a fish eye. 'Uggh, what does it taste like?' I said, 'Like a minty,' he grinned. 'Minty' is the word for all sweeties, particularly the black mints sold at every street-side stall.

After eating, and much belching and smacking of chops, the guests will rinse their hands, pouring water over them carefully, and mother will remove the bowl, whilst an elder daughter brushes out the spilled rice and discarded bones, which will end up in little heaps outside for the scratching chickens and goats. It was also a time for gossip and stories, news from visitors ('strangers' as they were called) from other villages, speculation about the harvest, the government, the goings-on in a neighbouring compound. And anecdotes like our turtle-rescue, which Ray was able to narrate with many gestures and grimaces and grunts of approval. Our turtle-rescue? Here's the tale:

One day Ray and I took Cameron and Jan to Sanyang. Jan was an exporter to Africa of agricultural and mechanical equipment, anything from water-pumps to fork-lift trucks. She was also an ardent animal-lover who, at home in Surrey, helped run an animal sanctuary and owned her very own Vietnamese pot-bellied pig. Tall, calm, competent she was, of course, a vegetarian, as were two other guests that week, giving me a chance to show off my vegetable curries, soups and peanut sauce with aubergines.

'Come with us to Sanyang,' we said and we all sprawled on the floury sand, swam in the silvery sea, sought out cuttlefish shells for the chickens and pretty pebbles for the garden. On the way home we stopped at Brufut to buy fish for the non-veggie guests, and that's when we saw the turtle. It was lying on its back, its flippers waggling forlornly, the sun stamping on its stomach, its eyes gaping upside-down at the clusters of fishermen and fishwives, children and goats and dogs.

No-one else was taking any notice. Marine turtles are a common sight; sometimes dead ones are washed up on the beach, perhaps after being caught in fishing nets, perhaps having come ashore to lay eggs and being trapped by low tide, I'm not sure. The sale of turtle shells for export is illegal. In fact, ironically, we have one under our baobab tree, because I frightened the owner, a German tourist, so much with tales of potential prosecution that he left the illicit souvenir here with us!

The Banjul Declaration, signed by the President in 1977, says, among other things: 'I solemnly declare that my Government pledges its untiring efforts to conserve for now and for posterity as wide a spectrum as possible of our remaining fauna and flora.' It's a fine declaration, but unfortunately hunters, woodcutters and sand-miners all help to give it a hollow ring. The Chinese and Lebanese, notably, like to go out and shoot small inedible birds 'just for fun' and have chased most of the antelopes over the borders into Senegal.

The turtle continued to look pathetic. Jan cried: 'Oh, oh, Ray, stop, please, stop! We can't leave it like that! We must put it back in the water.' She sent Ray to negotiate with the owner, an elderly and unsentimental Ghanaian lady who had just bought the creature from a fisherman and wasn't about to give it up without a lot of talk and the hope of a quick profit. 'I can sell the meat for three dalasi a portion,' she grumbled. 'But it's such a beautiful creature when it's in the water,' argued Jan. The Ghanaian raised her eyebrows at the crazy tubab. 'I have to feed my family,' she declared and turned her back, while Jan called after her salty

Me, Ray, Helma and Roel the far-travelled Dutch adventurers, Rodger and Chris from Cambridge and (front) brother Lamin and little Dutch Ian.

black shoulders: 'It mustn't be killed. There are not enough turtles left in the oceans. Please, please, think about this!'

A crowd gathered and began discussing the rights and wrongs of the situation. Carried away by Jan's oratory and the sight of tears in her eyes, most of the fishwives came out on her side and yelled at their sister to 'give the turtle to the tubab!' The turtle-owner agreed, reluctantly, to accept 50 dalasis — the sum she said she had paid — to yield up her blinking topsy-turvy captive. Now we had to get it down the rough road, where the bush-taxis turned and the women sold mangoes and melons, and across the beach and into the sea. Ray took one end, Jan took the other. 'Ouch!' she yelped. 'Its claws are sharp and it's jolly heavy.'

Two young fisherboys shrugged, sighed, grabbed the turtle's back quarters and, Ray leading the way, we all stumbled down to the edge of the water, the women cheering, the men muttering, and Cameron skipping alongside calling 'Poor tortoise! Tortoise going to swim now?'

The rotund reptile was deposited, flippers downwards, on the moist spot where the waves licked their sandy lips. It lay exhausted and confused by all this attention and we pushed it encouragingly into the deeper water. Would it swim? Would the shock and fear have been too much for it? The crowd waited, breathless, speechless. Then . . . the flippers were seen to move, the head bobbed doggedly up and down. The crowd roared. Cameron jumped and laughed till he got hiccups. The fishwives smiled and patted Jan's shoulder and said God would bless her. The little grey head bobbed further and further out to sea. It was a very emotional moment. I wiped away a tear. But I felt good. I may describe crises with relish, and as this book continues I may display pique, fury, sorrow and irritability many times. But when it comes right down to it, I'm happy with my life, and moments such as this.

Around the time of the turtle incident, there were a million butterflies in the garden, and a million more on the beach, and a million more around the brightly-lit signs for restaurants and hotels in the town. They were small white ones with charcoal traceries on their wings and they rose and fell like apple-blossom petals on the wind. Cameron tried to catch them, but never did. He called me 'Mariama-g'anny'. 'Hiya, Mariama-g'anny,' he would say in the mornings as he trundled his toy tractor over the bumps. Some local children still confused him with little Dutch Ian, who, back in the Hague, had just had a present from Helma, his mum: a new baby brother called Dominic, conceived right here in the back of the red Land Rover next to our wall festooned with mauve bougainvillaea tendrils. Something else to talk about over the evening meal.

Domestic Disturbances

Cameron talked about the turtle for a long time and to this day when we pass Brufut village, he says 'Tortoise place!' But he had also acquired another friend, a tame baboon which lived on the end of a string tied to a palm tree behind the casino. It appeared to belong to one of the building workers in the area and Cameron had struck up some kind of understanding with it. It checked his hair for nits and accepted bananas from him. Cameron yelled 'Bye-bye b'oon!' on his leave-takings and maintained that it waved to him. Ray said he used to have a pet baboon when he was a little boy, but the women in the village complained that it kept jumping on them and rumpling their hair. Otherwise, I have seen baboons only once in the Gambia, loping across the road on the way to Farafenni; but often in Casamance, at the quarry over the border from Seleti. Farmers dislike them because they cause damage to crops.

People's attitude to living things (and dead things!) varied. Devout white vegetarians devoted to preserving the lives of chickens and lambs would scream and stamp on spiders. Local kids would beat the huge harmless Nile monitor lizards to death for no good reason and hunt, with dogs, wild rabbits in the woods, then bring me the orphaned baby rabbits to nurse back to health. British visitors would look suspiciously at local chicken cooked in tomatoes and onion, in case it was of a different species to the bland white supermarket frozen birds they were used to. (It was; it had a taste. On the other hand, local chickens were so skinny, I too reverted to the imported ones in the supermarket). Some vegetarians would disdain meat and poultry but accept prawn and fish. Some were like Steve and Alison.

Steve and Alison were opposed to killing anything for food. I cooked them nice domadas (peanut stews) then learned that Alison was allergic to peanuts. But we managed to cater for them, and they were an interesting pair, obsessed by African music and dance. They were among a group Ray took to visit Pelican Island in south Senegal, where scores of beaky birds nest and hatch out their gangly young. An idyllic day of salt spray and wide open space; until my son and his friend produced their fishing-rods.

'Eeek!' said Steve and Alison. 'Uggh! You're not going to kill FISH! That's awful. Please, boatman, take us back to the shore.' They were very upset and I respected their views, though I must admit to enjoying watching Ray fishing, and also being very partial to a nice bit of butterfish or barracuda! I had become a pragmatist. In fact, I considered the lifestyle of the Gambian pig, sheep or cow infinitely more natural and therefore acceptable (in spite of the scrawny diet during the dry winter months) than that of plump pale beasts reared in sheds in darkness in Britain. I oppose factory farming, artificial fattening, inhuman methods of breeding, husbandry, transport and slaughter. But I cannot find it in me to get uptight about animals roaming and scavenging in wide open places and living (as they do in the Gambia) to a ripe oldish age before being killed. Actually, I think many probably die of genuine old age, as the ownership of animals, particularly cows, is much more of a status symbol than an actual food production-line.

After Jan and Steve and Alison we had a procession of carnivores. Indeed, some of them threatened to take personal pleasure from slaughtering Stanley who was going through one of his difficult phases, yelping and howling most of the night. I tried to catch him and kill him myself a few time, but he was very nimble on his paws.

Meanwhile, the summer, with its waist-high wet greenness, dark blue-grey dropping skylines, tiny calves cavorting among the tender grasses, birds bustling about in their gaudiest colours to attract new mates (and the evil attentions of Awa-dingding, unfortunately) . . . the summer had faded into our memories as the tourist season hotted up. I became, as usual, irritable and harrassed. You know the description by James Thurber? — 'She developed a persistent troubled frown which gave her the expression of someone who is trying to repair a watch with her gloves on.' That was me, or how I must have looked!

Daft, really, because I did have help with the loo-cleaning dishwashing, verandah-tidying and room-changing. Not just Mariama, wife of Mr M, but also a girl helper, the daughter of a local tradesman. It should have been a doddle. But it wasn't because I was such a fuss-pot. After they had cleaned the toilets I would do them again, tutting and sighing, sweeping the ignored cobwebs from behind the door, washing the base of the toilet-bowl, picking up the bits of paper and plastic that appeared from nowhere to drift among the grasses and wanjho plants like roosting birds.

One way to stop myself working was to flop down beside the tourists and have coffee with them, when I would find myself being pleasantly distracted for hours, airing my knowledge of Gambian politics and history, such as it was, or listening to their tales of travels in other climes. But then, as they wandered to the beach, I would begin niggling again, twisting the caps firmly on the marmalade, picking up crumbs, cleaning the toilets *again*.

Sometimes Ray would take me away from all that. No, not sweep me off for a champagne breakfast on a luxury yacht, but take me with him to Banjul to deal with one or other Government department. This was remember November of 1991. The roads of the capital 'city' were dusty and potholed and open gutters stank of rotten food, and worse, under black oily surfaces. The atmosphere was chaotic. If you were there just to stroll around and maybe buy some odds and ends, it could be fascinating. Otherwise it was oppressive. There were street vendors everywhere carrying bunches of ladies' knickers looped over their wrists, or gaudy towels or tee-shirts or tin cooking pots. There were strolling sheep and goats, wheelbarrows full of cement, rattling, rusting taxis and bustling Lebanese Mitsubishis demanding to be allowed through, quick, quick.

When we reached our destination, some office up a bare staircase with people waiting, sleeping, standing, sitting, in the hallway, on the balcony, in the waiting-room, we'd find that whoever we wanted to see was not available.

'He's gone home with a headache. He's visiting an office up-country. He's gone to the airport. He's in a meeting.' 'But *we* had an appointment with him'. 'Sorry. Come back tomorrow.' This was usually uttered lethargically by a large sleepy secretary bedecked in jewellery and cotton frills, who had been painting her nails or picking her teeth or reading a magazine and resented this interruption to her daily grind. We would go tomorrow and our files would be lost, or the man who was dealing with them was now transferred to a different department, or had resigned, or had died. Kafka would have been at home here.

For light relief, we went shopping. I had become rather fond of supermarket shopping, something which had begun properly to develop only in the previous year or so. You could even, by then, buy cheese, New Zealand cheddar (and, later, if you could afford it, Brie, Gouda and Danish Blue). But most of our supplies still came from the market, and Ray insisted that he could do it quicker and better because white people were asked for higher prices. I doubted this; I haggled harder and refused to accept bashed tomatoes and floppy lettuces, which he took uncomplainingly (usually because the vendeuse was his auntie or his cousin or a friend of his mother's). Anyway, I would sit in the 2CV while he foraged, thankful enough not to have to tramp through alleys of rotten fruit and fish scales, being plied with copper bangles, pink mullets, yellow sea-snails and 'nice batiks, tubab, very cheap.'

The drawback was that where we parked the car was also the unofficial public urinal, or that's how it appeared, for every man in Serrekunda with a loose bladder. As far as the eye could see there would be standing or squatting men ranged along the wall, fumbling under their djelabas or imported Levis. I averted my eyes modestly, but they were oblivious to, or disdainful of, my presence. The air smelled opulently of pee, but if I shut the windows I suffocated from the heat. Ray, the speedy shopper, seemed to take ages and ages, arriving back with his odorous plastic bag of prawns or fish with the potatoes dumped on top of the already bursting tomatoes, and enough lettuce to feed an army, most of which would have to be thrown out, brown and bedraggled, next day.

Carol, my daughter, had come to stay, and she helped at the huts, showing Awa and Mariama how to do hospital corners and reminding them to dust the mirror and check under the mattresses for ants. Often, though, we spent a great deal of time reminiscing together, scandalmongering about old friends in Glasgow and new ones in the Gambia, mopping Cameron's head when he tipped porridge over it and discussing ancient articles in *Newsweek* to keep, as we told one another, our brains active. Carol was job-hunting. Rab had already found work, in a school in the dockland area of Banjul. In the beginning, we ran him bleary-eyed to Serrekunda where he insinuated himself into the seething mass of commuters all intent on occupying the same bus.

Bus-travel is an education here. Loud conversations are held over your head in several languages, the people at either side of you are invariably enormous women with angular elbows, scratchy wicker baskets and a need to spit out of the window at intervals, or earnest schoolboys with jotters labelled 'Farming' or 'Social Science'. Something eventful happens on most journeys. For Rab, it was the apprehension of a thief. 'Thief, thief!' the cry went up and everyone on the bus battered and pushed the poor culprit up and down the length of the bus until reluctantly disgorging him into the hands of a policeman.

When Ray and I, or Carol and Rab, were away from the compound, Mr M could always be relied on to look after things in his own inimical fashion. His vision of himself as an executive type was actively encouraged by Graeme and Norman, two arrivals from Scotland, who found his personality hilariously engaging and egged him on in all kinds of mischief. 'I think I should take you back to Stirling as my butler', said Norman ingenuously. This made Mr M dream of a new life abroad and I swear he started packing and practising how to bow and scrape with a Scottish accent. Then BBC Radio Scotland arrived. I was out; Mr M was magnificent.

'Yessuh!' I am the garden-master', declared Mr M, while Norman and Graeme hid behind a palm-tree giggling. He straightened himself up, grinned to show his remarkable teeth and tugged at his dirty tee-shirt, patting his hair, in case, I suppose, there were any hidden cameras. 'Do tell me, sir', said the young radio reporter (researcher for a travel programme) 'what are you actually working on at the moment?' It was Mr M's finest moment. Coughing prodigiously he explained that he was preparing wanjho plants;, famous for their fruits used in making a special tea which was jokingly known as Vimto. It was indeed true that as time had passed, less and less of our soil was occupied by useful things like cassava and tomatoes, and more and more by his ubiquitous tea plantation.

'Fascinating,' said the interviewer, backing away from a cacaphonic cough. 'And how, tell us, do you prepare this tea?' Mr M almost burst a bloodvessel as he launched into a long, disjointed rigmarole punctuated by many a 'thank-you, suh!' The reporter left, looking haggard, while Graeme and Norman, straight-faced, assured our watchman that he was a star.

Meanwhile, I had been visiting the headquarters of Action Aid in Kanefing to hear about a visit from a group of Scottish Venture Scouts to an up-river village. The NGOs had mixed feelings about such trips. On the one hand the young people involved came with the most altruistic of intentions, and their families and friends at home raised large sums of cash for the work of the charity overseas. 'But it take a terrific amount of our staff's time driving around, using up petrol, visiting local chiefs and other officials to appraise them of the visit, arranging accommodation and food for the young people and checking that the equipment they've had shipped out is received safely!', explained one sore-pressed aid worker. The Scouts wanted to build some school classrooms for the Gambians; a very worthy and generous gesture. 'But we have an unlimited supply of labour of our own, Gambians who need work and know the conditions for local building. Really, it's money we need'.

The reason that so many youth groups come to the Gambia to do their good work is quite simple. It is only six hours away by plane, it is at peace with its neighbours, the official language is English and it has some very nice beaches for relaxing on between official activities.' You don't for instance get Guides and Scouts going to Latin America or the Pacific... too far, too dear, too dodgy', continued the cynical aid worker. 'So they all come here'. He sighed, but in fact the visits do serve a useful purpose, if only to foster good relations between two races and let the Scots kids see how the other half of the world lives. They were a super bunch, as I found out for myself. Action Aid drove me and Carol, with her camera looped round her neck, up-country to Pakali Ba where the Scots were based during the construction of classrooms in two different hamlets. Their tents, which were being shipped from Korea, of all places, hadn't arrived, so they were camped in empty existing schoolrooms and had erected their own latrines and camp kitchens. The bush surrounded them, flat acres of duty yellow land with accacia and palm and occasional clusters of round mud huts to break the monotony.

It's a shame that the road doesn't follow the amazing Gambia River but instead runs an angular route mostly well away from the sinuous

Daedalian course of the great geeny-fawn water where hippos bathe and the famous white crocodile lurks. A series of islands make the process even more intriguing — Elephant Island (no, none since about 1910!), Deer Island, Baboon Island (yes, the olive baboon and many monkeys; once there were chimpanzees, being re-integrated after captivity in Europe but I think they've all gone); and the giant island of Kai Hai, said to be haunted by a dragon which from time to time eats the occasional villager. I've never been there but the Insight Guide to the Gambia and Senegal says 'Visiting the islands by canoe, one can certainly sense an ominous atmosphere perhaps because of the overpowering foliage which casts a permanent shadow . . .'

In the village, the elders were assembled in force to welcome the Venture Scouts, and many long and fulsome speeches were made. These were made mostly in Mandinka, then translated, even more lengthily, into English. They went on and on. The sun grew higher and hotter. Carol wandered about photographing children and goats. Inside one occupied classroom, where rows of small black heads bent over their desks, a teacher's voice could be heard screaming: 'Shut up!" She sounded like I sounded when Stanley barked at three in the morning. We chatted to the young Scots; students, nurses, brickies, an amiable and undemanding bunch, and I wrote a feature about them for the *Edinburgh Evening News,* illustrated by Carol.

It had been hard for me to tear myself away from the compound. I peeled onions and potatoes and garlic and left them ranged beside the relative knives and saucepans with little notes explaining every step of the cooking preparations for Ray. Even then, I worried so much that he wouldn't be able to cope that I persuaded the Action Aid driver to leave promptly after the speeches and hurtle us homewards in record time. Mr M had become so full of his debut as a radio star, strutting his stuff in front of Graeme and Norman, being persuaded by them that he could become as big as Eddie Murphy, that it was difficult to distract him by such mundane things as opening the gates for us. I don't suppose Eddie Murphy ever gets asked to carry crates of Julbrew and sweep up leaves.

We all had to spring into action, though, for our next barbecue. We kept having these outdoor ordeals (as I secretly began to think of them), at which Ray cooked fish in aluminium foil over burning embers, usually after I had peeled all the potatoes and onions, laid out his herbs and tomato paste, set the trays of plates and cutlery, made the salad and cut up the bread. Afterwards everybody would cluster round him and say 'Ray, that was wonderful, thank you very much', as I cleared the plates away and washed the dishes. We did it partly to entertain the tourists, sometimes with local drums and dancing, or at least with some blaring cassette music, reggae or Bala Maal or Youssu Ndour or some other West African hero.

I found myself panicking before every one, though I usually enjoyed them when they happened. On this occasion, we decided to use the Braun food-mixer Carol had brought out from the UK. Ray switched on the generator early and we all eyed the appliance suspiciously. 'How do you open it? How do you start it? Why isn't it going?' This cackhanded ignorance about mechanical gadgets issued not from the Gambians, for whom there might be some excuse, but from me, the world's most untechnologically literate woman. I think I came to Africa to escape from gadgets, but they had followed me. 'Oh, my God', I snapped. 'The guests are arriving in half-an-hour'; and we all set to slicing and chopping and grating by hand while the mixer sat simpering emptily at us. Next day, Norman, the Mr M-baiter, who was a chef by profession and about to start a new job making tempting après-ski teas and stylish dinners in Val D'Isère during the Winter Olympics, came to our rescue and demonstrated the ridiculously simple methods involved in working a machine that most British housewives could use with their eyes shut. Ray ran amok delightedly mincing onions by the hundredweight and slicing enough cucumbers to make sandwiches for a Royal garden-party.

On the night of the barbecue, when we had gathered up fish-heads and foil from the hibiscus and oleanders, stacked up the empty winebottles and located the tapes of Bob Marley and Dire Straits, our exquisite and energetic friend Caroline trilled 'Let's go to a disco!' Me, I wanted to curl up in bed with my aching back and onion-flavoured fingers, but middle-aged wives of young husbands have to beware of showing signs of decrepitude and dullness. 'What a good idea!' I lied, and went to get changed and scrub my hands with toilet soap. 'I'll come too,' said sonsy Norman. 'You can show me the bright lights of the Gambia.' Bright lights?

We drove through the velvety darkness, through winding backstreets, searching for blaring music, flashing lights, bopping crowds. The posh disco near the Senenegambia Hotel had closed down while the German boss went home for medical treatment. The two normally very jolly discos in Bakau had inexplicably settled down into silent shadow.

Ray knew some low but lively dives, he said, off the tourist beat but they too were closed. Norman chortled. Caroline moaned. I thought gleefully we might all go home to bed. But at last, many miles later we arrived at Memory on the airport road, which, in spite of the name, we'd forgotten about. What a nice time I had, after all! The clientèle was allblack, except for us. Shadows gyrated in the moonlight, for the dance area was out-of-doors in a dark courtyard with just the odd glow from a lantern, insects waltzing round the beam, stars winking through nodding branches. The sound system had laryngitis but it didn't matter. Most of the customers were serious dancers who were there to dance till they dropped, not to show off their hairstyles or shirts. Music from Mali, Nigeria, Senegal and the Gambia boomed and twanged and rippled and reverberated. The dance-floor was concrete and the toilets were execrable but the beer was cheap and I was glad I'd come. Caroline ran us home, sticky with sweat and giggling foolishly as we tried not to waken Graeme (a devout non-dancer) or Stanley, always good for a night-shattering explosion of barks.

Inevitably, the morning after was less fun. I trudged around feeling like a chewed rag, a feeling which had been growing upon me since the season started, mostly self-induced. Carol and Rab advanced on me menacingly. 'You and Ray need a break. Go away. Take the day off. Leave everything to us.' I began to remonstrate. 'What about the guests' supper? Can you work the generator? Will you find the chilli pepper and the paper napkins? What if . . .?' They listened to me blankly then roared 'GO AWAY!' So we did. As we drove out of the garden, my daughter had mockingly lined up Mr M, Mariama, Awa, Cameron and Eliman into a guard of honour. They all saluted stiffly, grins cracking their faces, as we left, waving back like the President and his Lady. Go south, young man, I ordered Ray and we bumped and rattled through Bijilo village, saluting swarms of children. The road was a rosy, gritty ribbon between towering stalks of maize and millet and whispering elephant grasses. Squirrels and mongooses darted from one side to the other and ospreys and fish-eagles hovered overhead, scanning the ocean, ready to plunge. We stopped at Tanji to buy some copper-brown smoked fish, and by the time we reached Sanyang I had forgotten to worry about whether Carol would clean the rooms properly and whether Mr M would fill the feeder tank and whether Rab was really as good a cook as Carol said he was. The beach was pale powdery yellow and the sea flat and almost still. I lay on my back and floated: yet another of my skills acquired in Africa. I forgot the smell of urine behind the market, the obfuscations of Gambian bureaucracy, the mawkishness of Mr M. Lebanese, German and Gambian picnickers cavorted on the beach and pirogues drifted over the surface of the sea like floating sticks in the distance. On the way home in a misty mauve twilight we presented Ray's mum with a large ladyfish bought indecently fresh from a fisherman. At the compound we were forbidden by Carol and Rab to enter the kitchen so we sat under the baobab playing cards until Rab's chicken curry was ready. I resolved, dreamily, to be calm and serene on the morrow.

My little patch of Africa is about an acre-and-a-half of weeds, wanjho, tropical flowers, cassava (yam) plants as big as rhododendrons, accacia thorn bushes, lacklustre bananas and youthful lemon, orange, mango and mandarin trees with dark green leaves. Red-cheeked cordon bleu, tiny birds of vivid turquoise with crimson splashes either side of the head, gossip on thorn bushes. Pied crows, horrible noisy birds which push the yellow weavers away from the leavings in the cats' food bowl, clump about on the corrugated roof so that we never have silence. Even if they aren't around, the mourning doves are alternately chuckling or sobbing, 'coo-roo-roooo'. The cats clamour for food constantly. Calls of greeting come from the lane. 'Salaam Aleikum. Na nga def?'

At this time, I was cooking on a double gas-ring, with water carried in buckets. We had no TV and the generator's behaviour was hit-or-miss. But it was, and is, home. People liked it, seeking not to lounge by opulent pools or eat in restaurants but to share our fish and rice under the tree, walk to the village or to the beach, sit serenely reading or dozing or watching the birds. I would drift around, (on days unblemished by visits to offices in Banjul or failure to find prawns in the market or pangs of loneliness when Ray took visitors off to Casamance or Tendaba) and I would realise how much I had grown to love this place, these people, my African life. The day after the beach idyll was, at first, a day like that.

Then I realised that the screams and snorts and thumps emitting from the hut that Mariama and Mr M now occupied (built specially for then to manoeuvre them out of our tourist hut) were human noises and not merely the caws, cackles and coos of various feathered and furred species. 'You are a donkey!' thundered Mr M, in that powerful and resonant voice. 'Then that makes two of us!' counter-blasted Mariama. For a man to be called a donkey is the ultimate insult, even if Mr M thought it acceptable thus to define his wife. There was another thud and a yelp and Mariama scuttled outside lopsidedly with a large bruise dulling the silken brown of her thigh. I don't believe I have mentioned that Mariama was several months pregnant at this juncture. She was a tough, sturdy, lovable girl who treated her pregnancy casually, without fuss, as do most African women. I continually nagged at Mr M to get her fruit and vitamins and milk. He would say 'Yes, yes. Look, I bought her some Sprite!' He treated her condition even more casually than she. She gardened, washed, pulled water from the well, carried big bundles on her head. But now this! It was, I swore, the last straw. 'He's got to go!' I cried.

Wife-beating is not uncommon in the Gambia, but not in my backyard, not if I could help it. Carol came across and scowled at Mr M and swept Mariama off to her hut. 'You'll spend the night here,' she commanded. 'Have a cup of tea. Don't cry.' The few tourists in residence gazed at Mr M disapprovingly coolly, even his big pal Norman. Mr M muttered to himself and skulked about clucking like a blackcap babbler (I just can't resist these ornithological asides!) and we decided he must go in the morning. Mariama spent most of the night weeping, cursing the ill-fortune that gave her such a husband, and then being made to laugh by Carol, who has often been heard to say 'All men are bastards; don't let it get you down!' and no doubt said it this time too. In the morning, still limping but dry-eyed, the defiant little Jola girl announced that she was going to relatives in Serrekunda and never wanted to see 'that pig' again. She packed her most treasured possessions, notably her plastic washing bucket and basin and her Thermos flask and some clothes, balanced them all on her head and marched off down the lane, leaving her spouse open-mouthed at the door of their hut.

'As for you,' I said coldly when she had disappeared from view, 'You can go! Go!' I pointed dramatically into the distance like a bad actor in a Victorian melodrama. He trudged off, looking pathetic, and re-turned later with a donkey and cart on which he placed his broken chairs, a sofa with no seat-cushions, his bedding and a sack of empty bottles and tins collected from our rubbish-heap. I watched his and the donkey's heads bobbing along the other side of our wall and I fretted about Mariama. Would she be all right? Would her relatives take care of her? Where would she have her baby? What if Mr M sought her out and walloped her again because she had, by his way of thinking, lost him his job?

'Look on the bright side,' said Ray, always seeking to make a little profit. 'We can tidy up the hut and use it for tourists.' I looked doubtful. It fell just about as far short of luxury as you might imagine. Still, we moved Mr M's mattress out, discovering that it had not been turned for all the months they had slept on it and that the sacking had been eaten through by ants so that soggy chunks of straw dropped everywhere. It was what was called a local mattress, which we had bought new for about £5, being assured it was filled with the cleanest best-quality straw. We brushed and scrubbed the concrete floor and poured toxic fluids into the crevices where ants seemed to enter. We whitewashed and installed a foam mattress, a bright bed-cover and a basket chair. None of these disguised the fact that it had a corrugated roof with no ceiling panels, unglazed windows covered with mosquito-net and a tin flap and considerable proximity to the lane where the trucks plied their smoky noisy paths on the way to the sand-mining operations. Who would want to rent it? But then Karen came along.

She was a very young, very intelligent German student of journal-ism with spiky hair, colloquially excellent English and a three-month placement with Radio Gambia. She needed cheap accommodation. We had it. To be sure, in time she began to appreciate the distinct disadvan-tages of the ex-watchman's hut, but at least no-one could say it wasn't a bargain. Sharing its romantic simplicity with her, within a few days, was Werner, hot-foot from Dakar. He was a large floppy mechanic of whom her parents didn't approve because he was 'not good enough for her'. They snuggled in like squirrels and became — as Helma and Roel had before — part of our lives for many months. Under that awful rippled roof they were to share malaria together, have rows and make up, collect batiks and little blue and red enamelled attaya tea-pots, drums and bags of herbs and peppers so that when it was finally time for Karen to go home (Werner having left weeks before to go back to mending cars) she was told that her luggage was so overweight she would have to pay hundreds of dalasis surcharge.

'Keep it all, then,' she wept at the airport staff, but Ray dug into his own pocket and borrowed from various friends in the vicinity and they got her through, drums dangling, fabrics flopping, strings of little tea-pots tinkling like bells. We, meanwhile, were once again watchmanless, which has advantages (no foolish prattle, no wife-battering, no sleeping in wheelbarrow as Musa, for example used to do), but also disadvantages. Once again, together or separately, we hauled up countless gallons of water, filled the tank next to the tourist toilets (a matter of Ray clambering up a home-made ladder and tipping buckets into a 200-litre oil-drum. Unfortunately it doesn't last long). We raked up garden waste and ran to open the gate for cars, and we flashed torches bravely when Stanley barked in the dead hours of night. It was tiring but there was a certain satisfaction in it, and as always when we did things ourselves, the place seemed neater and smoother to operate.

After a mere few days, a pair of big skelly eyes and a mouthful of disorganised teeth appeared over the wall. The eyes were moist with remorse, the teeth were glinting with hope. 'We are very, very sorry,' Mr M ventured hopefully. 'We cannot sleep. We miss you very much. Allah knows our hearts and our hearts are full of sadness.' He smiled sadly. 'We?' I echoed. 'So you have been with Mariama?' 'Oh, yes. She is sorry she called me a donkey. We have compromised. And' (for he saw my steely glare) 'she has forgiven me for my little offence.' Pah! Some women never learn. We supposed that, if a true reconciliation had been effected, we should be pleased. Later Mariama arrived, smiling, shaking hands, crying tears of joy when she saw Carol and Cameron. They'd only been gone a few days but you'd think it had been six months.

'Is it true? Have you forgiven him?' we asked. 'Are you sure you want him back?' 'Ach, that pig!' she spat dismissively on to the charred earth. 'What else can I do. He's all I have.'

We learned later that Mr M had originally planned to marry Mariama's younger, prettier sister, who had been promised to him as a child. The family had reneged on the deal and given her to another, richer suitor. Mariama had been given, not having had any say in the matter, to an old and impotent man, who had subsequently died, leaving her a very young but poor widow. 'Why don't you just make do with Mariama instead?' the family suggested obligingly to Mr M, being anxious to get her off their hands. Thus came our odd couple together, but it could scarcely be described as a union made in heaven.

In the beginning he tried hard to make up for the nasty behaviour of a few days before. 'Please to give me time off this afternoon,' he asked importantly. 'I want to take my wife to see the sea.' Yes, it was true; Mariama had never seen the ocean, even though it roared and trembled and breathed its salty breath into the air jut seven minutes from where she had been living with us for the past six months. She was an up-country village girl and the sea was as foreign to her as the desert to a forest-dweller.

When she saw it, she was ecstatic. 'Oh, it's big!' she breathed. 'It roars with such a loud voice. I like it very much, but I am afraid of it.'

We decided after a cough-filled, 'Yessuh'-punctuated discussion with Mr M, that it would now be more sensible for Mariama, who was drawing nearer and nearer to her delivery date, to give up working for us and stay with the family in Serrekunda, near to the clinic and (we reasoned privately) watched over by others should her husband get violent again. Now that Karen was in the hut, and not specially wishing to have Mr M back as a live-in fixture, we told him he could live with the relatives in town and come to work for us daily, on sufferance, as a watchman-gardener. Which left us with the problem of someone to do night duty, if we ourselves were to get any sleep at all. Someone always turns up in the end, and this time it was Ibrahim.

He was Senegalese and we conversed in awful French. He huddled in a blanket and, from time to time, patrolled the compound, passing his torch-beam over the toilets, the generator hut, the verandah.

Stanley hadn't properly made Ibrahim's acquaintance. Every time our new watchman started his tour around the compound, the dog went crazy. Werner appeared from the ex-watchman's hut, blinking without his glasses, hair tousled, fulminating in very explicit German about what he would do if he caught that **** sweinhund. Who could blame him? We were all hollow-eyed. But we solved the matter in the end. Stanley was lured with morsels of fish and attached to his collar and lead, which poor Ibrahim clutched all night, trailing his canine shadow behind him whenever he went on the move with his torch. Stanley seemed to like the feeling of partnership, togetherness. It made him feel important.

Life would flow smoothly now, I persuaded myself. But would it? In a few weeks, after all, it would be Christmas . . .

Life, Death and Marmalade

Sheila, the sheep Ray brought me as a present from up-river the year before, was sick, and so was her little lamb. The baby had no name, because then I would have become personally attached to it, which wouldn't have been a good idea. Sheila was a pet but she was the first in a dynasty, we planned, of potential mutton stews and chops. She was a nice sheep, amiable tail-wagging, recognising my approach and waiting for scraps of pizza or pieces of bread. But we had grown apart a little for Ray had insisted she spend most of her time in the village with the other sheep, because he believed, perhaps correctly, that sheep were gregarious creatures, but also so that her carnal impulses might be satisfied and she might coincidentally get pregnant on a regular basis.

This lamb was her first, but now both were brought round to our compound showing signs of illness. It was just before Christmas. It always impressed me that Ray's uncles and aunties could so swiftly and accurately recognise their own sheep and mine, for fond as I was of Sheila she looked pretty much the same to me as all her ovine contemporaries. Today, however, she was very sorry for herself and the baby looked awful, weak and tottering and listless. 'We must take them to the vets at the ITC,'' said Ray and lifted them into the back of the Land Rover. Later he returned and said they'd been given injections and had to stay in our garden until they were well, and have a series of baths in a solution of a powder prescribed to get rid of parasites.

'You've to mix 24 milligrams of this stuff with three gallons of water,' he said helpfully, handing me the little package, while the sheep bleated mournfully. At that particular time I was carrying a tray of cups in one hand and a tray of jams and marmalades in the other. I had an order for fried eggs from our Germans, and more hot water for tea for the English couple. My female 'helpers', young Awa, 'assisted' by a very pretty girl called Sukai, now that Mariama had gone off to have her baby, were sitting chatting animatedly by the well, while I rushed around gathering up banana skins and breadcrusts and dirty plates.

The last thing I needed right then, I explained with what I thought was commendable restraint, was to start shampooing a sheep. We talked little brother Eliman into doing it instead. The mother emerged looking soft and white and demanding breakfast but the lamb became sicklier and sicklier, shivering in a dull corner by the rubbish heap. Eliman lit a fire to keep it warm. Perhaps callously, I urged him to burn some of the rubbish while he was at it, for the heap was growing as high as the house. Now, though, we were choosier about what we dumped there. Carol had initiated a compost heap. She lectured us solemnly about the importance of saving bio-degradable items such as cassava peelings and old rice. It was a good project. I think possibly it demanded more scientific knowledge than either Carol or I possessed, for the business of stacking vegetable matter in heaps or digging it into pits to allow rotting and fermentation and the release of nutrients, while pathogens are destroyed, is remarkably complex. You could combine, I read in a farming feature, residues with a high C:N ratio, such as rice straw, with material of a low C:N ratio, such as animal manure. There must be sufficient air and moisture and the heap must not be too dense.

We didn't have rice straw, and I didn't think the droppings of the dogs and cats would count as animal manure, but we did our best. Most of our leavings went to the pets, including the sheep, or were snatched by the pied crows that clomped about heavily on our roof but I hung a plastic bag in the kitchen for peelings and egg-shells and old tea-bags. At times it burst like a boil and dropped its stinking matter all over the floor at which point I would curse the entire conservation movement, but I was assured by Carol that we would, in due course, have a splendid mound of organic fertiliser and that she would be able to grow lots of crops for us, as a change from the cassava and beans and ubiquitous wanjho plants. Mr M's 'master gardener' claim seemed to have faded somewhat, especially since his tea plants had been discussed with the BBC reporter. (We never told Mr M that the interview was cut from the eventual programme that was used on Radio Scotland. It would have been too traumatic for him). It was only much later, incidentally, that I learned that the leaves of the wanjho plants, known as 'bissap' were a sort of sorrel and full of nourishment.

Had I known that then, perhaps I would have been less scathing about the dense rows of green which marched all over the space behind the huts. I would have gathered the leaves and chopped and boiled them to add to stews and soups and peanut sauce. But Ray never thought to tell me. 'I never thought you'd like it,' he explained when I finally made the discovery. 'It's a local vegetable.' I wonder what other local treasures I am missing. I see the women in the market buying all manner of roots and leaves and seeds, but finding out exactly what they are and what they are for is difficult, for Ray only knows the Wollof name and is hazy about their preparation . . . cooking is woman's work, after all!

Rab was no help to Carol in her horticultural pursuits because by the time he came home from his daily teaching job in Banjul he was exhausted. Just going to Banjul is a wearisome prospect; actually to work there all day must have been hell. Once, long ago, it was mooted that the Gambia should build a completely new capital city at Sukuta, the nearest small town (or large village) to Bijilo, where once Ray had travelled to school. The scheme was abandoned for lack of cash, but I am often tempted to think that the only thing to do with Banjul is bury it. Then I look at the Portuguese colonial buildings in the back streets and the almost Venetian aspect of the Bund Road (if you ignore the night-soil dumped there and the rusting boats) and I sense the elegant history that lies behind and beneath the surface decay. It would be a shame to let that go. (Indeed, nowadays roads have been surfaced, drains have been cleaned and trees have been planted — not before time!)

We had stopped taking Rab to Serrekunda in the mornings, partly because we were committed to coffee-making, jam-replenishing and the usual toilet-cleaning grind, and partly because we had discovered that our Finnish neighbour, Essa, had a workers' bus leaving from near our compound at 7 am daily. Rab, therefore, would sprint across the garden, dodging wanjho plants, tucking his shirt into his trousers at one minute before seven, clamber over the wall by the generator shed and gallop across the football field to leap on to the bus just as it was pulling away from Essa's yard.

The Continuing Education Department for which he worked deserves a mention. It was founded fairly recently by a group of eminent retired headmasters, concerned about the many children who dropped out of regular schooling.

There were may reasons for the high drop-out rate. School fees were beyond the reach of many families for more than a few terms. Parents often encouraged children to stay home and help with the peanut-sowing, hoeing, cooking and washing, or tending smaller children while the mother went to work. Some children simply couldn't keep up with the stream, either through long absences or lack of conventional intellectual ability, and remedial teaching was seldom possible. They simply fell by the wayside to become semi-literate adults with no hope of any but the most unskilled jobs. The C.E.D., started in a vacant primary school building in the depressed dock area of Banjul, sought to remedy this situation, bringing youngsters back into the classroom and encouraging them to catch up with the mainstream and even join it again. Rab found it tough going, as, naturally, his pupils' understanding of English (in which all text-books and test-papers were written), was often minimal. He also taught a Friday afternoon class of A-level students, and even there he found the English usage often under par. It was hard going for the kids too for their syllabus, devised by the West African Examination Board, included such choice items as

Coriolanus, Wilfred Owen and T.S Eliot, none of which can have had much cultural, linguistic or historical relevance to the life of an African teenager.

Rab bought a motor-bike to ease his commuting. It broke down after a couple of days. Most things do. It is the uncharitable belief of some residents that the reason mechanics mend things so badly and ineffectively is so that customers must keep returning time and time again. The enthusiasm is there. Any chap with a spanner of his own will claim to be an engineer and spend many hours tapping and poking and fiddling in the hope that by luck he'll hit on what is actually wrong with your vehicle. But few have solid theoretical and practical training and reliable spare parts are equally hard to find. Many parts are imported from Nigeria and their lifespan can be unnervingly brief.

My own flirtation with technology was merely in my relationship with the new food-mixer. After circling it warily and having had lessons from Norman the chef on how to open it, start it and stop it, I had learned to love it. It sat oddly in my utilitarian kitchen with its bags of rice and onions, lack of laminated tops, stainless steel or slick appliances. A small white beacon of labour-saving smugness.

In it, provided we could get the generator to work to supply the electricity it needed, I made the ingredients of courgette-and-green pepper soup with mint, tomato, cassava and bean broth, or smooth and creamy peanut sauce. I felt guilty at the speed with which I could pulverise vegetables into submission, while the women in the village pounded for hours at peanuts and grain and cassava with their big wooden pestles and mortars. I never had a food mixer when I lived in Glasgow's Merchant City. But then, neither did I have a sick sheep, a watchman with his own tea plantation, or twelve people sitting on my verandah waiting for me to produce a satisfying meal. Not that I didn't make the odd mistake. Once the fruit fool I'd concocted tasted inexplicably odd and the guests surreptitiously slid their untouched plates to one side. 'What did you put in it?' asked Ray suspiciously. 'Just watermelon, banana, imported apples and some of that papaya you brought back from the market,' I answered innocently. 'Papaya? Papaya? That wasn't papaya! that was pumpkin,' he snorted.

Christmas was nearly upon us. This may be a nine-tenths Muslim country but everyone likes Christmas. I tried to describe to Ray what a British Christmas was like, but it was difficult. On the one hand I would talk of crackling log fires and boughs of holly and sparkling snow with robins and beaming snowmen and children skating and chestnuts and hot punch and happy carollers. Then I would erase the picture-book Christmas-card fantasy from my word-sketch and tell him the real truth of irritable, pushing crowds in shopping centres, drizzling chilly rain, horrible debt being accumulated in seconds, tacky electronic toys bankrupting parents, greedy supercilious kids, who would be appalled at a sock full of tangerines and nuts.

Either picture, or even a gentle compromise between the two (for hadn't I sat in front of a crackling log fire at my friend Irene Auld's house in Ayrshire? Hadn't I laughed and cried emotionally at the carollers in George Square?) . . . seemed as distant and unreal as the surface of another planet. I had to force myself to seek out Christmas cards in the few places that sold them, and had to shake myself by the scruff of the neck to invent Christmas and Hogmanay menus like a good seaside landlady.

Any old festival, never mind the inspiration behind it, is an excuse to laugh and dance and play the drums. At Christmas, the children make boats or houses from delicately cut-out paper made from wood-bark, as intricate as a paper doily, and they place a small oil-lamp inside and tramp round houses and businesses in procession, followed by a bevy of drummers. The 'fanals' as they are called can be anything from eighteen inches to eighteen feet in length, carried by anything from a few small children, begging for butut coins to a host of young men and women dancing and singing and begging for much larger donations.

Small shops selling Islamic pictures, robes and slippers don't mind hanging up some scraps of tinsel paper, and the bars all hoist up faded decorations, some of which they forget to take down so that they are still flapping there, bleached white, in mid-July.. There are special discos and restaurant menus, and the incredibly talented singer-musician Youssu Ndour and his band Super Etoile traditionally do massive concerts in Bakau Stadium. The Senegambia Hotel, a couple of miles from us, and a number of rich Lebanese home-owners always let off magnificent firework displays at Christmas or New Year or both. Meanwhile by day, the sun blazes down and people drink sparkling wine and pull crackers (brought with them in their holiday luggage) wearing bikinis and reddening tans the colour of Rudolph's nose.

Our own Christmases tend to incorporate catering for any tourists who are in residence, plus any friends who just pop down and any kids from the village who turn up hoping for paper-hats and sweeties. We ourselves don't buy these — benign visitors usually bring them along. We don't have turkey and pudding. We have barbecued barracuda or tuna and fruit salad. Not fruit fool - once was enough!

And we have Big Sara and Choam, my friend the tailoress, from the village, who bring a batch of kids to dance and sing for us. The event is not always as happy and peaceful as it should be — but then, neither were some Glasgow Christmases I remember.

This time, war almost broke out. Everyone was sitting around drinking and giggling, or dancing frenetically, while I dashed about replacing glasses (of which we never had enough) and watching uneasily as my son and his friends from Glasgow secreted splashes of the Famous Grouse into their glasses when they thought I wasn't looking.

I caught sight of our Land Rover driver, dancing with astonishing vigour, leaping and prancing and twirling like the star of a Russian ballet, but with less precision and more abandon. In fact, he kept falling over. Only then did I realise that he was as pickled as a walnut. Later I discovered that he was a reformed (or now unreformed) alcoholic and had been swallowing copious amounts of home-made African gin all afternoon. He might have handled that, but my generous son had insisted he try 'a wee hauf' as well. I called him over and sat him down and lectured him on the responsibilities of staying sober when he was supposed to be driving our drummers and dancers home at the end of the evening. 'Sh'no problem, Mariama,' he hiccuped, and I sent someone to fetch Ray's young brother Lamin, a total abstainer. Ray appeared and found out what had happened and asked him to hand over the key. 'Sh'my key,' he slurred. 'No-onesh going'a drive exshep me.' Voices were raised. Ray tried to grab the key and the driver tried to punch him. Next thing they were lurching at one another, while Ray yelled: 'He insulted me! He insulted my mother! Did you hear that? Let me get at him!' and several strong black hands were hauling them apart. He swayed from side to side with a bleary baleful expression insisting he could drive even if he couldn't stand and that Ray was a **** and a ****.

His new wife wept loudly on the side-lines while her baby, born sometime before their nuptials were legalised, howled its support. I ran about smiling fixedly through tears of embarrassment and telling the guests not to worry, just a little tiff, a mere misunderstanding, ho-ho-ho. In the end, the driver was hauled away by a bunch of villagers, still hurling imprecations at Ray.

'Don't ever come near this compound again,' Ray called after him. The guests said next day they'd enjoyed every minute of the party. Later we heard that this man's behaviour had antagonised half the village. His drinking bouts got longer and longer and one night he staggered into Ray's dad's compound and began insulting everyone there, in very obscene language, including goggling grannies and bewildered toddlers in his tirade. Most of his spleen was, however, aimed at Ray's Uncle Ebou, who eventually got fed up listening and punched him so that he collapsed in an unconscious heap. The police were only then summoned and they, very sensibly, thanked Ebou and shovelled the body into their clapped-out car and took him to the police-station to sober up. Needless to say when we meet our ex-driver now, we greet each other with forgiving Gambian courtesy.

The village, for all its Muslim beliefs, is not unused to this kind of spectacle. A few years ago, Ray told me, a fugitive from a well-known family in Newcastle came to lodge in his compound, far away from an English wife and inherited business responsibilities and determined, it appeared, to drink himself into oblivion. The villagers offered him hospitality and sympathy; Gambians, even the most devout of them, are blessedly tolerant of other people's weaknesses. But even the most open-minded of them began to look askance when he staggered home with two satin-hipped trollops at a time, and they worried, with some justification, when his alcohol intake began to include the deadly local gin and on occasion substances like metal polish and, Ray swears, bleach.

In the end he dropped dead one day in Banjul, leaving debts, speculation about the cause of death (even murder was mooted by some, but it sounded to me like alcoholic poisoning and malnutrition) and a few grieving girls of an athletic disposition.

Life went on as before. Such grisly tubab interludes are mere whispers on the wind of African life, which has its own urgent concerns such as drinking attaya, sowing peanuts, giving birth and borrowing enough money to pay for next month's rice.

Births, deaths and marriages are always in the air. On New Year's morning, as we sat (having been there all night) still drinking and listening to tapes and being very Scottish, the watchman came to tell me my baby sheep was dead. He took it away and buried it and Sheila and I stood in companionable grief for a while. Perhaps lonely, Sheila baaed loudly for many nights, shutting up only if I went out and spoke to her and gave her some bread. In between times Stanley would yowl like a werewolf. He too was lonely.

Maradonna, his uncle and playmate, died in my arms under the tree where the weaver birds hang their pretty globular nests and butterflies dart and glance off the leaves. A spitting cobra deep in the bush ejected its poisonous saliva at both dogs, leaving them with swollen painful eyes and temporary blindness but it was Maradonna who died, and later we found two holes in her side where the fangs had struck. In time Stanley did settle down a little and seemed, ironically, to enjoy being the only dog around. The spit left his eyes more vacant and askew than ever before but he could see OK now, and he hadn't taken a chunk out of anyone's leg for months. Instead he sat coyly outside the tourist huts looking cute and cuddly and being fed scraps of biscuits and leftover prawns.

He got a little confused sometimes. We tried to explain that his job was to bark if someone came in uninvited. Instead, he yowled plaintively if anyone left. Thus when Rab set off on his sprint over the wall and across the football field, Stanley would mourn his departure with a noise like a wailing banshee. When Carol took Cameron out for a run on the back of the bike, where he sat in his kiddy-seat like a little emperor, Stanley squeaked in a piercingly sorrowful voice, distraught at being left behind. He was a very emotionally insecure dog, but I guess if your best big pal had been clobbered by a cobra you'd feel upset too.

Suddenly, as though to compensate for the dead lamb, Awadingding demonstrated unmistakable signs of pregnancy. This was very promiscuous of her since it was only eight months since we'd found her under the table in the Swiss Restaurant.

We assumed, but with some puzzlement, that Penny was the father. Penny was called Penny because we thought it was a girl, and even when, through time it displayed small but undeniable signs of being otherwise, it always seemed more androgynous than anything else. We were never quite sure about the whole matter, but the pregnancy itself was all too obvious. Awadingding, always a scrawny, spindly animal like a furry stick insect, bulged in the middle so that she was like a football on skinny legs with a little sharp head at the end and resigned, hungry eyes.

The guests opened a book on how many kittens she would have, with six being the odds-on favourite. I didn't NEED any more cats. As well as Penny and the mother-to-be, there was Norman-Kashmir. I called it Norman after Norman who taught me how to use the food-mixer, but Cameron called it Kashmir because his first kitten in Glasgow was called that and he thinks all cats are Kashmir. I disliked it intensely. It stole, vandalised, scratched and clawed its way up and down walls, mosquito nets, washing and people's legs.

'But, Mum ', Carol would say reasonably when I complained, 'it was you who came in one day with this dear little fluffy white bundle and said diddums ickle-wickle prezzie for you, Cameron!' `I did not!' `You did SO!' I did actually, but we all make mistakes sometimes. Sheila the sheep, recovered from her bereavement, had become the most sociable, amiable and trouble-free animal in the compound. The night-bleating had stopped and she chomped away at the weeds, tethered at a different spot each day, eating crusts and bits of cold pasta and wagging her tail at me like a dog when I approached. She never scratched, barked, stole prawns from plates or jumped up on people. But Ray said she would have to go back to the village soon to meet other sheep and get pregnant again, and Eliman came and took her away on the end of a string and I felt very sad.

Other things soon occupied me. Cameron started nursery school. A year before when he came for a holiday, we had tried him at the village day-care centre, but 200 village kids, unused to tubabs, swarmed around him poking and prodding and gazing at his blond head and it was too disruptive, for him and for the teachers. So we enlisted him into Miss Anna's little school in Kotu. There were about eighteen children, all African, in the class, but they were more used to seeing white people and also they were much better-behaved under Miss Anna's benign but beady experienced eye. For the first couple of weeks when we took him in the car, in his little grey shorts and shirt with his red and yellow schoolbag containing his flask of orange juice, two hard-boiled eggs and a chunk of bread, he howled and sobbed. 'Please, leave him. He'll be OK,' Miss Anna assured us, and of course she was right. I'd drive off trying not to howl and sob too, but when we went back to collect him, sneaking up to the window to peer through, we'd see him sitting surrounded by new friends, drawing or singing or counting.

In his absence, Carol taught accounting and bookkeeping to a 14-year-old English boy and basic English to three rich Egyptian kids. The life here was very good for Cameron, even though Carol was perpetually hard-up and they lived frugally in our two-roomed hut, cooking outside and without benefit of toy-shops, television or trendy clothes-shops. Instead, my grandson scampered about in flip-flops wearing a cotton African shirt over his bare bum and picking up more Wollof than I'd learned in over two years. He was brown and fit and totally at home. Family life is always complicated, though. Rab, Carol's 'bidey-in', as we say in Scotland, was not Cameron's Daddy, though he tended his cut knees and sore tummies with considerable patience. But now Cameron's real Daddy, Tich, was here to see his son. It was very touching because the two of them were devoted to one another and Cameron was basking in being allowed to miss nursery school and go with Daddy to see the crocodiles and swim in the hotel pool. Meanwhile Carol was wandering about looking wan and bereft, but pretending she was enjoying the break from motherhood. Such are the exigencies of modern relationships.

To take her mind off it all, I sent her to collect grapefruit and oranges so that I could experiment with marmalade-making. The citrus fruit were dripping green and gold from the trees and it was a shame to let the season pass without making use of them.

In the beginning, I made a total hash of it. This was a lot to do with the fact that I started at ten o'clock at night when I was tired out after a day of sweeping, washing and worrying about Sheila in the village, the cat's pre-natal condition and Carol's separation from Cameron. I had cooked dinner for eight, cleared the tables, washed the dishes and now I was peeling and squeezing fruit and wishing I wasn't. The generator went off half-an-hour after I'd started, so I was working by candlelight. I grazed my knuckle on the grater, dropped peelings all over the floor, and set up a domino effect. Picking up the peelings I knocked some empty wine bottles into the cat's dish and in trying to retrieve them I knocked the recipe against the candle-flame and it began to burn merrily. I quenched the flames, cursing, rinsed off the peelings and started simmering fruit and sugar, while Ray snored on the sofa, grunting occasionally at all the rattles, clangs and rude oaths coming from the kitchen. The pale yellow liquid simmered away but seemed never to reach setting point. Ray went to bed. I sat down and resolved to shut my eyes for five minutes and then give up, switch off and follow him. Two hours later I wakened up to find liquid toffee encrusting the gas cooker and dribbling to the floor. As it cooled, an army of grateful red ants paraded, pirouetted and waltzed in ecstasy around the sweet sticky mess. The pan was as black as licorice. I attacked it all with Vim and vile temper and went to bed at 3 a.m.

Next day, feeling like a fool for being so inept the night before, I tried again and it all worked beautifully, because I threw the charred recipe away and relied on instinct. I now had rows of jars of delicate platinum-coloured marmalade of fine clear texture which had cost me about one-fifteenth the price in the shops for imported brands.

For a while, I became obsessed, creating blends of lemon and grapefruit, adding a little cashew-fruit, mixing banana and orange. I only later recognised in myself the symptoms of a phase I had gone through once before in my life, some fifteen years earlier. Then, I had given up the strenuous and stimulating role of editor of a Scottish magazine called *Woman's Way* so that I could spend more time with my children and try to patch up my crumbling first marriage. I became briefly an Earth Mother. I gathered blushing rose-hips from the hedge-rows and made rose-hip syrup. I baked bread and smelled its yeasty warmth all over the house on the exposed, salty shores of the Firth of Clyde. I made jams and jellies and pies and tarts and pizzas, filling cupboards and the freezer. I dug the garden and planted lettuces. It is significant that this period of back-to-nature saintliness lasted only a short time before I began to yearn for something to write, someone to interview, something to research. It is also typical of me that I always went to one extreme or the other. I was in danger of doing the same thing again. While I shopped and boiled and blended, my typewriter lay gathering dust.

I had enthralling conversations with Werner, the tousle-haired German who shared the watchman's hut with Karen about his mother's jam recipes. I purred when guests commended me for my creamy vegetable soup cunningly flavoured with ginger. I forgot to buy *Newsweek* or listen to the news on radio. Yet inside me a little worm of discontent was gnawing away. This is the paradox of womanhood. When we are expanding one side of our natures, we are squashing another side into an explosive tight corner. Men don't have this dual personality to cope with. And most women manage it better than I did. Only recently have I learned to balance the two halves of my psyche and I still don't know when a new crop of mangoes on the one hand, just asking to be made into jams and juice, and an idea for a short story, just begging to be battered out on this old machine, may tip the balance once more.

For the moment though, as 1992 opened its eyes and stretched its limbs, I was too busy to notice that I was on the brink of a small but significant crisis. Not the everyday crises of Gambian life, for I was becoming used to these, but a subtler one within myself.

Unhappy Is the Bride

My attempts to concentrate on such cerebral matters as jam-making and reading stories to Cameron (his favourite, as a matter-of-fact is called *Adventures of Dragon*) were always short-lived. Around the turn of the year I had been perplexed to find a pretty girl, who with Sukai, helped us to clean and wash for the guests, regularly bursting into floods of tears.

She would sit on a low stool by a big bowl of dishes and cooking-pots, dropping desultory splashes of washing-up liquid on to them, and rivers of tears. She and Sukai would abandon completely their apathetic dusting and brushing to have long earnest discussions which would just make her cry even more. When I asked what was wrong, I was answered with a strangled snort and a martyred 'Nothing . . . it is nothing.'

In the end Mr M, always fond of a bit of gossip, told me the problem. Her father — the solid tradesman, a very holy and prayerful pillar of the mosque — had decided she must be married. This had, it seemed, been tried before, on which occasion the girl, not liking the man chosen for her, had also wept and had swallowed some potion which she hoped would kill her or at least cause her to be sick enough to gain sympathy and a reprieve. Her father was not at all pleased since he had already received from the prospective husband the customary gifts, including a television set and a sizeable sum of money. Now he had to give back the loot and gaze instead upon his wan and stubborn daughter.

This time, his mind was made up. 'You marry this man or you are no longer my daughter,' he ordered. 'But you don't love this man?' I asked, patting her ineffectually on the shoulder and telling her to leave the dishes to me.

'Of course I don't. He is old. And he is my uncle,' blubbered the reluctant bride. 'He's what?' Yes indeed, it transpired that the groom-to-be was the blood brother of the girl's father, a very nice chap I'm sure but how could he condone this? It says in the Koran: 'Forbidden to you are your brother's daughters' among various other categories. Yet, strangely, no-one in the family seemed at all shocked. Indeed, her mum was delighted at the prospect of a wedding and said she was just being a silly girl and she'd soon settle down and behave herself. The local elders were also in full agreement that the girl should be married to her uncle and the whole village was getting geared up for the ceremony.

Perhaps at least they'd let her stay at home for a few months before moving in with the husband, I suggested, but no, she was to go to him on her wedding night and stay there. In cases where the girl is very young, or where the husband has no job or source of income to build her a house, it is not uncommon for her to stay at home for months or even years before the marriage is consummated. The ceremony of taking the bride to the husband's compound therefore, is often bigger and more festive than the wedding itself. In this case, all was to happen on the same day. Meanwhile bride-to-be was being dragged along to the market in a bush-taxi by her mum to get measured up for her wedding-dress and white shoes, still snuffling and looking like a kicked puppy.

I asked Sukai what the man was like. 'Oh, he's a very good man,' she said crisply. 'Everything will be fine after the wedding.' We boycotted the ceremony as a matter of principle, but no-one seemed to notice. The Shuff family, mum, dad and two boys from a Scottish island, were invited and loved the whole thing, eating coos-coos with sour milk and sugar, which gave them diarrhoea later. They said there was a huge procession with the bride in a frilly frock looking miserable amidst a horde of laughing, dancing people and drummers beating out a message of matrimonial bliss. They took photographs of everyone and sent them later, all nicely arranged in an album as a present for the happy couple.

Long afterwards, when I met our lass and asked how she was, she'd bite her lip and scowl but in due course she got pregnant and, after a long, hard labour, and in spite of all my fears that she would produce some mentally or physically affected baby, she was delivered of a beautiful healthy son, of whom she is inordinately proud.

And what of the lovely Fatou, she of the limpid eyes and sumptuous body clad in expensive clinging clothes, for whom our brother Lamin had developed a passion? We, and all the rest of the family, had donated money and goods to help him 'buy' Fatou as his wife but in the end nothing came of it. I hadn't seen her around for many months, and Lamin was morose and sulky. Eliman filled me in. 'Oh, that one!' he sneered. 'Every time my parents went to Bakau to discuss things with her family they said, oh Fatou's not here. They always asked for more money, and they wanted the wedding in Bakau in] of in Bijilo, and in the end they married her to another man.'

I had my own, much more mundane irritations to deal with. Sukai had asked for two days off for the wedding, then not come back for a week, by which time I was in such a bad mood I snarled at her to go away and not bother coming back. Later of course, I felt ashamed and wished I hadn't said it, but by then it was too late. The bride had already handed in her tear-stained 'uniform' (wraparound cotton skirt and top).

Carol was around to help, but it wouldn't be fair to expect her always to be there with a wet cloth in her hand. The thing that had made me mad with Sukai was the fact that she'd sent word she was sick, then Eliman had seen her in her compound, pert and fit-looking, having her hair elaborately plaited. These operations take hours or even days, as braids of artificial or imported hair are woven into the short woolly heads of vain young women and coiled and whorled into incredible patterns and shapes. The braids can be black, or variegated black and gingery-brown so that they create a colourful pattern as they are shaped and twisted. Hair-dressers are busy people here, doing business in small shops barely as big as a phone-box, or just in the back-yard. Carol took a young friend for a short-back-and-sides the week before and he had to wait for ages because the barber was working on six other creations — none of them being attached to women's shoulders, as all of them were wigs. These are set into glossy bouffant black waves in 'European styles', very popular with the women who work in government offices and banks. Vanity is rife.

A few weeks before she left, a visitor was reduced to floods of tears by Carol giving her a stern lecture on the evils of skin-lightening, which practice she had secretly been indulging (or perhaps not secretly, as I heard her mother used to do the same thing). This is a foolish and dangerous thing to do, and you see many girls with ugly orange blotches and sores as a result of it, and many articles in newspapers warning of its perils. Even the risk of skin cancer doesn't seem to frighten those who buy the tubes and bottles of bleaching cream in little shops all over the country. I blame the men. If they didn't, in so many cases, ogle at white women and treat their own wives and girlfriends as second-class citizens, then skin-lightening wouldn't seem like the only way of winning their love.

No wonder they often feel resentful and competitive. A mere word or smile from a white tourist can be enough to make a Gambian desert his African lover, convinced that he is now adored by a tubab. Our own guests, some of them single young women, will come back bemused and ask advice on these matters. For they will, out of politeness, chat for a moment to a chap who stops them on the beach, then find that he follows them here, lovesick and dreaming of marriage, and handing amorous notes over the wall. Usually Ray sends them packing.

Now my mind was not on hair-styles, skin-dyes or love letters, but on what to do to get a decent watchman. Yes, Mr M had gone, finally and absolutely, for good. Things had reached a peak when we found him selling packets of his wanjho tea (from the plant that now covered the whole compound) over our garden wall, to streams of local women. This kept him so busy he was visibly annoyed if we asked him to fetch water or open the gates for the car. Then we would find him tucked into Carol's outside kitchen making free with her coffee and milk and so busy chatting importantly to Rab that working for us was beneath him. I blamed Rab for encouraging him. Things came to a head when I begged him to do some weeding behind the house and he shrugged and went off to sit down and drink coffee. 'Ray! He's driving me crazy!' I exploded, and Mr M was told to leave. He came with the donkey and cart again. This time it was laden high with his wanjho plants which trembled green and rose-pink in the breeze as he set off. Long afterwards he would pop back, smiling his wall-eyed simpering smile, and demand to dig up 'his' cassavas and collect 'his' pumpkins, all of which I distinctly remember him planting for me.

Next we had Ibrahim by day and old Musa by night. The idea of a day job, doing a little gardening, appealed to Ibrahim very much and in no time at all he had scraped up all the weeds, burned the rubbish, planted tomato, lettuce and onion seeds and cleared paths to all the huts. He was so good, I was afraid something would go wrong, but kept my fingers crossed desperately.

Old Musa (not Musa our first watchman, but another) was a lean, silent figure who sat solemnly under the baobab when our guests went to bed, lighting hurricane lamps and in the morning, filling up our temporary water-tank and watering the garden. He prayed conscientiously in between times, and we never spoke to one another, since he knew no English and I knew no Jola, but we smiled in a dignified manner when we passed one another. I sent him plates of whatever was left of the tourists' suppers — garlic prawns, chicken curry, beef stew — and he seemed to enjoy them.

But I still had no-one to help with cleaning the huts and doing the washing (remember there was no running water, no washing-machine or spin-dryer, not even an old-fashioned mangle). But I supposed I would manage. I always did, in the end.

And suddenly, we were leaving these mundane worries behind and we were in Glasgow. Right in the middle of our busy period, and the weather in the Gambia was beautiful while in Glasgow it was cold damp, windy late January and I wished I was home in the sun.

But we were to be on telly. Scottish TV producer-presenter Kaye Adams wanted to use me as a subject for her series on six women whose lives had changed dramatically. She agreed to fly us both over to Glasgow for some of the filming, if we would let them come to the Gambia for the rest. Lots of wheeling and dealing went on between her and a package holiday company and the Ministry of Tourism and everything was arranged — at least from her point of view.

From my point of view, it was a mixed blessing. It would be good to go to Scotland and see my Mum, get my teeth fixed and my eyes looked at and, more urgently, my womb looked at. For some time, as my monthly period had faded away with the onset of my second half-century, I had been suffering terrible back-aches and discomfort 'down there', as my mother would call it. Sometimes I wakened weeping with the pain in the mornings, making it hard to smile and chat to the tourists, not to mention changing sheets and brushing floors. I was snappy with everyone including Ray.

A quick check-up would be useful, I told myself. But on the other hand leaving Carol in charge of the huts filled me with fussy apprehension. 'How will you manage?' I whined. 'The beer stocks . . . the accounts . . . the menus . . . the bookings?' I found myself telling her how to boil an egg and dust a table. 'Mum,' she drawled, 'I have a Higher National Diploma in Hotel and Catering Management, don't you remember?' Yes, of course I remembered, but this was the Gambia. They didn't teach you at college how to handle frogs in the toilets and weevils in the flour. Still, it was only for a week, so off we flew.

At Manchester Airport, I went through EEC Passports, Ray went through Others. The guy at the desk looked at him with that blank, emptily hostile look certain British officials appear to save up specially for black visitors.

I went to the loo, collected the baggage and made a phone-call. Ray was still standing at the desk, being glowered at. The immigration officer was staring suspiciously at him then down at the letter Ray had shown him. It was a letter from Scottish Television confirming our flights there and back and our accommodation in a small Glasgow hotel and outlining the filming schedule. It had seemed like a good idea for Ray to have it so that twitchy officials could see that he really was just over for a flying visit, and not planning to stick around and darken the selective air of the United Kingdom.

'Is there a problem?' I eventually went over and asked in my Ice Queen voice, cold and hard and ready for a fight. 'Hmmm. Maybe YOU can help us here,' he said in a tone that implied that Ray was not just incompetent and illiterate but deaf and dumb as well. 'How many people is he travelling with, then?' he jeered, stabbing the top of the letter, which was addressed to Rosemary Long/Mariama Faal. 'Just me,' I sighed, explaining that the first was my maiden and professional name, while the second was my married Gambian name. I wanted to slap his smug face. 'Oh, yeah? And why should they want to make a programme about YOU?' he demanded witheringly. I longed to say I was a psychotic killer who specialised in murdering and dismembering white men in uniform, but I restrained myself and tried to explain Kaye

Adams' ideas. 'She wants to 'sit on my shoulder' while I toddle round George Square and revisit my old flat and my old office,' I said crisply. The technical phraseology impressed him and he let us through. We spent a night in the impersonal disorientation of an airport hotel then flew to Glasgow. Our room in the Terrace House Hotel off Great Western Road was as big as a Gambian family compound, with mirrors as tall as a palm tree.

They gave us breakfast in bed and we watched TV and I had three hot baths in a day, just for the novelty of it. Hot water! A bath to lie in! We tried to think of something else to put in the trouser press. The old Colonial restaurant had gone Indian and my corner delicatessen had changed hands and there was a backless wall towerlng over Ingram Street like a theatrical backdrop, but otherwise everything and everybody was much the same. And we weren't there to lounge about and look at the scenery anyway. Telephone calls at night: 'Please, wear the same clothes you were wearing today when we start tomorrow. For the continuity, you know.' Tomorrow was stunningly cold and I shivered and borrowed a technician's gloves whenever the cameras were off. We were filmed in the *Glasgow Evening Times* office, where I had been a creaky pillar of the establishment for so many years and I felt as though I was seeing it through a glass screen; it didn't seem to have anything to do with me any more and new young faces stared blankly and wondered who I was and why I was being filmed. I rather wondered the same thing.

We walked in and out of the front reception area three times till the director was satisfied, back and forward along corridors and streets, over the suspension bridge, along Argyle Street. There, Kaye thought she would stop and ask me some really deep, searching questions about my emotions and longings and fears, but the mood was interrupted by wee boys jumping in front of the camera shouting 'Ra polis is bastards' as wee boys in Glasgow so often do. Nothing changes.

There was a lot of cuddling on and off camera, and my mum and my sister were filmed visiting me at the hotel and taking tea with us. 'He could have more than one wife, you know?' my mother confided cutely to the TV crew and my sister laughed and said, 'I think Rosemary would be quite enough for any man.' Ray nodded in unflattering agreement . . . or was it flattering?

Somewhere in the middle of all this, when the pain in my lower regions had me sobbing in my bed at dawn, I arranged to see genial gynaecologist Bobby Lowe in a private clinic (something that went against all my political principles but I was now an ex-pat, a non-payer of NHS contributions, just like an Arab prince or an American jet-setter, except that they have money and I don't). Bobby poked and prodded while gossiping grossly about mutual friends, and said: 'Och, you've got a fibroid the size of a football.' It didn't sound serious but he said

'Next time you're over come and see me and I'll take it all out.' All? I decided to grin and bear it for a while and think about it (not to mention the cost which would be near enough £2000). But I got new glasses and had my dental plate fixed. I felt like an old car going in for an MOT.

All of a sudden, it seemed, we were back in the Gambia, peeling off woolly jumpers and watching our chilblains vanish in the soft orange sunlight. A day later, Scottish TV followed us out. This was the first time we'd seen John and Steve and Dave and Jack out of their regulation anoraks, heavy trousers, woolly gloves and chubby-soled shoes. They were toting their gear on raw red shoulders and exposing their little pink knees under cheeky shorts. Kaye was wearing flimsy cotton and a lot of sun oil. 'Just do that one more time,' John the director shouted encouragingly, as we drove the 2CV in and out of the compound, over and over again.

Ibrahim was baffled. Every time he closed the gates for us, John, hiding on his hands and knees behind the wall, tugged at his trouser-leg as a signal for him to open them again. Stanley gave up yapping at the crew and sank down on his haunches to watch our strange antics. The Shuff family from the West Coast island obligingly took breakfast at noon to fit in with the crew's time-table. They even said, very loudly several times, 'the prawns last night were lovely,' without being coached.

One morning we bowled along the Badala Highway with Steve's head poking through the open roof as he filmed palm-wine tappers and gaily-dressed market-women with a look of pure joy on his face. 'I usually do news,' he said. 'This is terrific!' When a herd of cows blocked our way he went into ecstasies. I never knew cows' bottoms were so photogenic.

At the junction with Kairaba Avenue, two gendarmes with their Ton-Ton Macoute sun-specs waved us down menacingly. 'What you doing? No filming!' they shouted grimly. The crew produced their authorisation from the Minister of Tourism and their whole demeanour changed. 'Have a nice day!,' they smiled cheesily, hoping to be on film, but they weren't.

'Let's film in the market,' decided the director. 'Well, let's check with the Council first,' said Ray diplomatically. Gambians get irritated at people with cameras and video recorders treating them like bits of scenery. The Council sent a market security man with us. His approach was useful, if hardly gentle. To any stall-holders who griped at being filmed he barked 'Shut up or I'11 arrest you.' Most didn't complain anyway but smiled and joked and enjoyed the attention. Many of the scenes that were shot during these few days were unused. But the market scenes stayed in and were beautiful. Wide beaming grins, scampering children, heaps of scarlet, gold and green fruits and vegetables, the jolly old man who sells the prawns, women holding aloft multi-coloured fabric, chickens, peppers. Lovely stuff. No wonder Steve was

Serrekunda main street where you can buy everything from kerosene and candles to keep you lit up, to ju-jus (protective magic) to keep you safe.

in seventh heaven. Not that it was all fun for us. And not that all went smoothly.

At one junction we met Big Mary our Glasgow friend, formerly employed by Glasgow Procurator Fiscal's office and as tough as an old boot. She was fizzing mad and in terrible pain. 'Ah broke ma ****ing ankle,' she told me, as I tried to signal to her that the microphone looped round my waist was switched on. 'Ah went tae the ****ing clinic and the ***ing doctor said he couldn't X-ray me unless ah gave him thousands of dalasis up front. He's a ****ing ****.' I looked sympathetic and backed away before the sound man swooned from embarrassment.

On Sanyng beach we were having a row, Ray and I, while smiling through gritted teeth and scampering in and out of the waves on command. He was upset because we were too late to go to his Dad's compound, where we and the crew were expected. 'They'll blame me,' he grumbled. 'This is very rude.' Steve went on and on filming sand and waves and our semi-naked bodies and it was dusk by the time we got home. 'Too late for the village,' said the director. "We'll do it tomorrow.' Ray was livid and narked at me, and I scowled at him. Thank goodness, none of our grimaces showed up in the programme. And next day, far from being in the huff, the whole family were out, dressed up to the nines, to be on the telly. The smiles lit up the air and the word 'welcome' resounded from every corner.

We were filmed walking, talking, sitting, standing, running, cooking, cleaning. Ray was caught in the flickering firelight barbecuing fish. Rory Cuthbertson, the Scottish architect and also a skilled piper who has taught members of the Gambian Police Band the skirl of the bagpipes, blew for all he was worth, the glow of the embers behind him, the music haunting . . . and that was the end of the programme Scottish viewers saw several months later.

For us, it wasn't finished. A frantic fax arrived from Kaye. 'The sound's not good. Can you get into a radio studio and record the answers to all the questions I asked you, spontaneously as though I was there with you?' George Christiansen, owner of Gambia's new Radio One FM station leapt to our aid. I sat in the studio, talking to myself, for an hour, and two Scotland-bound holidaymakers were kind enough to take the tape and drop it in personally to the station in Cowcaddens on their way north.

The experience was educational. I learned that 'two blondes and a redhead' is a lighting man's jargon for two big yellow lights and a smaller red one. I learned how to stroll about nonchalantly with a miniature microphone clipped to my bra, the wire snaking somewhere between my breasts and my bum, the pack bouncing about like a colostomy bag. But I was still a seaside landlady. There were duties to be done, people to be fed and I was not entirely sorry when they all packed up their gear and headed back to the editing room in Glasgow.

One really fascinating fact emerged while I was at Radio One FM and it was nothing to do with sound or lighting. I discovered that George had created a fabulous garden behind his studio, crammed with neat rows of coriander, garlic, tomatoes, onion, beetroot and herbs. I came away with a big bag of plump pink tomatoes.

George's secret garden would still be flourishing long after the television programme had been shown, repeated and forgotten. And in my day-to-day life, tomatoes play a more vital part than microphones!

Love Conquers All

Now Peter from Prestwick had arrived and it was as though he'd never been away. It was Peter who helped Caroline launch the community project at Tanji Village down the coast, and on many occasions we had found him there up to his waist in hot dry earth shovelling along with the men from the village. But a lot had happened since then.

The romance which had blossomed between Peter and Caroline as they worked together, living a truly Gambian life learning Mandinka, catching typhoid and dysentery and sharing in the compound's bowl of rice, earth toilet and open 'shower' (merely a basin of water and a jug screened from view), sneaking off for tennis, building up contacts with government officials and other NGOs, had come to an end before he left for a new job in Pakistan.

Much of Peter's time on our verandah now was spent in analysing the situation, bitterly assessing what had gone wrong, while I, fed-up with being a Mother Confessor, finally told our good old chum to belt up and stop being sorry for himself. We got him to talk instead about his new job, with Health Unlimited in Quetta, on the Pakistan-Afghanistan border, where there was enough excitement and drama to take his mind off any faded love affair (and also a Finnish nurse who was to become his girlfriend, but that was later. At this stage, it was just the occasional casual reference which made me suspect he would soon have someone who could make him forget all about Caroline!)

His life in the shadow of the bleak, fierce mountains of war-torn Afghanistan was eventful enough to keep us talking well into the night, takes of mujahideen kidnappings, warlords on horseback swathed in turbans and robes and brandishing rifles, local feuds and vendettas, corruptions and scandals. His own job involved sending medical personnel under armed escort, over the border into Afghanistan to try to offer even the barest of health care to the oppressed and exhausted people falling sick in the shadow of war. The sides in the battle changed but the people went on suffering. Theoretically Health Unlimited had no official right to go into Afghanistan but unofficially they were accepted and welcomed.

It was of these things we were talking, in the small hours of the morning, and calling up old times in the Gambia, the times we would all go fishing on the beach by night, the many rousing games of Crazy Eight we'd played. And it was then that Awa-dingding decided to give birth. She sang and shouted and raced across the red tiles of the verandah looking irritated and impatient. Then suddenly she flopped into a box I'd left ready in a corner, and, as the stars grew higher and sharper, and Peter and our other friend, Irish Brendan, reminisced and argued and grew philosophical on my red wine, three tiny skinny objects like dead rats were being licked furiously by their skinny under-age mother. When I announced the happy event to Peter and Brendan they grunted, 'Ummm' and went on dissecting Muslim politics and international aid policies. Ray had long since gone to bed, exhausted by such heavy conversation.

As day broke I went out to clear away the debris of our meal and sweep the tiles, and there were three more new arrivals. Within no time at all they were frisking around among the detective novels and *Newsweeks*, piddling on *Hello* magazine and tearing old *Observer* colour supplements into confetti. Whatever was I going to do with them?

Awa-dingding was eating for seven, voraciously gulping down supermarket cat food, leftover rice (at which she normally turned up her sharp nose), and all my old bread (once given to Sheila the sheep) soaked in milk and water. I tried encouraging her to go and seek out her own fodder. 'I'll baby-sit for you,' I told her. There are creatures known as 'veggie rats', I'm told, large non-carnivorous rodents which scamper about in the bush near our boundaries just asking to be caught and eaten, but Awa-dingding had no time to go foraging; her babies constantly clung to her teats and she looked like an over-worked soup-kitchen worker trying to keep up with demands which always exceeded her supply.

We had decided that poor asexual, celibate Penny was not the father. We had seen a big, tough feral cat hanging about which, instead of fleeing when I shouted and ran at it threateningly, came towards me on legs like tree-trunks hissing and drawing its ears back like a lynx. I called on Ray's brother to chase it far out of my sight. I didn't (cat-lover as I am) even mind too much if they hurled a clod of earth after it to speed it on its way. Neither did Awa-dingding.

Natural selection tended to solve my problem of what to do about all these kittens. Ray opened the French door one day and there was a frightful squawk as one got caught in the hinge. It was killed outright and Ray was in tears and couldn't look me in the eye. Then Kabu and Pascal came to see us, and she fell in love with the prettiest of the litter, a silver stripey tabby with white bib. Kabu is our Senegalese tour-guide friend and Pascal gets lonely when he has to go to Kafountine or Dakar with coachloads of French tourists. The kitten would be company for her.

She also gets jealous. I could sympathise. It was totally unreasonable, and we both knew it but I also knew how disconsolate and bitter I felt when Ray went off with Europeans for excursions, especially if they were young and female! In my heart and in my head I knew he was simply doing his job, showing them the fishing pirogues, the crocodile pools and the cotton-silk trees and the mangrove creeks. But I developed, in these few months at the beginning of 1991, a terrible fear of losing him, a terrible sense of depression and irritability, which mostly I kept hidden, but which sometimes plunged our relationship into deep abysses from which climbing out grew harder and harder.

At the back of it all was the pain in my back and pelvic area, gnawing like a rat at my composure. Our different colours made it harder to get through this tense time in our lives. My snappishness made him, an immensely touchy and occasionally neurotic individual, attack like a cornered animal and we would say things to one another that make us both now, as we look back, feel ashamed. Through it all, we still had our love, but it was being battered on many sides.

And that was when I met Magali. And France and Valerie. The three of them, all from Paris, came to visit us out of the blue, with Nicole (Mama Karamba, of the campement in Kafountine). I cooked chicken and lemon for them, wincing at the pain in my pelvis, and we chatted and heard a little about their lives and they decided to stay the night. All were school-teachers. Magali taught English and Spanish. They had come to Nicole (whom they had met in Paris the previous year) laden with homeopathic medicines for the village, for Magali was a healer.

I only found out by accident. I was talking, tiredly, to France, a gentle grey-haired woman about my own age, and I was saying that, soon I must go to Britain for a hysterectomy. Her face puckered in concern. 'Oh no, no, you must not do that, cherie. No, no, you must speak to Magali. She helped me; she can help you! Magali! *Attention! Viens parler avec Mariama.*'

France told me that she too had fibroids and had been told to have an operation but Magali had treated her and she was absolutely fine now. And her son, she said, had been badly injured in a terrible car crash which left him covered in deep and ugly wounds which seemed not to heal. 'Magali, she went to him and she laid her hands on him and spoke to him, and it was amazing. The wounds, they disappeared. I saw it with my eyes.'

Did I believe in miracle healing? No. Did I believe that Magali, slender with a cap of dark shiny hair, wide wise eyes and a slender brown body like a bird, had some special gift of tranquillity and knowledge? Yes, I did without quite knowing why.

There were other people around, visitors, friends, Ray, but Magali shooed them away like chickens. 'Leave us in peace!' she commanded, and made me lie on the day-bed in our living-room. She placed her hands gently on my stomach and over my womb area and her face twisted as though she was feeling pain 'Ah, yes, yes, yes, it is here. But it will go. It is big because you are so tense, so strung-up, under pressure, feeling that you are not appreciated, that your creativity is being stifled.'

Always a bit of an egotist acting humble, I felt that she was saying something I had sensed all winter. My initial plans to come to the Gambia and write books had been submerged by our agreement to open this little holiday business. Had I been less fretful and conscientious, I would have let a couple of Gambians get on with the cleaning, cooking and customer-relations but I couldn't do that. I was never good at delegating, and I had always been thus. When I was involved in running charity projects in Glasgow I used to build myself up into a peak of exhaustion, temper and self-pity, trying to do everything instead of sharing it around. I would blame others for what was, intrinsically, my own fault

Now I was blaming Ray because I wasn't writing books, though it wasn't his fault. But how did Magali, whom I'd just met and with whom I hadn't discussed any of it, know all this from placing her hands on my body? 'You must begin to do the creative things you want to do,' she said calmly. 'And you must learn to relax. Then this thing will go, you will see.'

She massaged my back, my front, my legs, pulling gently on my toes, tugging the strain, it seemed, right out of my body. And she said: 'Come and see me again. Don't go to Britain and have your whole womb pulled out. It is your body; don't let them talk you into what is not necessary. If you want to come to Europe, come to Paris with Ray and stay in my house and I will treat you.' I never went to Paris. There was never any money for such a trip. But I did see Magali again, as you will see. Meanwhile, I felt quite remarkably soothed and encouraged by her presence for a few long minutes in our living-room.

I have thought about her 'gifts' long and carefully since. Can she heal just by placing her hands on the right place? I don't know. She didn't 'cure' me. But she did make me think about the casual manner in which Western doctors say 'Let's just take it out, or off, or away.' And she made me think about my own state of mind which had become, often, sulky and self-pitying and resentful. You would see me scurrying around, sighing, carrying huge trays, my back curved in the antithesis of sensible posture, my face contorted in a frown. I fully believe still that a combination of physical and emotional stress can cause not just fibroids but probably many other conditions, to become aggravated.

I tried therefore — though it hasn't always worked — to become less neurotic about the domestic arrangements. I abandoned tablecloths and let people eat from the scrubbed table-tops. I abandoned side-plates and let them eat French-style, using the same plates. I stopped having a tantrum every time the loos weren't spotless or there was some dust on a chair, I walked slower and taller and looser. I began writing more, and, the following year, I began painting. I have occasional relapses of fretful worrying and subsequent pain but I know that if I stay calm and stop over-working and carrying heavy weights, the pain will go away. And I still have my womb!

I might be depressed when Ray went off with tourists for one day or two days at a time, but I tried to look on the positive side and regard it as a period when I could read and write to my heart's content or just sit and think. There was always plenty for him to tell me about when he got back. Once, for instance, he took some people to Kartong, far to the south, on the mangrove-fringed creek which separates the Gambia from Senegal, and they got stuck in the mud.

They all had a wonderful time. 'Oh yes, there are crocodiles here,' teased Ray, 'but they don't often eat people.' Alison and Sam and Ann and Derek were wading through brown stuff like chocolate pudding at the time, aiming for the island in the middle of the mangrove swamps where they were to have their picnic.

The plan had been for them to go by pirogue, paddled there by a sinewy local fisherman. Unfortunately the tide was out, so instead of a channel of water there was a channel of mud. Everyone regarded it as a hysterical adventure, except Ray and the boatman who had been urging the boat furiously on in an attempt to move it, only to find their paddles sticking deeper and deeper into the goo. The mangroves straddled the surface on their fragile sinister roots and swayed softly, casting dark green shadows over the skin of fawn water that lay on the mud, and birds of ridiculous hues appeared and disappeared. Roots are cut and stacked by the locals and used in building. They form, for example, a very beautiful rippled golden-brown ceiling in the reception area of a large hotel on the coast.

Across the creek of Allahein is Senegal, so the tourists had to report at the police station beyond Kartong village. The policeman wrote down all their names and the time of their arrival, so that if they didn't reappear in a reasonable number of hours he'd begin to assume they'd smuggled themselves over the watery border or been eaten by crocodiles. The Shuff family had gone part of the way, but had been dropped off on Sanyang beach, where they planned to play at survival: gathering twigs for fires, building shelters and swimming with their snorkels. This is because Mr Shuff runs a survival centre on a Scottish island — where young people including sometimes those from deprived or criminal backgrounds, can pit their wits and endurance against the elements. The balmy beach at Sanyang is less challenging.

He'd probably have enjoyed another excursion conducted by Ray a few days later with the same quartet who had been trapped in the mud. This time they thought they were going to get trapped in a military rebellion. Ray came back looking extremely alarmed. 'We had to turn back at Sukuta because all the taxi-drivers there said the soldiers were blocking the roads. We drove about a bit and someone else said it was possible to get through to Banjul. So we did, but the military were everywhere.'

The story behind it relates to the Liberian back-pay fracas. Members of the Gambia National Army were part of the ECOWAS peace-keeping force (ECOMOG) in the desperately unhappy and dangerous country of Liberia, riven by civil war, frequently a bloodbath, mostly ignored by the West. The lads came back, tired and shocked at being so close to such brutal events, for the Gambia itself has no real experience of such horrors. They were due to get certain monies appropriate to personnel who are posted away from home but the money had never been forthcoming. Other grievances had also been simmering and on one occasion the army and the gendarmerie had to be stationed around State House and key buildings and cross-roads for fear of trouble from the Liberian returnees. In time it all simmered down but it was unpleasant to see so many guns bristling in our insignificant little capital city.

The tourists thought it was all wonderfully exciting. In between goggling at guns, they managed to see Banjul museum which is full of fertility symbols and fierce masks and sepia pictures of former colonial bigwigs. At night they would go for a 'Serrekunda at night' tour incorporating a visit to the wrestling. Gambian wrestling makes Sumai wrestling look dull. There is lots of roaring and strutting about, drumming and cheeky remarks, for it is the provocative posturing of the combatants before each bout that is the real centre of entertainment, and supporters can start their own unofficial battles too. The noise is incredible and the sport never loses its appeal. It is held every Saturday and Sunday in Serrekunda, regardless of the season, and white visitors are tolerated but not at all necessary. Wrestling flourished in West Africa long before the tourist trade.

Ray also took the group through the dark streets, where they sell fish pies and pancakes (globules of batter deep-fried in oil), kebabs and eggs, and then to the cinema to see some kung-fu movies. They went to the New Vision bar and drank beer and disco-danced, while I stayed at home and convinced myself I was oblivious to Ray's absence. But my dreams were disturbed by Ray anyway, for there he was beside the bed, having deposited the guests quietly outside their huts, and he was waving a torch and whispering 'Mariama! I think there must be a thief trying to break in! I can hear funny noises and flashing lights.' It turned out to be a totally unseasonable thunder-storm. Later, it actually rained, something it wasn't supposed to do for another six months. In the morning, the compound was moist and fresh and the tomato plants were looking surprised.

I was still working on my 'stay calm, stay cool' technique. But it wasn't always easy. I found myself muttering and stuttering from time to time. If people MUST bring food into their rooms, I'd think, you'd imagine they'd at least have the sense to screw the lid tightly on their jam-jars so that they don't have ants crawling all over the place. Why, I'd wonder, do some people bring enough medical supplies to tackle a full-scale national emergency? It's the Gambia not Somalia; diarrhoea is probably the worst thing you're going to catch. Why, I'd speculate, do people come to a place like ours with lounge-suits and high-heeled shoes and hair-dryers? And so on, and so on. I would fold things up, brush things out, wipe things and wish I had a good chambermaid so that I really could take Magali's advice and learn to relax. But we were drifting towards the Spring, which would mean fewer tourists soon, so I could manage, I told myself.

And at least I had Ibrahim. As day watchman and gardener, he was great. He even grabbed dishes from the verandah and washed them, surely above and beyond the terms of his employment. I'd also caught him trying to wash our clothes and mop our tiled steps. I'd seen him running to open the gates for cars in a country where running is something reserved entirely for athletic meetings. It had to come to an end sometime. It was too good to be true. We communicated in bad Wollof and bad French and lots of hand-signals.

And Ray too was ready for a rest from being a tour-guide. 'I miss you, Mariama,' he said, and I resolved again to stop nagging and count my blessings. (I make this resolution regularly; how I wish I could keep it!)

There had been brief periods when severe alienation had, to be sure, chipped at the unconventional and — some would say — impetuous foundations of our marriage. But for each little sliver that was chiselled away, another solid rock seemed to form. Every argument climaxed in a passionate reconciliation and every misunderstanding conversely increased, in the end, our understanding of one another.

Ray's method of dealing with these tempestuous times was very Gambian. While I was wrestling within myself analysing my own faults and exaggerating his, reliving scenes in my head, torturing myself with if-only, why-didn't-I, how-could-he? . . . he was looking not inward but outward. 'I know what's wrong, Mariama,' he would say at last, serious and angry. 'Someone is trying to split us up. Maybe some man would like to marry you and he has asked his marabout for a spell to spoil our love. But he is wasting his time. We are too strong for that. We will show him . . .'

There was no 'him', at least none that I knew of. But it WAS a perfectly normal thing for people to put a hex on other people's good fortune. Joe, our Sierra Leonean artist friend and confidant, educated and reared in England, by no means a simple, superstitious peasant, told us seriously one night. 'You know, you two are special. You have a good marriage. You may not be well-off, but you have your little business and you love each other and it shows. Some young men, people who went to school with Ray or worked near him on the beach, they see all this and they are jealous. Instead of being happy that he has found a good new life, they want to spoil it. Believe me, Mariama, they would do it if they could. This is Africa. You have to believe in things that would seem ridiculous in England or Scotland.'

A spell to stop us loving one another? Let them try! It would take all the marabouts in West Africa to make even a tiny dent in the phenomenon of the Faals.

One Saturday we left our guests to fend for themselves and fled, with Caroline and Julius, to the beaches of the south. Julius is a handsome, charming Gambian with massive shoulders and a blazing smile. He serves in the Episcopalian cathedral in Banjul and his family are Akus — descendents of slaves who were taken to Britain where they assimilated many British customs and returned to West Africa to enter the higher echelons of public life. In fact, Julius's mother didn't think Caroline, an English rose, good enough for her son. She would have preferred an Aku girl. But love conquers all, and Julius and Caroline continued to be a couple — so much so that Ray and I, solid, married folk that we were, would sigh and raise our eyebrows at the amount of billing and cooing and cuddling they did at every opportunity.

We bounded along in Caroline's silver Suzuki jeep till we came to a deserted spot, where we spread blankets and towels on the sand. Caroline had made prawns in wine and cream sauce, chicken wings with pasta and we had champagne and proper plates and cutlery — definitely a step up from our usual bonga fish eaten with the fingers and washed down with warm beer! Birds as green as new leaves were skipping about in the woods. Parrots, maybe; Ray only knew their Wollof name. We gave the leftover prawns to a thin feral dog but it turned up its nose and walked away. It may have been a Muslim dog and sniffed the wine. Caroline and Julius kissed as they stood in the lapping waves of the Atlantic Ocean. 'Look at these two,' said Ray and shrugged and kissed me. Then we walked along the edge of the water hand in hand looking for shells. The Muslim dog followed at a distance. It probably disapproved of my bikini.

Romance and Rascals

A fortune-teller friend told me once I would always live near the water. No matter how harassed I was, the sea soothed me like embrocation, never mind if it was angry and dark like broken pewter, simperingly blue like a predictable postcard or James Joyce's 'snotgreen' sluggish and soupy.

The best time to walk from our house to the beach was five o'clock in the afternoon. We would set off in procession, sometimes, past the cows whose sweet dung-smell had softened as the sun had dipped. The attendant clouds of flies had floated off to rest.

On this particular afternoon Cameron was in the lead, two-and-a-half-year-old bottom wiggling importantly as he plummeted pell-mell down the path by the forest. Eliman wobbled daringly behind on Carol's bike, sitting doubled like a hairpin on the baby seat, because the actual saddle was too high for him, showing off, look no hands, feet askew, leaping the bumps like Dirty Harry. Ami, aged five-and-half, pattered along demurely beside Carol and me, wearing a straw hat with flowers bobbing on its brim, her sheeny black skin shimmering over her lime-green cotton skirts.

'Monkeys!' we all whispered and tip-toed to the fence to peer between the creeper-garlanded palms into the mahogany-dark recesses behind. A colony of colobus stared back at us wise-faced, long tails hanging like upturned question-marks, eyes round and wistful. Then they scattered like leaves in the breeze to their secret places.

At low-tide, the sand was firm and fawn and washed clean by the foaming breakers, into which I could now plunge and duck and show off, one time scaredy-cat, now Bijilo's answer to Esther Williams. Eliman and Ami tiptoed in suspiciously and refused to wet more than their insteps. Modou the third oldest Faal brother, with the same high cheek-bones and curling lashes as Ray and Lamin and Eliman and Janqui and Ami and Mariama, trotted towards us on our grandfather's brown horse, bare-backed. As horses went here, it looked fit enough.

Sometimes I had seen painfully thin nags being hauled along the beach carrying tourists who weighed almost as much as they did. They reminded me of Ginger in *Black Beauty*, winded, ribs poking through sagging skin. But succulent bundles of hay are not easily come by here. The cows too looked perilously thin, especially in winter when eight months of dry weather rendered the bush scrawny and barren of fodder.

This horse looked solid enough and Carol, whose equestrian experience was limited to a pony-trek in Innellan, county of Argyll, at the age of nine, decided she wanted to ride it. There was some discussion then about whether her short wraparound skirt was going to create a shameless display of thigh as she was pushed aloft, Modou and I hoisting a leg each, the horse staring into space, oblivious to us all like a Glasgow police horse in the middle of a rammy.

She made gee-up noises and bounced about on the tough textured back trying to get into first gear, while the horse stood serenely still mesmerised by some unseen view across the unruly Atlantic. 'How do I get it to move?' Carol begged Modou. 'Say: Aitcha!' he answered and at the Wollof equivalent of the F-word, her steed sauntered forward, silhouetted against silver sea and pearly sky, followed in outline by Eliman on the bike, Cameron now stately in the baby-seat, Ami tripping along behind. I wanted to be a film director and record the scene, shading the edges with the lilac of dusk.

In the distance, the local youths were limbering up, doing press-ups and squats and push-ups and asking their friends to kick them hard on the stomach to test the iron flexing of their muscles. I supposed that was how our visiting fire-eater had begun learning his tricks. For he was much more than just a fire-eater. He would come with the drummer to entertain our guests. After he had rolled a flaming torch up and down his arms and chest, swallowed gulps of fire and ejected it in yellow belches of sparks, he would next lie on the ground and invite tourists to place a large wooden bowl on his belly. He would then instruct them to pound the inside of this vessel as hard as they could with a wooden pestle as big as a baseball bat. 'Thunk! Clunk!' the pestle would go, the tourists looking embarrassed, all of us wincing on behalf of the horizontal fire-eater, who laughed with each blow then bounded back to his feet.

No matter how often I saw this, it made me shudder. A week before our perambulation along the beach led by grandpa's horse, we had introduced a slight variation to our usual drums, fire-eating, belly-bashing programme. Pete was there from Glasgow. He was Cameron's adopted Grandpa, being the live-in partner of Granny Lue. He was a busker, and rather famous, for, in the year of Glasgow Garden Festival the security people tried to remove him and his flutes and whistles from the Festival bridge where he had always drawn a big crowd. The

Glasgow Evening Times took up the story and Pete became a hero fighting against bureaucratic bumptiousness.

Pete played the flute while Sidiki played the drums. It was a spontaneous marrying of African rhythms and fragile Scottish airs that worked impeccably, each musician humouring and enhancing the sounds of the other. When Ray took Lue and Pete and some other guests for a pirogue trip through the silent green fringed creeks of the mouth of the River Gambia, Pete produced his whistle and strewed silvery sweet notes of music like stardust over the ripples. Everyone said it was a magical experience. Scott, our poet friend from London's Soho, said he cried, it was so beautiful. Scott liked a good sniffle sometimes.

He was a big muscular bald young man with a rich mauve nose which he later had modified by expensive plastic surgery. He was a homosexual only just coming out of his closet, with pale baby-blue eyes and a dashing turn of phrase. 'Oooh,' he said the first time he arrived at one of our huts. 'It's WICKED!' Ray was confused till I explained that it was praise of a high order. Scott had trained in method acting in New York, run a wine bar in Paris and an art gallery in Manhattan, and now he was a waiter in Soho. He had a granny in Knightswood, Glasgow. He juggled oranges for the local kids and he wrote poetry.

One day I was cleaning his hut and, being an undeniably nosy landlady, I glanced at the open pages of his notebook beside his bed. He had written 'Thank you, God, for sending me here.' He was one of our favourite guests, with willow-green cream on his nose to deflect the sun, and a hundred charming and philosophical anecdotes to tell.

Our other favourite guest (well, we liked most of them, really) had been, of course, ribald Roel the devastating Dutchman who was, we knew, urgently needing money to help rear his expanding family. 'PLEASE try to sell the red Land Rover,' he wrote, 'Just get what you can for it.' We could understand his impatience. It had been lying outside our window now for ten months. The demand for quirky converted veteran vans with beds in the back and Dutch number plates was pretty limited in the Gambia.

But at last we managed to sell it to a fish trader who said he wanted to use it to carry ice and fish from the sea to the salt-water-fish-starved residents of Basse. That seemed a worthy enough occupation for it, after these years of lumbering through Europe and Africa, but we felt sad to see it go; it had become a sort of mascot and a reminder of our friendly Frauenfelders. Not that the sale went completely smoothly, for nothing ever does, here. 'I will give you some of the money now, and the rest next Tuesday,' promised the virtuous fish trader. 'Don't worry. You can trust me.'

We believed him. We were so innocent. Tuesday came and went. After a week, Ray phoned the man and said politely that we were rather surprised that he hadn't appeared with the money, particularly as Roel was arriving within the next few weeks. 'Oh, my brother. I had a problem at Basse. One of my lorries broke down. Things have been very difficult. But, don't worry. I will come to you with the money in two days.'

No, he didn't. This situation went on until our patience was utterly exhausted and Ray had heard himself getting more and more vituperative on the phone until everyone in the office could hear him shouting and swearing at the fishy fish man. We drove to Brikama, where his depot was. Lorries were standing outside being loaded or unloaded. The smell of fish filled the air and there was a general aura of busy prosperity. But when we found our man, he once again spun a tale of hard luck and penuriousness calculated to melt the heart of the hardest creditor. But we were not for melting. Oh, we were so tough. 'I am shocked,' I said, 'that a man like yourself should break his word to a respectable person like myself. I am hurt, saddened . . .' I turned away from him in disdain, trying to keep a straight face.

'Our Dutch friend is coming. He is a big tough mafia,' said Ray. 'When he doesn't get his money, aieee! He turns very nasty. I have seen him beat a man almost to death because he owed him money.' This was pure fabrication but fairly effective. The man began opening drawers and cupboards and plastic bags and cardboard boxes from all over his cramped office. Each contained bundles of fives, tens, twenty-fives, fifties, grubby and tied in elastic bands. One bag was tipped on to the desk and contained hundreds of tinkling coins. The man sighed and spoke of how we would ruin him, but the money kept coming and we sat, implacable, arms folded, until every butut was paid. I felt like an actress in a TV movie. 'Thank you so much,' we said sweetly. 'Bye bye,' and drove off giggling.

Perhaps we would have a special barbecue in Roel's honour. If so we would ask old Musa to dance. Last time, he was striding ponderously into the compound to start his six o'clock shift, his long blue gown flapping round his bare ankles, his face solemn as he viewed us and our guests jumping about and stamping and clapping to Sidiki's drumming. His woolly hat was pulled down over his ears, but he heard me say, jokingly: 'Why don't you join us, Musa?'

Suddenly, he hitched up his skirts and, after carefully laying down the plastic bag containing his water-bottle and torch, he dipped his head, flailed his arms and kicked his feet like a can-can dancer. We gave him a huge cheer; he straightened his clothes and his limbs and his face, took an upright position and, carrying his plastic bag, paced towards the corner behind the baobab tree where he performed his evening prayers. He was a very dignified chap, normally. He was, for instance, a staunch believer in the dignity of labour. But only if he was standing nobly watching someone else doing it. It had been arranged that Ibrahim would water the plants in the late afternoon and Musa would do it in the morning at the end of his shift. Both would share the irksome task of filling our temporary water-tank.

As it was, it was always Ibrahim I saw watering, filling, watering, filling, while Musa strolled behind him offering stately words of advice and occasionally deigning to steady the wheelbarrow (in which buckets of water were carried from the well or the standpipe) or flick a fly from the surface of a pail. This was because he was older than Ibrahim. Age is far above intelligence, diligence wit or wisdom in the pecking order of things. 'The elders are gods,' wrote one Serrekunda poet. 'They sit on top of everything.' Ray might rant at Ibrahim, who is, on the whole quick of foot and anxious to please, because Ibrahim is younger than he is. But he would hesitate to make any gentle criticism of Musa, because Musa is his elder. A bit like the old Ronnie Corbett-Ronnie Barker-John Cleese sketch: 'I know my place; I look down on him, but I look up to him.'

One thing neither watchman could understand, no matter how often we tried to explain, was the theory of the compost heap. Carol's obsession with gardening at this stage bore no relationship to the actual amount of produce yielded by her assiduously-tended plot though we all oohed and aahed when she pointed out tiny specks of green she said were coriander seedlings, and admired, with her, a shaky row of tentative lettuces. But she was creating the biggest if not the only compost heap in the Kombos. I would get stabbing guilt pains if I accidentally threw a banana skin or a fish head into the plastic bag for non-degradable rubbish. Instead it must go into the other plastic bag of putrefying gunge which still had a habit of exploding all over the kitchen-floor. Usually it did it when I was frying doughnuts or carrying a tray full of breakfast dishes.

Every so often I would take my contribution over and add it to Carol's mouldering tip. I would often find plastic bags and catfood tins among the festering fish-gut and decomposing cassava peelings. 'It's all rubbish,' Ibrahim would say, 'Why don't you go and buy some nice fertiliser in the garden shop in Kanefing?' It's against our principles, we would explain, but he couldn't understand. This is the odd — rather sad — thing about my adopted country.

Planters prefer chemical pesticides and fertilisers to natural methods. Young men disdain the elegant African robes of their fathers to wear imported Levis and imitation Lacoste tee-shirts. They clamp a Walkman to their heads rather than listen to the rhythmic djembas and talking drums. If it's from the West, it must be better. Gradually, perhaps only the tourists will buy the traditional hand-made batik and watch traditional dancing to traditional music. But no. I can still ask any village child to dance and play 'drums' (usually empty tomato tins) and he or she will oblige. And there is still — among the women at least — strong preference for the swirling cotton wrapped skirts and waramba and elaborate head-ties of their grandmothers. And the Ministry of

Agriculture is trying to educate farmers about the benefits of organic cultivation. There is hope for us yet. And SOME good ideas come from the west. Iréne, an astute and vivacious woman came to the Gambia for the first time three years before the events in this narrative to help to publicise an international educational project. She also began to campaign for re-usable bottles and other practices which would reduce the environmental degradation of West Africa.

But something else happened. She met a serious, intense Gambian bird-watcher and together they strolled through forest and along river-bank gazing at orioles and cuckoo-shrikes. Iréne's strolling was done on crutches, because she had had polio as a child and later her condition was aggravated by the breaking of a hip. But she walked and talked in a determined and businesslike way, every gesture saying 'Don't pity me.' She ran her own high-powered business in Europe, but for perhaps the first time, she experienced a delicious passion for the pratincole-watcher, the hornbill observer, the man who made her feel like a complete woman. She went home to her business but they corresponded. She, a cautious type and insecure because of her disability, wrote circumspectly of weaver-birds and flycatchers they had seen together, hoping he appreciated the deep feelings between the lines.

Perhaps he didn't. They met again recently, and that's when I first met her. We became instant friends. She had short bouncy grey hair and a subtle sense of humour and she was, she said, ready to put her business into other hands and come here to live, for here she experienced none of the embarrassed pity with which her restricted mobility was viewed by strangers at home. Here she just felt warmth, both in the people and in the kindly climate which soothed the ache in her body. She and her bird-man met us and within minutes the old romance was reborn. But this tale had no happy ending then.

'I want to meet his family but he always makes excuses not to take me to his compound ,' she confided, bewildered. 'He's keeping something from me and it's driving me crazy.' The showdown came in our house one day at dusk, while the fine-spotted wood-pecker (crimson stripe, yellowish underparts) laughed unsympathetically outside the window. 'Piu-piu-piu,' sniggered the campathera punctuligera, while on my sofa Iréne sobbed 'boo-hoo, boo-hoo,' and I clucked like an old mother hen.

The birdman (bidden thus he insisted, by his bossy Muslim father) had taken unto him a wife in Irene's long absence. Not a local wife, even, but an English woman. 'But,' he pleaded, 'it's you I love. I will get rid of her. She told me lies about her age. I will divorce her.' It was a very emotional evening. Ray had been in Casamance and as he climbed wearily from the Land Rover I filled him in on the unfolding drama. I made some omelettes and we all picked at them dully then abandoned them. I took Iréne into the bedroom and gave her a hankie and tried to talk like a problem-page auntie (one of the many facets of journalism I have, in fact, explored in my time). I find this happens a lot. Women write to me or visit me to seek advice which I am seldom qualified to give. I tried to explain that African men regard marriage differently to us; or rather they regard it somewhat as Europeans of times past regarded it, something arranged by the families for territorial or financial reasons, nothing to do with love.

Ironically, the birdman had first brought Iréne to meet us as an example of how well a marriage could work out between a black man and a white woman. 'Look at Ray and Mariama,' he'd say, peering at us as though we were a pair of buffalo weavers or flappet larks. For he had surely been fond of our dear friend, and perhaps he had thought he could continue the relationship without mentioning the small matter of the English wife. Was he just insensitive, or was he callous? I've never been quite sure.

I soothed and scolded and sweet-talked until Iréne had stopped sobbing and applied fresh lipstick, while Ray conversed solemnly with her once-beloved in the living-room. An understanding was then reached. They hugged and wept together. Later she went home once again to wait for him to inform her that his other inconvenient union was dissolved. Then she planned, she would come back here, crutches and all, and make her nest here among the violet-backed sunbirds and lavender firefinches. I now know, many long months after this story first unfolded, what the ending was to be, but perhaps I will save it for another time, another book, for my mind is still roosting in 1992.

I had become, as you can tell, passing fond of ornithological jargon in these days. We received quite a number of twitchers for this is one of the prime sites of the whole sub-region for spotting species of rarity and beauty. The twitchers would be instantly recognisable, even without the aid of binoculars for they all carried very small back-packs (clothes being unimportant to them) and very large tripods. They rose at dawn and set off into the forest without breakfast. They came home to roost late and when they talked it was distractedly, with their eyes roaming over your shoulder all the while, until they broke off in mid-sentence to stare, entranced, at a spectacled weaver or red-cheeked cordon-bleu. In other words, they were wonderful guests. You could have fed them on sawdust and slept them in sheep-pens, I sometimes thought, and they would barely have noticed. They sat outside their huts with their *Field Guides to the Birds of West Africa*, scribbling in their notebooks. They went off up-river, impervious to the bumps and police-stops and seats crowded with old men and chickens and bales of rice, with the harmattan wind blowing or the summer humidity dribbling down their faces, never mind, just so long as they spotted a hammerkop or a shoveler or, oh bliss, a grey tit-babbler.

Some more mundane species were being wiped out systematically by our cats. I pleaded urgently with friends to adopt a dear little fluffy kitten (blackish-grey plumage, white underparts) but I had no takers. Foster father Penny, of the uncertain sexual status, mother Awa-dingding and four progeny, now big enough to scamper and leap all over the verandah, overturning milk-jugs, decimating my fern plants, scrabbling up guests' trouser-legs and yowling for food every five minutes.

They had been installed in a small hut across from the house which was once a storeroom, then became the breakfast room, and was latterly a bicycle-shed. It now smelled terrible and was full of fish-heads and bread-crusts and colonies of black ants come to collect the kittens' leavings. It was odd to think that once we had sat here with Werner and Marianne, Helma and Roel, Chris and Rodger, eating bread and marmalade and swapping travellers' tales. Now people ate on the verandah or under the baobab tree. Mostly on the verandah, which was a damned nuisance. It was nearer to the kitchen, that's true, but it was also right next to our bedroom so that we could never retire until the very last guest had drunk his last glass of wine and staggered off through the darkness to his little hut.

On the other hand, it did mean we could keep an eye on the cold-boxes and the gas-canisters. Carol and Rab, tucked away on the other side of our acre-and-a-half had wakened one morning to find two gas bottles spirited away overnight. The dog had, apparently barked furiously, but by the time old Musa of the distinguished bearing had stirred from his distinguished blanket-draped prone position on a beach-bed under the baobab, the thieves had long gone. Thieves, while no more prolific than in any other country, are a favourite topic of conversation, speculation and amusement.

One morning, for example, brother Lamin was supposed to come early to take us and some friends to Abuko to watch the monkeys, antelopes and crocodiles in the cool of the dawn when they are less fickle and stand-offish than in the mid-day heat. When he didn't turn up, Ray, expostulating loudly, went off to the village to find him. On his return he reported, matter-of-factly: 'He has gone with my uncle and my father and some other men to catch some cattle thieves.'

Some cows had been driven off in the small hours and an uncle who owned a gun (a kind of homemade blunderbuss, I believe) led a posse in pursuit. Lamin also owned a gun, at least a kind of a gun with no ammunition and no history of ever firing. He carried it anyway, menacingly, pointing it into the shadows and looking — he hoped — like Arnold Schwarzenegger whom he had seen in the cinema. They tramped south through the bush for many hours, their legs scratched and dusty, their feet aching, until they found the cows. The rustlers had vanished.

On the road to Kafountine in Casamance, South Senegal, a mother and children offer cashew fruit for sale. The nut is embedded in the sweet golden fruit.

It made a fine story to tell our friends when we apologised for not coming to pick them up at the pre-arranged time. It is much more convincing to say: 'The driver was stalking cattle-rustlers,' than to say 'we slept in' or 'the battery was flat.'

We got to Abuko eventually, and we did see monkeys, hundreds of them, perched on trees or at the sides of the shimmering, silvery paths through the primordial forest. For by now it was evening which always seems to me the time when roles are reversed, and the monkeys become the tourists, gazing intrigued at the strange ungainly species which trips and trudges on swollen feet in silly sandals, making odd hooting and squawking sounds and often accompanied by its young which demands drinks and rests and stops for the toilet at inconvenient moments. In fact, it was blessedly peaceful, few tourists to be seen and we spoke in hushed voices and squabbled in a whisper over whose turn it was for the binoculars. And that night we made plans to leave everyone behind and sneak off to Senegal, for word had reached us that Magali, my hands-on saviour, and her two Parisienne travelling companions, were having a good-bye party at Nicole and Sebastian's place and we were invited. We got packed, imagining drumming and dancing and succulent chicken and fish cooked by Nicole, and animated conversation in French. It turned out rather differently.

The Pharmacist's Tale

Two days later. I was lying on a bed in a round hut under a moonless Senegalese sky. Magali was passing a hot-tipped joss-stick back and forward, back and forward, an inch above my aching spine. Magali may have been — and to the best of my knowledge still is — a Parisienne healer, but she was at home in Africa. Already the Kafountine villagers had come to her in droves, with their boils and back-aches, menstrual pain and ankle sprains.

My own back-ache was now, I think, merely the result of too much bending and lifting and carrying water and trays and boxes of supplies, and, today, falling asleep on the beach near the campement in a clumsy position in the hot sun, and wakening with an 'Ouch!' The discomfort in my womb and pelvic area had virtually gone since my first meeting with Magali. Coincidence? I cannot tell. That very day I'd seen a backpacker's migraine dissolve under her touch.

Occasionally while she dealt with my spine, she left me and pit-patted through to a recess where a black-headed gull with a broken wing was also ensconced as a patient. The round house belonged to Sebastian and Nicole. Outside, France and Valerie sat at their large gnarled table under their large gnarled tree eating fish, cooked over hot wood embers with garlic and herbs, the roes distributed on top like little succulent parcels. But the atmosphere was as taut as the strings of a kora. Where was the party? There had been a certain contretemps between hosts and guests. It was all rather petty and I tried not to listen. I think there was also a contretemps between Nicole and Sebastian. She sighed and allowed tears to fill and illuminate her pale china blue eyes. He shrugged and ignored her. Conversations started and stopped abruptly. We had taken a bottle of brandy for Sebastian, so much cheaper in the Gambia and he sampled it once or twice. There were sniffs and snobs and stifled whispers and I was glad when we could disappear back to our little cell-like room in Situkotu Campement. We had come for the party, but also to have some time alone, hand-in-hand on the beach, cheek-by cheek in companionable silence. I don't know why we ever plan anything, because our plans never become reality!

Next day, we forswore our planned lunch à deux (fingers touching across the table, eyes meeting, sipping wine and nibbling fish) because we felt we ought to take *les trois dames* to lunch. The only actual restaurant in the village at that time was a few tables in an open yard with a latticed roof looped with some climbing leaves. Chickens and goats pecked and snuffled outside the open gate and it was recommended that you order food the day before. We ate rice with peanut sauce and cassava, since we had been remiss about ordering fish. We took our own wine, from the village's only grocery-shop. The reason we felt we must take the ladies was that, early that morning, they had appeared, tear-stained on our doorstep and claimed that Nicole had thrown them out. The brooding atmosphere of the night before had obviously exploded into a storm of accusation and counter-accusation

We negotiated with Diack, the amiable manager, who gave them a three-bedded room. Our own morning, meant to be a lazy one under the white mosquito net followed by an intimate breakfast of coffee and bread and honey became thus a morning of explanation and indignation, voices all around us, sympathy to be dispensed in several languages. Tut-tut, but not too much, for we had known Sebastian and Nicole much longer than we had known the ladies. Enough, though, to quench their tears and make them feel righteous.

'Zey 'av trone us out of zair 'ouse!' they repeated. 'Shhh! Never mind,' we said several times. They bought us the next lunch in return for our 'kindness'. In the evening we all ate together in the campement refectory. On the final morning, which had been intended to stretch idyllically into the afternoon, with time to watch again the ospreys soaring and plunging, the Chinese wreck outlined against the sky, instead we rose at 6 am so that we could drive *les françaises* to Banjul airport for their connection to Dakar and Paris. We looked at one another sadly. It was not how we had planned it. But we could not abandon the ladies, not now that their former hosts had washed their hands of them. We began to pack.

Oh, little Deux Chevaux! The 2CV deserved some kind of trophy for what it achieved that moist grey morning. Such a little car; such a remarkable amount of luggage. Was it, perchance, coming cavalierly to the aid of its own countrywomen? Their balafons and djembe drums, their bags and cases and boxes, our bags, a hundredweight or so of oranges produced by Diack as a goodbye gift. It ground slowly forward plunging gamely in and out of and around potholes and hillocks and troughs, its shock absorbers singing melodiously or croaking indignantly, its much-welded exhaust system puttering and wheezing until we arrived safely at Yundum airport. At the customs and immigration post between Francophone Senegal and Anglophone Gambia, there were certain minor difficulties. Nicole had brought the three ladies into the country 'by the back route', the unofficial one plied by certain bush-taxis, wending through rugged lanes between woods and remote hamlets devoid, usually, of uniformed officials. This route, like the one across the creeks at Kartong, was much used by people carrying bags of cement and suchlike, to avoid paying duty. It also meant that the three French passports had not had their entry stamp. Now an indignant immigration policeman eyed the documents suspiciously and it took all Ray's powers of Wollof winsomeness to persuade him that these good women were mere innocents abroad, unaware of the intricacies of the regulations. In the end, a few notes having changed hands, he allowed them to cross the border.

At the airport I enquired politely of one of the girls at the desk: 'When is the plane for Dakar connecting to Paris?' She glowered at me. 'What?' 'Dakar in Senegal. On to Paris,' I articulated helpfully. 'Mmmm. Maybe Wednesday?' she offered unwillingly. 'No, there's one today,' I insisted and she snarled at me for my impertinence. 'I have to go and check,' she grunted at last, and disappeared. I waited for a while then crossed to the airport Gamtel and phoned the Uniclam office in Kanefing. 'Oh, it's due to leave at twelve,' said a helpful voice. 'Thank you, thank you so much,' I responded.

It has always been a puzzle to me that there are so many sweet, helpful, smiling Gambian girls around, yet the ones who are employed in positions where they will meet the public seem to be chosen for their dourness and dullness of spirit. Sometimes I make a point of smiling fit to burst and smothering the girl with pleasantries, just to see if I can draw some ripple of reaction from her. 'What a pretty dress! What a nice day! My goodness, you must be very busy, blah-blah-blah . . .' It works sometimes, but not always.

Helpful doesn't mean accurate, mind you. Twelve o'clock came and went. One o'clock came and went. Groups of puzzled French people clustered in the tiny airport and the little bar over the road. A Uniclam rep skulked around looking harassed. 'He is trying to find a plane,' our friend Kabu revealed. He, being a courier, was trying his best to soothe some of the Gallic would-be travellers. Find a plane? What did he mean? Find a plane? Had they lost one? We asked Kabu how Pascal's kitten was. He looked blankly at us. Obviously cats were the last thing on his mind. '*C'est pas problème*', we heard him murmuring unconvincingly as he made his way from table to table.

Our three ladies slumped over their Pepsis and smoked Gauloises and waited trustingly for us to make everything come all right. Eventually the Uniclam man found two small planes, which shuttled the sweat-soaked, dusty, hungry passengers towards Dakar at 2.30 pm and 3.30 pm respectively. The Paris connection there was due to leave at 4 pm, but we assumed hopefully that they would hold it back for them. *C'est la vie. C'est pas problème.*

When we reached home my daughter asked: 'Did you have a nice romantic weekend?' and wondered why we answered 'Hah!' in such rasping tones. But she had had her own problems to cope with. Before we left we had filled the 1000-litre water-tank (a sky-blue moulded glass-fibre tub which sits some 35 metres above the well) using our brand-new pump, a splendid device, shipped out to us by none other than Jan the Turtle Rescuer.

Perhaps I should recap a bit on our water experiences. In the beginning there was none. Musa, our first watchman, would tramp round to the cattle station and fill buckets at their standpipe, then carry them back on his head, his feet smacking the earth flip-flop, flip flop. We valued every drop, using the water from washing clothes to flush the loo, 'showering' with a sponge. Then, on our first visit to the UK in 1990, we brought back a water-pump. It worked magnificently . . . for about a month, then burned itself out. We tried to mend it. Peter from Prestwick took it back to Britain and returned it to the factory. They said that, because we'd tried to fix it, we had broken the terms of the guarantee. By this time, of course, we had our well, dug by Ketta the well-digger, all of twenty-seven metres deep. When the pump broke down, we went back to hauling buckets up, which made us appreciate water even more than when it was coming from the standpipe, conveyed on Musa's head. No wonder I'd such back trouble!

But now, hallelujah, we had our new pump, a brilliant piece of equipment which pushed 1000 litres of water into our pale blue tank in a mere 22 minutes. We had reckoned that quantity should keep Carol, Rab and Cameron in liquid comfort for the weekend, and had therefore left the generator (which powered the pump) safely locked up. In fact, a leaking pipe behind the tourist toilets meant that the whole damn lot had gushed out and left them with a severe drought situation hours after we'd left for our 'romantic weekend'. Oh dear. To make matters worse, Carol had developed a horrid bout of Banjul Belly, as it's known. She lay on the bed, groaning, in our absence, with sudden desperate dashes to the loo, cursing the lack of flushing water, cursing us, I guess.

Ibrahim trudged stoically back and forward to the standpipe, bringing bucket after bucket, while Carol, clutching her stomach, gazed forlornly at her kitchen-garden, whose frizzy carrot-heads and spiky onion shoots were drooping mournfully for lack of moisture. Even if there was water to spare, she wouldn't have had the strength to pour it. She was what we call in Scotland 'a puir wee sowel', and I felt guilty for having left her.

All the same, Carol had fitted into Gambian life with astonishing ease. A slender, freckled lass who never bothered much about make-up or fancy clothes, she took the dust and sweat in her stride and her easy-going, honest friendliness made her popular with everyone. Even more, Cameron, his little white-blond head bobbing as he trotted or tricycled along the paths, had become a firm favourite with the villagers. 'Cammy-RON! *Na kam? Fo do dem?'* (How are you? Where are you going?) they would call and he would grin and toddle onward. The only thing he hated was to be called 'tubab'. 'I'm not tubab. My name's Cameron' he would shout crossly, and everyone would laugh.

Dr Tom called and gave Carol something for her dehydration. Ray had the leak fixed and pumped up oceans of water. The taps turned on and gushed, the loos flushed, Ibrahim used a hosepipe to refresh the onions and carrots. And a fax arrived from Paris saying that *les trois dames* had arrived home safely and were ever so grateful to us. Now all we had to contend with were the everyday oddities of our guests, Like, for example, Peter the pharmacist from Skipton. Beatific smile, spaniel eyes, jaunty straw hat. All charm and dither. Lizzie, my TV announcer friend, had found him on the beach and he followed her here, panting like a stray adoring puppy. He never got anywhere with Liz, but he kept trying, and he was impossible not to like. He had lectured in clinical pharmacology in a prestigious Canadian university and written learned articles for medical journals, but he still dropped things, lost things, tripped over things.

I was crushing garlic with one hand and stirring groundnut sauce with the other when he shuffled into the kitchen. 'Er, em, just supposing, speaking hypothetically, one of your guests had sort of, em, lost the only key to their hut, and their hut was, er, sort of locked at the time, what, just speaking hypothetically, of course, would you do?'

'Speaking hypothetically,' I said, slicing through some cassava with murderous downward sweeps of glinting steel, 'I'd kill him.' He backed out of the kitchen, tripping over a cat, and flopped down on the sofa dejectedly. 'Oh, I see.'

We searched the beach and the forest path, upturning stones, digging in the sand, alarming monkeys and lizards. No key. We tried, fruitlessly, to open the door of hut B with each of the twenty or so keys in our possession, those for cupboards, toilets, bedrooms, storerooms. None worked. We set about the door with a selection of sharp and blunt instruments. By removing the inner part of the door frame we succeeded in effecting an entry, with merely a pile of shavings, splinters and sawdust, a busted lock and a bulging blood-vessel on Ray's forehead to show for it. Meanwhile one of our twitchers had arrived, hotfoot from spotting a violet plantain-eater, its scarlet wings and purple back skimming through the leaves like an exotic wind-blown orchid. He and Peter sipped vodka outside hut A (hut B now being defunct until we could find a joiner, a locksmith and a painter) and I sighed and decided I preferred scatty but lovable guests like these two. The efficient, unforgetful ones who arrive with matching sets of luggage, designer sunglasses and a habit of peering at the food and the bedclothes suspiciously always fill me with awe and apprehension.

The Peters and twitchers of this world will doss down anywhere, eat anything with relish and chuckle tolerantly if you forget to clean their rooms or replenish the toilet rolls or run out of bread. But they can create their own kind of gentle havoc. And Peter was the only guest we ever had who missed his plane (apart from my son David, but that's another story).

A day before he was due to go home, the befuddled pharmacist decided to go to Basse 'But it's at the other end of the country! It's too far. It's too hot. It's too late . . . ' we yelped, to no avail.

'I've thought of everything,' drawled Peter confidently. 'I've met this chap with a taxi who says he'll have me there by lunchtime, make sure I see all the sights, install me at the Apollo Hotel, then have me back here in time to pick up my stuff and go to the airport.' He gave the happy smile of a child who has watched Peter Pan and knows he will be able to fly if he flaps his arms hard enough. Talking of Peter Pan, I don't think our Peter had ever really grown up either. We gazed at each other ominously. Ray stomped off to pump some more water and I attacked more blameless cassava with an angry cleaver.

Next mid-day, no Peter. The afternoon expanded and the sun rolled inexorably west. His shirts and towel and books and bottle of vodka remained untouched in his room. Bleakly we watched his Air 2000 flight soaring after the sun. 'Should we call the police?' I wondered. 'Send out a search party?' Ray shrugged and said something rude in Wollof, just as a battered, bleary-eyed figure in frayed shorts and dust-caked shoes staggered into the compound and threw itself down on a protesting basket-chair. 'Basse!' It croaked. 'Grrrr!' Peter's tale was too long and too complex to relate in detail. It appeared to involve his accidentally bumping the arm of the driver, who swerved and hit a stone, bursting the tyre; arriving at the Apollo Hotel in darkness and sharing a room with things which rustled and scratched and brought him out in crimson bumps; waking to find the taxi-driver had vanished; finding another driver, running out of petrol, being stopped by the police and interrogated for an hour because the insurance was out of date, breaking down again because the radiator was dry. There may have been a few other incidents but that was the gist of it. It was calculated to bring tears to the eyes of any tour operator. One rep almost broke down in sympathetic sobs, and fixed Peter up with a flight two days later. For his remaining forty-eight hours in our care, he was greeted with compassionate admiration everywhere he went. 'You're the Peter who went to Basse! Tsk, tsk! Sorry, sorry!'

Poor old Basse gets a bad press sometimes. But it has a seedy charm all its own. The full name is Basse Santa Su. Santa Su means 'upper home'. Duma Su means 'lower home' and describes the riverside area, where buildings can be severely flooded in summer and prospective builders now think in terms of stilted floors. There are some ramshackle but atmospheric old colonial buildings, where whites in solar topees must once have watched the bustling port. Many craft used to ply from the coast to Basse, carrying animals, people and tradable goods, some destined for further afield, to Senegal or Mali. There are warehouses for groundnuts and a couple of cinemas, and at the time of writing there were plans to build public toilets. That's what I call progress!

Bird-watchers love it. I understand it bustles with black crakes, guddles of grey-backed cameropteras, swamp flycatchers and black-bellied bustards. There is even the chance of seeing the elusive Secretary Bird, with its huge stalking legs and unpleasant habit of pounding snakes into a pulp before eating them for lunch. Peter, however, had missed out on all of the sights and just wanted to go home. We wanted him to go home too, not because we were impervious to his charm, but because we couldn't cope with too many more excitements. And the bird-watcher was under the weather and needed our unobtrusive attention and gentle ministrations. For he was prone in Hut C, swathed in lotion and making harsh strident crying calls very similar to the black-bellied bustards mentioned above. This was because he had allowed himself to become so enraptured by the number of species he spotted on his first days in our compound that he wandered about in the sun without a hat or a long-sleeved shirt. He was now a striking rosy-red colour, usually seen in the body-feathers of a carmine bee-eater. It wasn't so much the pain that was troubling him, it was the frustration. The very thought that, as he lay there twitching behind his closed door, some wonderfully rare bird might hover overhead or dance cheekily past his door, knowing that he was as inert and tender as a braised pigeon.

Perhaps, we worried, he would echo the remark made by President Roosevelt in 1943. Franklin D. spent a night in a cruiser anchored off Bathurst (now Banjul) on the way back from the Casablanca Conference en route to Brazil. He caught a fever and blamed it on poor little Gambia, which he described in conversation to Winston Churchill later as 'that hell-hole of yours'. But Bill was made of sterner and more forgiving stuff, and, as later events would show, embraced West Africa with more than platonic fervour. Meanwhile, bye-bye Peter.

'Have you got your passport? Your tickets? You'll be sure not to lose anything? Will you check the time of the Gatwick Express as soon as you reach the airport? Please be careful. Don't do anything silly.' My maternal instincts flowed freely, while he said meekly 'Yes. Yes. No. No. Yes. Yes. Of course not.' He ambled planeward carrying bulging plastic bags full of oranges and bananas, bottles of vodka and bits of clothing which kept falling out. I knew he'd mislay something before he landed, but what was it to do with me? This was my problem. Room maids, for instance, were only meant to make the bed and dust round lightly. **Me?** I picked up soiled socks and underpants, folded shirts, re-arranged letters and books so that my poor guests probably couldn't find a darned thing. And don't think I only fussed over men. When Annie and Maggie where here from Glasgow, I fussed over them like a mother-hen pecking at would-be suitors, presumptuous postcard-sellers and feral fly-men. Daft really, since both of them had travelled the world and were well able to look after themselves.

In Uncle Dembo's a Rasta Romeo would swagger to our table and feel the sharp stab of my discouraging glare. 'Hey, Mariama. I just wanna talk to your beautiful friends.' To which I would indicate that he could get on his bike right now, or else. Or else what? I had no idea but it didn't matter; the 'bumsters' always wandered off amiably to seek out other victims. (Bumsters is a term now recognised sufficiently to be used formally in radio news broadcasts. I suppose it comes from beach-bum, confused with hustler, and it sums up the essence of the two words quite crisply). But more of that later, for we must go back to pink, peeling Bill.

International Relationships

Flocks of twenty or thirty pelicans had been passing overhead, pale-grey with, visible in flight, pinkish-wine back feathers and a wide-winged grace in the air quite unlike their comical waddling appearance on land. Had they come up from Casamance to say hullo? Did they, in their rare bouts of conversation (mostly clacking, grunting sounds) speak Senegalese-French? Or had they come from the Gambian hinterland, in which case perhaps they clacked in Jola?

I loved to watch them, necks stretched out, soaring and dipping. I had hated to see, once or twice, one dowdy dismal specimen on a chain, earthbound outside a border police post. But now Ray had pronounced a new species, henceforth to be known as the black pelican, which, even now makes me chuckle when I hear him say it.

The black pelican, you see, was first spotted by Bill, the lanky, shy, earnest ornithologist, fully recovered from his blisters and burning back. His skin, now more peachy-brown than raw red, was sensibly covered by a borrowed shirt of Ray's and his head was topped by my battered bush-hat as he set off on his peregrinations with field-glasses and notebook. In the beginning, he duly directed his attention to tinker birds (lemon-rumped) and bee-eaters (blue-cheeked), emerging dusty and sweat-stained from the bush or the forest at nightfall.

He was in Uncle Dembo's, however, when he discovered the common black pelican. He was, in fact, discussing the price of chicken and chips with Big Mary from Glasgow ('D'youse want tomato sauce, son?') when the bird perched on the seat next to him, conspicuously plumaged in large earrings, bright bodice and tight skirt. She was escorted by a local wood-carver whom she described as her brother. She was, she assured Bill, fascinated by nature, especially birds. He was a sitting duck. He almost left his binoculars on the table beside his half-eaten chicken. He crept home to bed in the small hours, and slept late in the morning. His tripod lay unnoticed on the floor. His *Field Guide* remained closed. That night, he brought the black pelican home with him, which quite rightly scandalised the watchman and put us in a very embarrassing situation. 'If you ask me, she's not a black pelican,' I whispered to Ray next day as I dusted the discarded *Field Guide* and changed Bill's sheets pointedly, 'she's a Senegal Puff-Back Flycatcher.' 'Eh?' said Ray. 'It says here,' I explained, leafing through the pages: 'A small noticeable flycatcher, always moving about and easily spotted . . .'

Should I have told Bill that she was indeed from Senegal and was, in Big Mary's words, 'one of the girls', that he could catch something very nasty from her, get ripped off and that there were, in the Spring of 1992, 150 recorded cases of full-blown Aids in the Gambia, mostly resulting from prostitution? Should I have said: 'Go back to your binoculars and find a few francolins or bulbuls to occupy your mind'? But Bill was besotted. 'She's taking me to see her family home in Senegal,' he chirruped happily. 'She's going to show me the best areas for birds.' Oh lordie, lordie. I visualised his being jumped by her cousins up some dark alley in Dakar, stripped of everything, including his field-glasses and his dignity. But he went anyway, his companion shimmying along beside him, rump rotating smugly, earrings swinging.

Four days passed. This was worse than Peter' pilgrimage to Basse. Should I call the police this time? But he was a free agent, over twenty-one and his sex-life was nothing to do with us. I tried not to worry, and of course he came back eventually, tired, scruffy, slightly shell-shocked but unharmed. He was almost broke and had to pay his bill in small denomination notes and scrounge the last couple of meals free but we were so relieved to see him we didn't mind, especially when he said: 'I'm so pleased to be back here with you. It feels like coming home.' Ah! I preened my dun-coloured feathers and crowed.

I assumed that he had donated most of his limited cash supply to the Senegalese Black Pelican Trust. 'Oh, you should have seen where I was living . . . the food I was eating . . . the beds I was sleeping on . . .' he broke off and gazed distractedly into space, not even noticing a palm-nut vulture cruising past. The girl had, it seemed, stayed with her family. But there were lots of others here to take her place with other gauche galoots like Bill. Some were stunning, with elaborately pleated hair and exquisite African dresses in riotous colours, lavishly appliquéed, embroidered and tucked and frilled. Haughty carriage, flashing eyes, bold conversation. Others affected buttock-shaping mini-skirts and jeans, bleaching their skins in the sad silly belief that male tourists lusting after the exotic experience of a black girl would fancy them more if they looked paler . . .

But if I felt exasperated by the girls, I felt positively apoplectic at times about the boys, the aforementioned bumsters who followed female tourists like vultures telling (I have seen and heard it) grossly overweight ugly Swedes and Germans that they were beautiful and they loved them passionately. I remember one exuberant Rasta describing the girl who had just left his table in Uncle Dembo's, where he had been stroking and sweet-talking her intermittently for several days. 'That one, she's weird,' he revealed in Mandinka. 'You know, her pubic hair is dyed green!' Everyone fell about sniggering. Inevitably the same young men — usually dashingly dressed and splendidly groomed — would be back with different girls every fortnight during the tourist season, murmuring the same sweet nothings over and over again, just remembering to change the names. 'Je t'adore, Annette,' 'Ich liebe die, Gretchen', 'I love you, Tracy'.

Some of the boys had ineffable charm and were, even while we disapproved, good friends of ours. Like affable Ali. 'I always make women very happy. Whatever they may give me, I give them a good time for it,' he said frankly. Others, I loathed. Like one Ousman, who would bring in his latest quarry looking like a fisherman who has netted a prize salmon. Others, to be fair, were perfectly nice chaps who fell genuinely in love with perfectly nice girls. Often they came to me for advice, but mostly I tried to avoid giving it. Even some of the nice boys had wives of their own race tucked away. And some of the wives didn't seem to mind their husbands having white girl-friends, presumably hoping some cash might spin-off in their direction.

Anyway, it was, at that particular time, all part of the free entertainment at Uncle Dembo's, a bar which has had a chequered career since it opened a dozen years ago. First it was run by our old chum Bakary Dembo, after whom it was named, at which time it was a cheap, basic, down-to-earth African bar, enjoyed by tourists for that very reason. We had our 'wedding reception' there - Julbrews and Fantas and chicken and chips and Bakary put up some bunting. The bar was always open but the catering counter opened and closed like a goldfish's mouth, with occasional grand appearances by young men who served elaborate food with napkins and tablecloths in profusion, dull periods when all you could get was a bowl of rice, and Ray's favourite interlude when Ali (yes Ali the ladies' man) made delicious *chawarma* wrapped in white paper and fiery with chilli pepper.

Since Big Mary and Wee Hannah had taken over, a reasonably cheap and varied menu prevailed, pretty lampshades dangled over the tables, danced round by exotic moths, and there were lively nights when local bands would play African jazz or Wollof drums and pack the place solid. It was the scene of some sterling human dramas. Marriages had been made and marred here. Fabulous fights had exploded and ended in blood or bawdy chuckles. Drug-pushers had been ejected by Mary with the classic words: 'See you, son? You're barred!' One doleful Englishwoman whose Mandinka husband beat her up regularly once a week came here for sympathy. Why didn't she leave the swine, I wondered? 'She loves the big bastard, so she does,' Mary would explain reasonably. Mary, as I have mentioned, worked for many years in a Glasgow Procurator fiscal's office; nothing surprised her. She had seen it all before, after traditional Glasgow Saturday nights.

She would break off in mid-sentence to lumber towards the doorway like an angry Sherman tank. 'Eric! Ah'm tellin' you wance more, if youse wants tae be liftit by the gendarmes, just you pit wan foot inside that door!'

Eric, our cute-faced little Rasta friend with the wild wardrobe (one night, voluminous African robes, another night, leather trousers and biker jacket; another night, hot-pants and hair twirled into a frizzy topknot) and a girl in every European capital (not to mention, he once claimed, a baby in Paris) was in disgrace. He was skulking on the other side of the wall where local lads who couldn't afford to buy a drink would sit and listen to the music. His hair tonight was oiled into a church spire, he was wearing one of his colourful African frocks and he was shouting: 'F*** you! F*** you!' towards the interior, over and over in a grim monotone. From time to time he picked up a stone and hurled it after his words. He was, Mary informed us, not only drunk on beer, but he had also been swallowing the poisonous local 'gin' and sloshing down certain pills with illegal implications. Someone ought to take him home, but it wouldn't be Ray. He was still fuming about the last time.

Then, Eric slumped in the passenger seat yelling and snarling to no-one in particular and Ray who, like me, always had a quite unwarranted sense of concern about his wellbeing, however badly he behaved, asked him, as he circled the dark alleyways of his village, 'Where do you live, Eric?' He asked him many times but Eric seemed to have forgotten. Local residents, when questioned about him, took one look at his rolling eyes, slack mouth and twitching limbs and disclaimed all knowledge of him. Ray came back in a foul mood. 'I'm never going to help that idiot again,' he vowed. But he would, I knew. This time, Mary was about to have him arrested, so Ray sprinted outside to try to quieten him down. He arrived just as Eric had spotted an old enemy and yelled an obscene challenge vaguely in his direction. The enemy clobbered him and blood spurted out, spattering Ray's nice Marks & Spencer trousers. He stormed back into the bar. 'Bloody Eric! Let the police take him!' Ray is very vain about his clothes. Blood-stains on his trousers were enough almost to ruin his evening.

I patted the miscreant on the arm and issued maternal advice. He looked at me virtuously, full of pathos and remorse saying: 'Yes, Mariama. You're right, Mariama,' then wandering off to hurl more epithets and broken bricks into the bar. He spent the night in the cells, seemingly intoning all the time his opinion of Uncle Dembo's and its clientèle, till, next day, sober, he was eaten by shame and remorse, as usual. We had stayed to enjoy the antics of the guests. Some were stuffy souls who found all the colourful activity unsavoury and unsettling. They soon found their ways to the staid and safe English-run establishment where English breakfasts and teas were available and the customers were mostly white. Others — notably Scots and Irish — relished it all for its entertainment value, a bit like a good Glasgow pub on Fair Friday or Hogmanay. The band turned up when Eric left and everyone tried the sensual bum-waggling, bosom-swaying, foot-stomping African dances. Girls of several tints and sizes nestled into strong black arms, old white men sat up taller in their seats on attracting the attention of lissome black pelicans, and a bunch of London teenagers chewed gum and drank lager and tried to look old enough for whatever was available but didn't quite manage it. On another night, the fanatical vegetarians (the ones who had hated to see fish being hooked) who otherwise were very interesting and convivial people, became the centre of a clapping, cheering circle of Gambians. For Alison's dancing was sensational, better, everyone agreed, than most Africans'. The rotating movement of the bottom, in harmony with certain wide-sweeping arm-movements, is something I have never got the hang of, but it is — as dear Scott would have said — 'wicked' to watch.

And on yet another night we went to see a very famous African band playing at the Tropicana nightclub, which has spacious gardens, lavish seating for up to 2000 and elaborate lighting effects. Waiters scurried around frantically serving somewhat overpriced drinks and there were dignitaries in the audience, government ministers and prominent bureaucrats and businessmen. Their daughters, young Gambian women of substance, were dressed up to the nines and bejewelled intricately. Sleeves like giant tulips, peplums like pelmets, headdresses like birds of paradise. The young men strutted in new shirts and jackets whose designs were initiated in New York or Jamaica and interpreted by eager tailors in Serrekunda and Bakau. If there were any black pelicans here they were overshadowed by the peacocks. I felt like a wee Glasgow sparrow. Here, because of the 'VIPs' in the audience, everyone was shy about dancing and sat instead clapping politely as though it was a Church concert. The inside disco was vibrating away and we tried to insert ourselves into that but it was like chiselling a hole in a solid wall, so we gave up. Clusters of butterflies and moths danced their own aerial ballet overhead. The moon, a slender crescent, lay on its back like a cradle waiting to be rocked.

In the hot light of day, a flitting took place. Mattresses and cooking-pots, Cameron's trike, bulging bundles of clothes and boxes of books were heaped into the back of the Land Rover. Cameron was yelling: 'Wanna stay at g'anny's house!' Carol and Rab were dusty and bad-tempered. Carol was almost in tears, not at leaving me but at leaving her garden, with its lacy rows of carrot-tops and coriander, not to mention the famous compost-heap. She knew I wouldn't remember to water the plants or replenish the heap and she was right. Within days weeds had skipped and scurried over it all and it was as though her months of work had never existed.

I wasn't sure if I was glad or sorry to see them go; for I must add quickly that they were only transferring a couple of miles away to a sensible set of rooms in a compound in Kololi, with a kitchen and a toilet. No running water, but that would come, the new Serahuli landlord assured them innocently.

In the morning Carol would bribe a neighbour's boy to go to the standpipe along the street and bring her buckets of water. There were bare concrete floors and several other, Gambian, families living in the compound, a bus-stop nearby and tar roads where Carol could cycle more easily to work. She would miss the space, the garden, even me, but how long could a young mother survive with two rooms designed by us as basic holiday space? Until now she and Rab had earned my admiration by managing to cook on a gas-ring between two concrete blocks outside under a screen of palm leaves, where wind, dust, rain and ants made culinary life marginally less luxurious than heating a billy-can in the desert during the war. They had tholed our unpredictable and sometimes non-existent water-supply, and Carol had gamely pushed her bike along the pock-marked sandy tracks through the field to reach the main road. But her new job as a librarian in a Bakau school, with prospects of teaching next term, made it necessary to seek more convenient, if less pastoral quarters.

It was all a bit tearful though. I had become used to barefoot Cameron banging the door at 7 am to demand 'b'ead 'n jam, g'anny'. I had enjoyed borrowing garlic and lending coffee and filial gossip. As for Eliman, Cameron's beloved adopted big brother (technically his step grand-uncle but at his small age that seemed too great a title to carry), Eliman was bereft, until we loaned him a bike and saw him pedal furiously off to Kololi every day to see his wee pal. Often, he brought him back here on the kiddy-seat, so that I didn't feel deprived after all, watching his diminutive blond head bobbing up and down as he flew his kite or chased the dog or tried to clamber up the broad base of the baobab. And he liked his new home too, which he referred to as 'my other house'. There were swarms of kids to play with and building sand to climb on and the family over the lane (a rich Gambian with two wives and many children) had a roomful of fancy toys and a video recorder. Mostly though, it was the downmarket brigade he played with. He would toddle after them when they followed tourists calling: 'Tubab, tubab! Gimme dalasis!'

What, I wondered did they think of the peach-cheeked, white-haired boy-child begging lustily alongside Alieu and Bintah and Modou, wearing flip-flops on little fawn feet and an African cotton smock? Carol and Rab found it very embarrassing. I thought it was rather funny. Finding the funny side of things is one sure way to survive in this 'dear little place' (Queen Victoria's epithet!).

Laughter and tears blended richly when we went to another Irish night, this time to celebrate or mourn Brendan's imminent departure back to his homeland. It was held in a very small bar in Bakau, with about a dozen of us huddled over Guinness and red wine, getting merrily maudlin over the usual guilt-inducing, gut-wrenching songs. Donal the priest was there, well-relaxed after being THE prime organiser in the visit that Spring to the Gambia of His Holiness the Pope. Great tales he told us, of how when the Pope decided he wanted to stop and pray in a little church en route from the airport, the entire cavalcade came to a confused halt, with himself and the Vatican security men talking frantically to each other on their walkie-talkies. 'Where IS he? What's he DOING?' It was a wonderful visit, enjoyed as much by Muslims and Methodists and me (a lapsed Episcopalian/Church of Scotland/Wee Free) as by the Roman Catholics. Choirs of Gambian children sang in Wollof and Mandinka, Fula dancers danced, drummers drummed and the President and his Holiness each made stirring, heart-warming speeches. At the airport, we heard, as the dignitaries of Church, State and Islam lined up to greet His Holiness, a string of porters joined the line so that the Holy handshakes went on and on . . .

Donal and everyone else sang sad songs and silly ones, and I was even induced to sing 'There Was a Wee Cooper Who Came From Fife, Hey Willie Wallicky, Ho John Dougal, etc etc', which elicited an understandably restrained round of applause. At 4am or thereabouts Peter the archivist from Banjul Museum stood up and poignantly paced the floor, reciting Andrew Marvel's ode 'To His Coy Mistress', with fine gestures and total recall. I wondered what nocturnal passing Gambians might have thought to hear him:

Then worms shall try
That long-preserv'd Virginity:
And your quaint Honour turn to dust:
And into Ashes all my lust . . .

A long-haired maiden (actually a volunteer worker at the local mental hospital) provided the foil to his performance, lowering her eyes and blushing and simpering appropriately. We all — Gambian, Irishmen and women, English and Scottish, not to mention the Swedish proprietor — howled in admiration and the Swede threw out one foolish Spaniard who had had the temerity to ask for disco music while Brendan, red-haired, red-cheeked and moist-eyed, was singing the kind of song that could get you lynched in Larkhall. (Lowland Scots will understand this reference; others may ignore it). In the end, shaking hands and hugging our Irish friend, we were all moist-eyed. Oh these continual partings; life sometimes seems punctured too often by goodbyes, so that all the compressed air of companionship threatens to escape.

We had a letter from Iman and Farid in Cape Town. Their moving had been drastic. Iman went via London, while Farid forged his way south, via, I think, Sierra Leone, Ghana, Botswana, until he was finally reunited with her and his South African family and a supportive Muslim enclave. This was what they had dreamed of. Gambian Islam infuriated them, with its loose interpretations of the Koran (as they saw it), superstitions and immodest modes of dress. In the Cape, they were sure, they would find real devotion and an efficient, progressive society far different to the leisurely, independent, haphazard hotchpotch of West Africa. Once Iman, a jolly, sturdy, outspoken woman of whom I had become extremely fond, had refused to bow to the judge in a court case she was observing in Banjul because, she said, 'I bow to no-one but Allah.' In the beginning, their new life was described in glowing terms, but as the months passed, the oppressive regime and high costs of, for example, health care, altered their once-rosy view. A year later, we were to open their letters and find sorrow and frustration both in and between the lines, and the words 'How we long to come back to the Gambia.'

Our circle of friends always had an ecumenical flavour. Monica, a born-again Christian, refused to speak to us for a long time after Stanley bit her husband Matthew on the leg (Understandable, I guess!) but her fury faded. Matthew had left Banjul for Yorkshire back in the Fifties, and in the decade following he was Masambula, the huge leopard-skin-clad wrestler who threw and was thrown by Giant Haystacks, Mick McManus and others of that ilk. A superstar in his heyday, but driven, or lured, back to Africa to set up the basis of a retreat for like-minded fundamentalist Christians. The building is there, just behind the graveyard in Bijilo, but no retreating Bible-thumpers have yet arrived. Matthew is now nearer seventy than sixty and a mild and mellow reflection of that wild champion of the ring.

Caroline and handsome Julius were Episcopalian in a desultory fashion. She was no longer working at the Tanji Community Project launched by Peter and herself in 1989/90. Now she was a high-powered power-dressed temporary staff member with the United Nations in Banjul, helping to initiate a poverty alleviation project which seemed to involve reams of paper laden with circumlocuitous phrase and an interminable number of clauses, sub-clauses and words like 'implementation' (my pet hate word! Why can't people just 'do'?). I knew all this because, as often as not, she would arrive on our doorstep while we were trying to prepare a meal for a batch of hungry guests and ask me to help her sort it out into reasonably comprehensible language. Being a sharp-tongued cynic I once said to her: 'Why don't you tear it all up and distribute a memo which says: There are a lot of very poor people because a few very rich people have all the money?' She said: 'Please be

Lunch under the baobab with Andrea Merryll, artist from Boise, Idaho, and Joe Lamsin, artist from Sierra Leone — and who brought the two of them together? We did!

serious. We're trying to implement expeditiously an ambitious and far-reaching initiative . . .' Oh, yeah.

We enjoyed our friendly debates. I regarded her as a cross between a daughter and a sister, and she, I think, saw me as a cross between a mother and a sister (I preferred the sisterly label) even though we both infuriated each other frequently. 'For goodness sake, stop looking at yourself in the mirror,' I'd nag. 'For goodness sake, START looking at yourself in the mirror,' she'd retort. She had a point. Since I came to live here, one by one, my bra, my eye make-up, my moisture cream and my high-heeled shoes have been abandoned. Yet I still feel I look better here, brown and flat-footed, than I did in Glasgow!

Julius smiled tolerantly at our exchanges. Built like an American footballer, with that dazzling smile and a responsible job as a marketing executive with a large petrol company, he adored every well-groomed high-heeled, moisturised inch of Caroline and they made a dashing couple. Her attendance at the Anglican Cathedral increased and I observed snidely to Ray that it was probably because Julius, in his high-necked white surplice, looked so cute. Both of them were present at our next, and surely most international so far, barbecue. Kabu from Senegal with Pascal, the French girlfriend, Tom and Joan, our infinitely kind and competent medical friends from Scotland, Joe the Freetonian artist, Andrea, a talented artist from Boise, Idaho, Darren, an Australian back-packer en route for Casamance, and Roel. Yes, the crazy Dutchman was back to collect his Land Rover lolly. When we met him at the airport he was pale and respectable with parted brown hair, as we'd never seen him before. But within a few days the hair was sun-streaked and tousled, the skin was brown, the shirt was off and he was drinking Julbrew with all the determined vigour he had shown a year before. He and Sidiki (Senegalese-Malian, I think) thumped the djembe drums together under the tree, brothers in beer, both beaming companionably.

It's good that people come back. It makes the partings less traumatic. I dare say one day Brendan will be back and we'll listen again to rebel songs in the moonlight.

Dumplings and
Dressmakers

I was feeling a lot safer at night, I said sardonically to Ray, now that Gorro our new watchman had armed himself . . . with a bow and arrow! Yes, another watchman. Musa of the noble bearing and well-worn prayer-mat had simply disappeared, never to return. As for Ibrahim our trusty dayman, who had planted flowers along the edge of the path and never let the banana go thirsty, he had received a message from his in-laws in Senegal that if he didn't go home to his wife soon they would annul the marriage. 'I suppose I must go,' he sighed, with notable lack of fervour.

Yet again Ray was destined to sit morosely under the baobab tree wrapped in a blanket, clutching the cutlass, and jumping when the dog snarled at a passing rabbit. Yet again, by day, we took turns to go shopping so as not to leave the place unattended, and Ray watered the plants, which took him about three hours. I longed to go to the beach but 'we can't leave the place unguarded,' he insisted. The actual rate of burglaries was probably considerably lower than in Glasgow. There, I recalled, if you didn't get done over at least once a year, the neighbours speculated that you must have bought all your furniture and leisure equipment from Oxfam. But Ray had never forgotten the dramatic nicking of the generator a year before and he was obsessionally determined it would never happen again.

Indeed, just before Ibrahim left something had occurred which had brought the whole incident back into sharp focus. We were lying on the beach beyond the forest, salty from the sea, sweaty from the sun, sipping warm beer and reading old *Newsweeks*. Suddenly Ray said, out of the corner of his mouth, 'Mariama, don't look now, but it's him! That bastard!' Tiny crabs scuttled back and forward across the creamy sand and whimbrels strutted and skipped at the edge of the surf. It was so peaceful; who was this person who had turned Ray into a black James Cagney? I sighed and mumbled, drowsy from the heat.

'It's him! The thief! The one who stole our generator then escaped from Yundum police station!' For all of twelve months he'd been on the run, except that I suspect he didn't have to run very hard as the police seemed to have forgotten all about him. Now as I sneaked a look, he was certainly not running, but strolling in a leisurely manner with another Rasta rascal, both of them animatedly chatting up a haunted-looking tourist. 'Go!' hissed Ray, whose favourite TV programme on visits to Britain had been *The Bill*, 'Run to the house and take the car. Go and get the police. I will follow him.'

I gathered up soggy towels and *Newsweeks* and empty Coke bottles, trying to look casual, and hirpled up to the house, sweating profusely on the sharp incline adjacent to the forest, waving a hurried greeting to the herdsmen who look after the ITC cattle, hoping that Roel might be sprawled in the garden with a Julbrew, for he would love to be in on this. Was it not he who had been with Ray on the night of the raid, flashing his torch and waving his cudgel? For months after the robbery, when I wrote to him I would start my letters: 'Dear Batman . . .' Ray, of course, had been Robin. On such silly shared experiences and jokes are friendships founded! Roel wasn't anywhere to be seen. Ray still had the house-key so I wrapped a towel round my swimsuit, grabbed Eliman for moral and linguistic support and drove panting and dishevelled to the police station. I spluttered out my story in English, with Eliman providing simultaneous translation in Wollof, and the duty officer with commendable alacrity bawled! 'Go with her!' to two delighted constables, happy to have some excitement to take them out of the office. I suspect if they visited Britain they would enjoy *The Bill* too. We all leapt into the 2CV and I hurtled along the road to the front entrance of the Senegambia Hotel. I have explained before that the police have virtually no transport, not even a supply of bikes. I have expressed many a criticism of the Gambian police in my time, but over all, I feel they have a thankless, ill-paid, badly-equipped job to do. The particular station my two straining-at-the-leash escorts came from had not even electric light in the evenings . . . often not so much as a candle, never mind a hurricane lamp. Imagine a British bobby coping with that?

I screeched to a stop and we all jumped out and strode purposefully through the hotel grounds towards the beach. I had an uneasy feeling the guests probably thought it was the scruffy white woman in the flapping towel who was being arrested, or the little black boy hopping frantically beside her. On the beach, the Rastas were just reaching the tourist area, with Ray plodding menacingly along behind them. As the policemen loped forwards Ray grabbed the wanted man and shouted (I swear!) 'Surrender!' I think he saw that in a video in Partick once. An interested crowd gathered round. 'What happened? Who is he?' 'What did he do?' asked the beach-bed attendants, bumsters and postcard sellers. I told again the tale of the stolen generator, how this chap in his police-cell, had asked to go for a pee, then bolted like a rabbit through the bush, with several policemen pounding behind him. You would think he would have had the sense to skip over the border to Senegal and stay there.

Inevitably, our Land Rover was commandeered to take Ray, the police and the unfortunate captive to Yundum police station, where Sergeant Jatta greeted him grimly with the words: 'Aha, we have some business to settle with you. And when you want to go to the toilet this time, we'll give you a bucket.'

Eliman and I were dumped unceremoniously at Uncle Dembo's, where, lo and behold, there was Roel, sharing some Guinness with Sidiki and watching Ray and the police driving off in the Land Rover. 'Who's the poor guy they're holding?' he asked. When we told him, he roared with laughter. We described the sighting, the tailing, the moment of capture and the response of the villain who had, after a sulky silence and a torrent of abuse, then uttered the Wollof equivalent of 'It's a fair cop'. We inserted many embellishment and thespian gestures and noises. Big Mary and Wee Hannah gave us some beers on tick, and Pepsi for Eliman, because I was still wearing a swimsuit and a towel and had no purse with me. 'Now I hope he'll go to court,' I said, feeling a mite sorry for him. After all, we'd had our generator back and for me, and him, it was all ancient history.

I was amazed at the response. 'Hah!' barked the normally gentle and peace-loving Sidiki. 'Hah! Court! If it happened where I live we wouldn't go to the police. We'd deal with him ourselves.' There followed a gruesome account of local methods of punishment, so grisly they don't bear repeating. Roel nodded approval; our big amiable friend from the liberal and progressive little country of Holland. 'Ya, it's the same in The Hague,' he said with relish. Sipping his Guinness sagely he explained. 'People are fed up with the police and the courts. If they catch a thief on their property, now they beat him and throw him in the gutter, and only then do they ring the police.'

A long loud argument followed with me taking the humanitarian view. 'What if' I expostulated, 'the thief was a very poor man with lots of children to feed?' Up piped dear little Eliman. 'Then he could go to the bush and cut some firewood to sell. If it was me who caught him I would get a big gun and shoot him and all thieves.' Oh, dear. What Draconian reactions. It must have been this brand of thinking among the good citizens of Banjul that prompted a recent announcement on Radio Gambia by the Inspector General of Police. Following a fight between two Gambians, one of whom died, the other was arrested. The police chief, aware that the assailant's mother and brother and sister lived in the city and could be menaced by relatives of the dead man seeking retribution, said: 'The police have the matter well in hand. Anyone taking the law into their own hands will be severely dealt with.'

There was plenty of time to discuss law and order lengthily in Uncle Dembo's because by this time, once again the tourist season was petering out. It lasts only five or six months, and seems over in a flash. Now again the rain hovered, waiting, a giant shadow with wings of water upended against the blue sky, ready to drop like an eagle. For three days a pall of yellowish-grey dust had also hung over the whole country, occasionally whipped up by the wind, stinging our throats, our eyes, our lips. If I dusted the furniture it bloomed with a patina of fawn in minutes. The verandah was permanently carpeted in dust, and so were the car, the garden chairs and tables. I coughed and wheezed and wondered if I should wear one of these smog-masks they use in Tokyo and Mexico City.

It cleared eventually and we went jogging along the beach in the early morning when the sky was still mother-of-pearl and the sea was stretching its muscles for the day ahead. This was a passing phase of ours, plodding along the damp sand, then swimming in the sea. My back, so long as I didn't carry heavy weights, was giving me little trouble and the fibroid appeared to have shrunk. The passage of time, the end of the menopause, or Magali's ministrations, who knows?

As we walked back up to the house, feeling virtuous and healthy, there was much crackling and crunching from the forest. 'Monkeys!' said Ray, delighted, for although he has been seeing monkeys since he was a baby he still experiences the same thrill of pleasure as I do when they appear like a conference of elders, glaring at us with round, calm eyes, drifting across the nooks between the trees and shinning up the trunks to peep from behind the leaves. The pair of ground hornbills which nests in the forest, large as turkeys, black and stately in their progress like a Glasgow matron and her man coming back from church, side by side, paced out their morning stroll. No jogging for them. A couple of ground squirrels, grey and sinuous, zig-zagged into the weeds and I reflected that life without tourists, even if it meant no money, could be rather pleasant. We held hands and walked home in silence, sedate and silent like the hornbills.

The huts might be empty, but friends still came to the Gambia, choosing the more cushioned accommodation of large hotels, but descending on us with hugs and news from home . . . and strange gifts. For example, I had lived in Scotland all my life before the Gambia, and I probably ate clootie dumpling three or four times in all these years. But within a span of a mere ten days we were given *two* gigantic globes of suet and fruit, the traditional pudding of Scotland. The nearest English equivalent, I suppose, would be spotted dick. It is eaten in slabs as heavy as engine-blocks, glorious to the taste-buds, and every true Scottish granny has her own unique recipe.

To find one in the Gambia is like finding a bowl of *mhabal* in a Glasgow kitchen. The first came from Andrew and Carol and their son

Justin from Gretna. Andrew runs a large and luxurious shop at Gretna Green, selling Scottish knitwear, salmon, cheeses and oatcakes, pottery and plaid tammies. He brought not just a dumpling, vacuum-packed, but a tinned haggis and a big plastic apron bearing a well-known: 'Wha's like us?' essay on all the things the Scots have invented from television to tarmacadam. Andrew is a rampant Scot. He is also, as you will see, a rampant Glasgow Ranger's supporter.

Ray wore the apron to barbecue red snapper for supper. Andrew positioned himself strategically in front of a litre of the Famous Grouse whisky and made swift decisive forays into it throughout the evening. Rory the Scottish architect who played the bagpipes on the Scottish television film, turned up this time with a massive bowl of tandoori-marinated chicken, which was grilled alongside the snapper. Andrew waxed lyrical about his regular holidays in the Atlantic Hotel in Banjul and particularly this one which coincided with a historically significant date in his calendar. Not the Queen's birthday or the Gambian Presidential elections or World Telecommunications Day. No, no, much more vital; it was the Scottish Cup Final between Rangers and Airdrie.

On the day of the match being played 2000 miles away, Andrew, Carol and Justin emerged into the blistering heat of the hotel pool area ignoring magnificent hangovers from the previous night's preparation for the mood the day, clad from head to foot in blue and white, Rangers badges, scarves and flags bristling from them in all directions. They then obliged the amiable staff in the vicinity to listen with them to every significant second of the game on BBC World Radio, managing to dispose of six bottles of whisky, helped by a number of other Scottish diehards. Thank heavens their team won, and they ended the day in a balmy haze of vicarious triumph. One thing about the Scots, they seldom do things by halves.

The next clootie dumpling was a real home-made one, brought to us by Roderick and made by his mother. It was bigger than a watermelon, rich as sin, bursting with fruit. We saved it and launched it with some ceremony at a little Scottish supper for Tom and Joan, with Ray wearing the plastic pinny again to create atmosphere. The soup was a Gambian version of Scotch broth, with cassava, aubergines and garlic as well as barley and carrots. The haggis was served with mashed potatoes and, for want of neeps (as the traditional big orange turnips are known in Scotland) carrots and more cassava mashed with pepper and butter. Tinned milk was poured over the clootie dumpling and Ray was heard to remark several times that it was a braw bricht moonlicht nicht the nicht. It sounds even sillier in a Wollof accent.

Roderick and Raymond from Perth have been coming to the Gambia so often they've lost count. Two immensely kind and couthy pillars of the Perth business and commercial world, normally to be seen there in sober grey suits, ties and striped shirts, they blossom here in gaudy holiday shirts and baggy shorts. They are welcome in many a Gambian compound and know more about the country than I do after living here for, as I write this, almost five years. They always come weighed down with gifts for us and for their many Gambian friends and I suspect if they could throw away the suits and ties and the need to earn a respectable living in the douce grey city of Perth, they would live here and grow beans or bananas in blissful obscurity.

They brought, among other things, a wide-brimmed leather hat for Ray, in which he looked like a black Indiana Jones and swaggered about unbearably. Poor Roderick had a tale of woe to tell. He had been relieved, while lazing on the beach, of his bag, containing his diaries and cash, by a shabby-looking chap carrying a knife. We were appalled that such a thing should happen to our friend and distressed to realise that very gradually, these incident are increasing in number. Small numbers compared with Britain, but still out of character for the country that calls itself the friendliest in Africa. Roderick shrugged it off with fortitude and it hasn't stopped him coming here, for it is in many respects his real home, and Raymond's too. They are like Tweedledum and Tweedledee; Roderick chunky and gingery-haired, Raymond slim and grey, bouncing jokes off one another like tennis balls. They have been friends since they sat in the same schoolroom at the age of 13.

Other Scots who turned up during this mellow month of May were Graeme and Angela. Graeme had been before, with Norman the chef. He didn't bring clootie dumplings but he brought packets of instant soups, chocolate drinks, stock cubes and marmalade. He and Angela felt obliged to explain their arrival together. 'We're just pals,' they both stressed. 'Old workmates. Nothing romantic.' It was true and I understood it, but it was hard for Ray to wallow. 'They MUST be sleeping together,' he whispered when they weren't listening. 'How can a man and a woman be on holiday together and not . . ?' I tried to explain that this kind of situation was common in the West, that in the old days most of my best buddies, to whom I could pour out the worries of the working day over a glass of wine in the pub, were not women but men. It doesn't happen here, except perhaps among very cosmopolitan Gambians who have studied and travelled abroad. Here, man plus woman equals sex. Platonic relationships? Tell it to the birds. That's what Ray says anyway.

All this Scottishness was making me feel — not homesick, for here is home now — but a bit sentimental. I spoke dreamily to Ray of Scottish history and politics and haggis and heather, until he snored loudly and I came back to reality. I don't let my nostalgia express itself in public displays of tartan and strathspeys, though, as some ex-pats do. Most of those who involve themselves in the Caledonian cult, with ball-dresses sashed in tartan, men in kilts, endless reels and Scottish waltzes to the skirl of the pipes, are actually English, but they all take it very seriously and the big St Andrews night dance is one of the social events of the season. Needless to say, we don't go. I understand rehearsals are held beforehand so that the steps of the dancers are correct on the night. No shuffling through a Gay Gordons twirling when you should be sashaying. Dash it all, let's do it properly, what?

The old colonial day are long gone, but I suspect that British wives (as opposed to Gambian wives like me) have to toe the line. Non-appearance at a High Commission cocktail party for the Queen's Birthday could cause some pursing of lips and shaking of heads. Bridge and gossip at the Club, tennis tournaments and gins and tonics on the terrace. Not my scene Although, to be honest, I would probably enjoy the gossip if it wasn't that we have enough of that on our own side of the track to keep us perpetually entertained. 'Did you know that —'s Gambian lover, the one she left her English husband for, was beating her up something awful? And that she'd seen out with a Lebanese? Did you hear that Big Mary and wee Hannah weren't on speaking terms for a week because of a row over Mary's Gambian boyfriend? Did you hear that Alieu was taking another wife, Assan's wife was pregnant again, and the schoolgirl who used to clean our toilets is also pregnant, Mariama and Mr M's baby had arrived, cute as a kitten, and E— has taken all the money his French girlfriend gave him for a flight-ticket to Paris and spent it on drink, clothes, and more girls . . . ?' Love and lust foment in the clammy pre-summer weather, black and white, white and white, black and black. Some are doomed. some are blessed. Meanwhile we were still together and still eating clootie dumpling

Outside Gorro the latest night-man dozed under the tree with his bow and arrow at his side. He was thin and slow of mind and hand and I could not imagine him as a William Tell character, but at least he didn't ask for a gun, as Mr M used to do.

What I wanted, I told Ray, wasn't tartan or tweed; I wanted tie-dye, batik, some succulent lengths of the locally hand-decorated cottons. 'I'll take you to see Musu Kebba,' he said.

Musu Kebba Drammeh, when we found her, sat on a large piece of faded Wilton carpet, which was spread out on the hard earth behind her batik business in a backstreet of Serrekunda. A large lady of some years, she sat like an empress.

Her minions scurried around on the fringes of the Wilton, like drones round a queen bee. She had a deep rich voice and sharp eyes which missed nothing. I called her Gorro, which means step-sister, because she was vaguely connected to Ray's family, though the relationship was so obscure I couldn't unravel it. (Gorro the watchman, incidentally, was so called by Ray because of another tortuous family connection). If you ever felt women were downtrodden in this part of the world, come and see Musu Kebba. She was a tycoon. Would any man dare to defy her? I doubt it.

The shop in front of the sprawling yard where the fabrics were dyed was small but brimming from floor to ceiling with tie-dyed bales in all the colours of Africa. The purple and lilacs of bougainvillaea and dusk skies melted into the gold of sun and sand, the turquoise of the sea, the rose-pink of oleander, the pale green of bamboo and baby corn, the darker green of the leaves of the citrus trees. In the yard itself all that happened was under Musu Kebba's beady eye. She was a big benevolent spider in the centre of a web of artistry and industry. Hunks of white cotton and occasional silks were tweaked and tied tightly so that they looked like fields of stalagmites, then dyed and tweaked and tied again until the colours ebbed and flowed into rainbow designs. Meanwhile serious young men stooped over banners of cloth carefully painting wax outlines which would reject the dyes leaving the intervening shape to greedily absorb the colour, making pictures of birds, babies, hoeing women, girl carrying jugs of water, old men talking, trees spreading, animals feeding.

If you didn't take care you would trip over a bath of indigo, the rich dark blue-purple grown here and powdered and mixed in the Gambia for the most authentic effects. Or you would, if you didn't duck, be slapped on the face by two-metre wide batik pictures dripping and drying on the washing lines. Pelicans trembling in the breeze, elephants rippling. It was a magical place and the chief magic-maker was as much a businesswoman as she sat on her old carpet in the dust, as any power-dressed city executive in London or New York.

They say she supplies fabric to top people, and they say the Mercedes outside is hers. Whether or not it's true, she creates many beautiful things. But she has her bad days too. One morning we called to collect some material from her and her face was slumped into a scowl. 'I'm sorry, beautiful step-sister,' she sighed (for she flatters me shamelessly; perhaps that's why I like her). 'Your green and gold cloth is not ready. There is no water here today.' And it was true. It was the rainy season and the roads were muddy, but the GUC had cut off her water for several days, and production had ground to a dismal stop. White damask flapped sorrowfully in the breeze like a model's face with no blusher, eye-shadow and lip-liner. The buckets were dry. The staff slouched around, eating rice in an absent-minded fashion, gazing into space or eying the dry cotton and unmixed dyes in frustration, waiting for the water which must flow like life's blood through their many-hued powders to bring them alive.

We shook our heads sympathetically and drove off to say hullo to Modou, the tailor. It was Rab who first discovered Modou, when he went to him to have some trousers made. His shop was a tiny space crammed between rows of other tiny spaces, all of them bustling businesses, throbbing and rattling with the sound of ancient sewing-machines, in the road that leads to Serrekunda mosque. It is a road that makes Oxford Street on Christmas Eve look like a country lane. It is crammed with bicycles, beggars, hooting cars and bush-taxis, donkey carts, women with babies on their backs and bundles on their heads, urchins darting between people's legs, dogs huddled in the shadows, stalls and barrows and trays loaded with underwear, shirts, bracelets, hats, shoes. Ray fumed and fizzled as he edged the car along, grazing the awnings of cigarette stalls and the elbows of billowing matrons. 'You fool! Are you blind? Get out of the way,' he yelped, blasting his horn at the world. The timing needed adjusting, so that the engine went off every time the car slowed to a stop, which was every twenty seconds. Driving in the towns of the Gambia is a complicated art form, demanding rock-hard nerves, a loud horn, the patience of Job, and incredible negotiating skills.

I have only driven the Mosque road once and afterwards I was a gibbering, quaking blob of jelly. Now we wondered where to park, which was like wondering where to park in the middle of the Champs Elysée only worse. Modou saw us and came to our rescue, throwing himself under hooves and tyres to reach us in the midst of the heaving mass, then holding his hands up like a traffic cop so that everything ground to a grumbling halt. 'Turn in here, quick,' he commanded. 'Into my compound.' The traffic snorted like a field of randy bulls, while Ray negotiated his way into a narrow opening flanked by bowls of peanuts and oranges whose venders shuffled back resentfully to let us past, so that we could park the hiccuping little car thankfully in the shade of a large mango tree. A flock of kids settled around us like starlings, all round eyes and outstretched hands, and Modou shooed them off and took us to his shop.

Inside I squeezed into the narrow space between Modou's machine and the wall, and perched on a bench with a row of waiting customers. I produced a batch of my old clothes and some amateur drawings and began explaining my needs to the tailor. 'Can you make a shirt like this?' — holding up a faded Miss Selfridge blouse — 'but with sleeves like that' — waving a little drawing. 'And then, shorts like these, but with pockets like that. A dress like this but one inch less in the hips and two inches longer at the hem . . .' and so on. Garments and papers kept falling between people's ankles and the set of instructions I offered him was intricate enough to bamboozle the most advanced computerised production plant in Europe, but when we returned two days later, everything was ready, immaculately stitched, pleated, tucked and ironed. The skills of local tailors are legendary. When my son was here he had a pair of Lee Cooper jeans copied in heavy tie-dye twill, perfect down to the last stud, zip and double seam. And the fabrics are fantastic. Forget the batiks even, and you will find in the markets bale upon bale of imported cottons, cords and organza in a multitude of colours and patterns. They come in from China, Holland and elsewhere and material that would cost five or six pounds sterling a metre in England is around 80p or £1 here. I would drool over pictures in *Vogues* and *Cosmopolitans* left by visitors. Then I would cut them out and take them to Modou with my bargain fabrics, and have a made-to-measure exclusive design all my own.

I didn't do it very often, for such extravagances were mostly beyond me, but it was nice to think about it, and visits to the tailoring quarter were always enthralling, especially before Muslim festivals like Tobaski and Khoreti. For then the tailors would work all night by the light of oil lamps, stitching elaborate gowns for both males and females, with machines which produced lavish embroidered panels and edgings of gold thread, appliqué, cut-out designs, frilled collars and sleeves, dazzling diamonds and hearts of contrasting colours, no contrast too bold, purple plackets on lime-green, lemon satin laced with royal blue net, white broderie anglaise inset with rose and yellow linings. In a damp, grey European street such splendiferous splurges of colour and texture would have been vulgar. Here they were delicious, filling the holiday celebrations with exotic display, glorifying God perhaps, but also extolling the Gambian's love of brightness and self-decoration. Against silky black and nut-brown skins the colours looked superb and the Gambia bloomed like a garden of glorious flowers.

Getting to the
Grass Roots

Gorro never shot his bow and arrow, either in fun or fury. He had other things on his mind. Each night, one or other of his two wives would come along, smiling coquettishly, and the watchman would disappear inside tourist hut C with her. She would go off an hour or so later, picking her satisfied way through the moonlight, and Gorro would sleep through the night immobile, unblinking, even when the dog was howling and we were yelling in his ear. Callers came and hammered on the gate blasting their car-horns and flashing their lights on and off until we ran out to greet them. Gorro slept. Goodbye, Gorro.

Abdoulaye was marginally more wakeful by day, but Abdoulaye even for a watchman was lacking a lot upstairs. Ray would see tyre-tracks when we came back from the beach.

'Was someone here?' he would ask. 'Ah, eh um. Y-e-e-s.'
'Who was it who who came?' 'Er — umph - aah.'
'Was it one person or two?' 'Er -.'
'Was it a lady or a gentleman?' 'Ummm - '
'Was it a car or a taxi? A big car or a small one?'

It could have been a double-decker bus full of Red Indians and Abdoulaye would have been unsure of who, what or why. Good-bye Abdoulaye.

Senegal again. We hadn't been back since Magali, France and Valerie had flown to Dakar. It was night-time, black as Guinness, and the air hung heavily on us like a soft sticky blanket. The village hall in Kafountine is made of corrugated iron and palm rods. Inside the atmosphere was as dense as peanut soup and smelled of sweat and musk and the occasional wave of ganjha. Ganjha: marijuana. There were gardens nearby where a few straggly cassava or tomato plants around the borders acted as accessories to positive swathes of ganjha plant. 'It's infuriating,' grumbled Diack's Parisienne girlfriend Nadhia. 'You go shopping and you have to search the market for one or two tomatoes. Sometimes there isn't a single vegetable to buy. All the people are too busy growing that stuff.'

We were at a disco. It didn't start till after midnight and the mosquitoes were gathering in clouds in the purple-dark air. The men stood around in groups drinking soft drinks and talking loudly. Not loudly enough to be heard clearly over the music which was played at maximum volume on execrable speakers, screeching, croaking, booming, drilling holes in my head. Soon the women began to strut in, wearing African dresses all frilled and flounced and flashy, or European jeans and shiny tops. I was in a resentful mood because they all wore gold high-heeled sandals and I was in rubber flip-flops. 'You never told me there would be a disco,' I hissed heavily at Ray. 'What?' he yelled over the multi-decibel reggae. He was looking, belligerently, for a man with a dog. The last time he had been there in that hall, he had been with my son David and a bunch of tourists he'd driven down from Bijilo. He had had a fight with a drunken Senegalese because the man insisted on bringing his dog into the hall. The dog knocked Ray's beer over. Neither the man nor his dog turned up this time, but there were children, darting in and out among the swaying, stamping legs of the dancers. 'They should all be home in bed,' I growled. Nadhia waved merrily from the floor and I waved back, trying to smile.

Nadhia had smooth blonde hair swept back from a high forehead and cut short round her ears. Large pale, pale blue eyes and fluent English. She wore hobble skirts and overtops made from the heavy local indigo tie-dyes, or baggy pants and smocks in other shades of navy and purple and black. She looked incredibly French, très chic, I thought enviously. I said so to Ray and he snorted. 'In these clothes! My mother would only wear clothes like that to go hoeing in the fields!' Men don't understand these things. To a Gambian man, it's the frills and the shine and the colour that count in his woman. The natural cottons, grown and dyed here, are discounted while, ironically, fashionable French and German girls seek them out as eagerly as if they were exclusive silks. 'She looks like something out of Vogue,' I explained to Ray. 'Then Vogue must be stupid,' he said, 'You look wonderful. Much better than her.' We danced.

Nadhia and Diack had met a few month earlier. In fact, she was the girl whose migraine disappeared under Magali's fingers during the weekend of the schism, when Sebastian and Nicole had ejected *les trois françaises*. We had barely spoken then but now we were becoming friends. Nadhia had lived for three years in Brazil. Before and after that she had worked in a Kenzo shop in Paris, hence the band-box smart hair and her habit of wearing only shades of deep blue. She and Diack laughed and hugged a lot but the relationship was thorny. They lived in Diack's little oval hut a couple of furlongs away from the campement, and Nadhia was painting it inside and out, gloss white with green and blue designs delicately drawn round doors and windows. Diack was growing peanuts and they were having a well dug. But the cosy atmosphere was occasionally cooled by Nadhia coming back from a trip to Ziguinchor to find Diack's old girlfriend, a sturdy Senegalese, in the little house that she, Nadhia, had cleaned and painted and made into home. Or there would be a letter from another old girlfriend, a Frenchwoman or a German, promising to come soon and visit. 'E say 'e loves only me. But 'ow am I to believe zis?' she would ask me as we sat having girls' talk on a bench outside their tiny picture-book house.

Had I been she, I'd probably have screamed and cried and leapt at Diack with my claws unsheathed ... or at the Senegalese girl. But Nadhia was cool and calm and had long serious talks with Diack and tried to believe him when he said he had reformed. They were dancing now, bodies bobbing and bending to the urgent Senegalese mix of brass and drums, and both of them were laughing, eyes on eyes, fingers on fingers. Several hundred other people also danced and the sweat dribbled down my face and into my mouth and into the dip between my breasts, while the mosquitoes feasted greedily on my feet and ankles. Hurricane lamps provided an orange glow which flickered on cheekbones and teeth and gold chains. Outside shadows emerged and broke up as groups of youths smoked and gossiped and wandered back to the dance. Wollof and Jola tongues rose and fell with the music. Thunder rolled somewhere inside the black-purple blanket of the night.

Once again I was struck by how different this area was to the Gambia. A few white people come, but they are not the excited families and married couples who come to the Gambia wearing new holiday clothes and sandals and carrying suitcases and cameras and hotel vouchers. They are travel-stained French and German back-packers who have seen more of Africa than I have, and many come for the ganjha as much as for the tranquillity of the countryside and the sense of being hidden from the rest of the world. The only other white faces at the disco belonged to some off-duty French soldiers from Dakar, looking the way off-duty soldiers do anywhere in the world. Oh, and one more white face — Sebastian's. 'Jolly nice, isn't it?' he drawled as he passed. Nicole wasn't there. She may have been at home cursing a dead pig.

He and Nicole killed the pig the day before because, they said, they had met a party of French school-teachers in Ziguinchor and they were all coming for a special pig-bake barbecue. They scrubbed hundred-weights of sweet potatoes and gathered piles of firewood and Nicole found herbs and oil and borrowed plates and bowls but when the school-teachers arrived they said they weren't hungry. The pig was stuffed into the neighbouring campement's fridge, which cools down a little during the evening hours when the generator is on. Nicole flounced about firing thunderbolts at the French visitors from her pale round eyes then went home early. Sebastian shrugged and came to the disco.

The following evening the teachers still hadn't eaten the pig. I worried about its viability in that climate, humid as a steaming kettle. They gathered instead in the campement refectory playing French rock and roll on their guitars accompanied by the Senegalese cook on drum. Nicole was there too, smiling, so she must have stopped worrying about the pig. We all spoke in French, naturally. It was challenging to say the least. I could remember the past pluperfect of various obsolete verbs and my grammar was excellent, if archaic. I could remember the words of silly French songs about shepherdesses and cheeses that we had learned at school, a passage by Dumas about a chap dying in quicksand, but for ordinary everyday words my mind went blank.

Words like shoe, funny, sheet, skirt, they disappeared out of my brain and into the darkness beyond. Naturally, as I type this, they all leap out at me easily and obviously. But I got better as the conversation expanded. I gave up worrying about verb endings and concentrated on being understood. It was distressing to realise how long ago my French had been taught to me . . . longer than Ray's lifespan. The stuff I remembered, if spoken aloud, would sound the way it would sound if you said to an English teenager: 'I beg of you, young sir, would thou be willing to walk with me for a moment, would this not presume too much upon your kindness?' Imagine the response *that* would get in a street in Greenock or Hull or Ballymurphy!

Next day we walked a couple of kilometres and met Guindo, who was a lecturer in accountancy and business methods in a university in Paris. He had opened a small new *pension* on the beach to be looked after by a friend when he was jetting off to work. A slim, cynical Senegalese (who spoke good English, thank heavens) he told us about the time he went to Los Angeles to do his Master's degree. 'At the airport,' he smiled bitterly, 'a big prosperous looking American businessman said to me: "Hey, boy, what yuh doin' here?" I told him I was there to study and he roared with laughter. "Why does a black boy need to study?" He gave me a lift and every time we stopped he'd point me out to his friends and tell them this big joke.'

Next time he met him, Guindo was with some of his own friends, 'high-powered' fellows, VIPs with a lot more clout than the loud-mouthed businessman. 'He fawned all over me then and offered me the use of his Mercedes for the rest of the visit, but I said no thanks,' said Guindo with a lop-sided grin.

A kilometre in the other direction, a Frenchman was building a hotel, but although the outline of pretty little chalets could be seen in a lush woodland setting, progress was very slow. Nadhia said this was because the Frenchman drank all the money meant for bricks and mortar. His African wife was young and beautiful with an olive-skinned baby, but she cooked and cleaned with tears in her eyes.

Sebastian and this man often formed a merry alliance, drinking an talking endlessly, making grand plans, giggling, winking, whispering. No wonder their wives wept.

In the evening we walked along the beach to the wrecked cargo-boat once more, for it seemed to beckon to us like a friendly ghost. The air was transparently bronze as the sun melted away to leave space for the stars. Crabs scurried through the iron ribs and pelicans perched on what remained of the deck. When we walked back, the French school-teachers were sitting on the sand playing their guitars. It began to drizzle but no-one took any notice.

Later, as we slept, the drizzle became a torrent. I wakened to find water slopping in through the unglazed windows. Ray slept on. I went back to bed and dozed on soggy sheets as the thunder crashed around my ears and the lightning flashed secret signals to the gods. We left next morning. We never heard if the pig was eaten. And it was a long, long time before we returned, for every time we thought about it, something happened to scare us off.

One late afternoon we met Kabu the tour guide in Uncle Dembo's. He was shaking a little, gulping his Julbrew nervously and sweating over his expenses. 'How am I going to explain this to my boss?' he asked in exasperation, writing down the sum of 5000 CFA (Senegalese francs, equivalent to about a tenner). He described how he had been shepherd-ing a bunch of bright-eyed French tourists through the village of Abène, about an hour's drive past the Gambian border post at Seleti, when the rebels stopped his mini-bus and demanded money. They might call themselves freedom fighters but right then poor Kabu was calling them something much less noble. 'These bastards!' he groaned. 'They have guns and they are asking the villagers for their cows, their rice, their wives . . . they took money from me, but will my boss be sympathetic? I doubt it!' Diouloulou, the main town in the area, was, he said, bristling with soldiers, all toting guns. The atmosphere was charged with hyste-ria and sulky suspicion, and we decided we'd give Casamance a miss for a few weeks till things settled down.

Meanwhile, in the Gambia the police had been rounding up illegal immigrants, helped by the gendarmerie, also packing guns. Sullen Senegalese, Guineans and Malians, Mauritanians and Freetonians with-out proper papers were being rounded up in the alleyways of Serrekunda, Banjul, Basse, Farafenni and Mansa Konko, described in the local Press as 'undesirables' and crammed unceremoniously into trucks, army lorries and buses. Police-stations were packed with skinny Mauritanian grocers and money-lenders in their long delphinium blue robes and white turbans; pouting Senegalese girls in jeans and short skirts, inter-rupted in the pursuit of their profession on bug-ridden mattresses and against crumbling walls in the seamy sides of town; skinny hollow-eyed 'almudos', the little beggar boys sent out by their Koranic teachers to recite holy verses they didn't understand and shake their rusty tin cans to encourage the charitable to give them coins.

Many of the street traders, hookers, urchins and wheeler-dealers could be spied speeding silently like shadows up the backstreets, away from the arms of the law.

'What will happen to the ones they catch?' I asked Ray. 'Oh, some of them will be able to bribe the police to let them go. Others, with no money, will be taken to the border and dumped there — many of them will find their ways back in a few weeks.' The big round-up happens once or twice a year but there always seem to be plenty of immigrants around to take the places of those who've gone.

They add to the rich and volatile life of the town, with their skin-tones ranging from pale peachy-gold through copper brown to pur-plish-black, their accents and tribal languages adding to the amiable hubbub.

At home, I had my own illegal aliens to deal with — the frogs again, carolling at top volume all night and crapping on the verandah. Two insisted on sleeping under the mattress of tourist hut B, presumably managing to wriggle through the half-inch space below the door. No matter how brusquely I tossed them into the garden they always sneaked back. Most of the human residents probably didn't even know they were sharing their beds with two frogs. *'Merde!'* I grumbled as I swept clusters of little olive-green squatters from the breakfast area. *'Allez-vous en!'*

A few days later Ray and Lamin went of in the Land Rover in search of grass. Not the kind that flourished down in South Senegal but the kind we use on our roofs. It's not just any old grass, but special reeds cut and bundled and woven by Manjago and Jola villagers in remote areas — so remote that my husband and my brother-in-law spent hours, driving around the rural villages of the south seeking a spot where, according to Uncle Ebou, grass was to be had in profusion. They plunged into cobwebby woods and up narrow tracks into dense bushland past coconut groves and rice fields into places Ray said he'd never known existed, but still they didn't find the roofing grass. 'Oh, we use corrugated metal for our roofs,' said some sleepy Manjagos and Jolas. 'Or if we can't afford corrugate, we use palm leaves.' Sure enough, there wasn't a thatched roof to be seen.

We ourselves had used the long splayed fingers of the fan-palm, which fade from bright green to a soft creamy-brown colour, to roof the under-the-baobab bar area. They cast a cinnamon glow and fronds hung like lampshade fringing all around. I thought they looked pretty but Ray had decided that grass thatch would not only look more attractive but would also be more waterproof when the rains came battering in from the Atlantic. He was full of vim and vigour, while I slouched about wiping rivulets of sweat from my forehead and wishing it was winter again. In winter you have a mere, mild 90°F and nice cool breezes in the evening. In summer, all you do is steam like a lump of new-made bread. Ray seemed impervious to it.

Eventually someone remembered that all the houses either side of the Senegalese border had grass roofs and deduced that there was a fair chance the grass actually grew thereabouts. Carrying the material across the border is illegal, but on the Gambian side Ray and Lamin finally pinpointed a village surrounded by tall brown reeds. Many hours of chopping and gleaning and bundling followed until they returned with their cargo, from which several field-mice scuttled in terror, hotly pursued by Peter, Patch, Tubab, Nyet Kunyul and their mother, Awadingding.

A squad from the village was coerced into helping the roofing operation to proceed. Ray's two brothers came, and Nabi the nervous Guinean, Pa Jobe the football fiend and Assan, Ray's soldier cousin. Provided we gave them plenty of green tea, sugar and tinned milk to make their attaya they worked cheerfully for hours in the sweltering heat, stripped to the waist, skin gleaming like polished teak. This is the anomaly of the Gambian work ethic. On the one hand, a man — or woman — will sit gazing emptily into space while all around there are urgent jobs of work needing to be done; when prevailed upon to do them, they will do so in a desultory fashion so that, for example, one hotel manager told me his staff-guest quota was four times as high as in similar hotels in Europe. But on the other hand, when there is something to be done to which the Gambian can relate, something he perceives a useful, practical and logical, like harvesting the peanuts, digging up a field to plant cassava, putting a wall round his home or constructing a new roof . . . then he will work with muscular fervour and enthusiasm while white wimps like me look on in awe. Not that our roof emerged overnight. Every day Ray said, 'Tomorrow it will be finished,' tugging scraps of straw from his hair and brushing insects and sweat from his shoulders. It took about a week, while reeds fallen from the bundles dropped everywhere and the whole garden looked like a stable floor.

The fan-palm leaves, abandoned, formed a mountain next to the baobab tree. 'Can't we take these away and burn them?' I asked innocently. 'Burn them? Don't be silly. Lots of people will want them for their houses,' said Ray. And sure enough, at dawn next day, we heard repeated calls of 'Salaam Aleikum', as a procession of old men came with wheelbarrows and took the leaves away to patch the roofs of their huts.

We began raking and scraping and gradually gathered up all the broken reeds until the garden looked as it had before — awful, a wilderness of weeds. I cleared my throat to begin nagging about this when, before I could open my mouth, Nabi and Modou materialised with two donkeys pulling a small plough. They'll break all the jasmine and laurel plants, I fretted, but they didn't. All day they trudged steadily up and down between bananas and shrubs, with stops now and then for Nabi and Modou to drink yet more green tea, and for the donkeys to munch the weeds.

Again I suggested to Ray that we should have our own donkey, but he wouldn't be budged. 'Donkeys are nasty, bad-tempered beasts,' he declared. 'Not if they're treated properly,' I parried but I was wasting my breath.

He was implacable. 'Maybe a horse,' he mused. 'Maybe one day we'll find one up-river, where horses are cheaper.' I couldn't ride, but I could learn. I basked in a vision of myself trotting elegantly through the forest and along the beach, the wind blowing in my hair, my eyes sparkling, my back straight, Meryl Streep in designer beige cotton. At one point I conjectured that we wouldn't need to go up-river, for it was perfectly possible that a seller would turn up with a pony because he had heard or guessed that we wanted one. This kind of thing happens so often.

'I think we should get a plumber to come and put a stand-pipe in the garden and a new shower-head in the tourists' loo,' I was pondering one morning, thinking out loud. That afternoon, Joe Silva the plumber was there. No-one had called him. He'd simply been short of cash and decided to pop by and see if we needed any little jobs done. These coincidences are almost uncanny. 'I wish we had a few more bougainvillaea plants to plant beside this wall,' I'd sigh to Ray, and a gnarled old man would turn up at the gate with a box of plants for sale. My thought-waves can't have been quite powerful enough because I still don't have a horse. I don't really NEED a horse, don't know how to look after one and wouldn't have time to ride or groom it very often, so perhaps that's why it hasn't happened.

I also hadn't, at that time, managed to wish up a flame tree. 'They're so beautiful,' I'd hint heavily at Ray. 'We really should have one.' Soft fringed green leaves and scarlet blossom which dazzles the eye for month upon month in spring and early summer. No genie appeared with a sapling under his arm, so I dragged Ray to one of the 'garden shops' which have sprung up on the Badala Highway. There are several of them, not shops at all but plots of ground packed with plants to sell to hotels and people like me. In the beginning, we had paid five dalasis for everything.

No matter whether it was a straggly African marigold or a frangipani (which grows into a huge tree with silvery trunk and branches, long tough leaves and glorious waxy creamy-pink flowers), the price was the same — the equivalent of about 35 pence. This time we discovered that the more exotic species, those likely to grow into beautiful tropical trees, the frangipani, the scented jasmine, the flame tree, all of them about two to three-feet high in their pots, had been priced at D25, about £1.80. Horticultural inflation, but I to me they were still a wonderful bargain.

Not quite Tesco's!
Shopping-time at Banjul market. Bitter tomatoes, sweet potatoes, cassava,
sea-snail ... whatever madame wants!

Ray, though, was horrified. *'Ngarr-fuka jurome! Pour benna garrap!'* he spluttered. 'I've never heard such a thing. They're just trees, they grow everywhere. Let's go.' I sulked and he fumed and the plant-seller smirked because he knew who would win. We brought several plants home and Lamin, the latest watchman, dug them in. 'You should have waited for the rains,' he scolded, 'before you plant new things.' But they thrived anyway, and as I write this, only a couple of years on, the flame tree is as tall as our tourist huts and casts rich lacy shadows over the pale hard earth. Lamin's logic was suspect anyway. If I told him my little rose-bush, a birthday present from Carol which had never really settled in its tropical home, was looking wan and droopy, or that the marigolds were dying for lack of moisture, he would say: 'No need to water now. This is the rainy season . . .' even though there hadn't been a downpour for three weeks and the soil was as dry as a bone.

We were now able to cut down the occasional bunch of bananas from our own plants every couple of weeks. Each bunch held some twenty or so small yellow-green fruits, floury-tasting and quite different to the kind I used to buy in Glasgow. Our aubergines were burgeoning too, pale speckled violet shading to white, small and succulent. But nothing else very edible was growing in our garden, except the fiery red peppers whose flesh could inflame your palate for a fortnight. In the markets vegetables were scarce and expensive but there were mangoes by the million. How I wished someone could process all these wasted fruits to make drinks and preserves for export. As it was, they grew in such prodigious numbers there were always rotting fruits on the ground, studded with flies like blue-black diamonds.

Fish, in summer, is also scarce, though the prawns are bigger and more mouthwatering than ever. We went fishing to try to catch our own. We were unsuccessful as usual, but spied a glint of silver at the water's edge. Ray galloped toward it and grabbed a three-foot-long ladyfish. It was alive and bucking frantically, but with a snagged cheek where the German fisherman along the beach had almost caught it with his fancy rod. We scurried off, Ray carrying the fish on a large stick over his shoulder, the fisherman looking after us and scratching his head. Eliman and a bunch of the village kids met us as we scrambled up the steep slope past the forest. 'Ooooh! What a big fish! Did you catch it?' they asked Ray. 'Er, yes . . . yes,' he mumbled, which I suppose was true in a manner of speaking. We cooked half of it and had a feast with Eliman and the watchman. We gave the other half to Mary and Hannah at Uncle Dembo's. Mary was stitching sequins on to a pair of sandshoes. This was her hobby. She covered shoes, peaked caps and waistcoats in meticu-lously applied sequins like the scales of a fish, shimmering now in the twilight, silver and lavender and rosy pink.

The Old
Black Magic

And still the killing in Casamance continued. Genuine rebels tussled with Dakar soldiers while Mandinkas and Jolas tried to beat the hell out of each other. Politics and tribalism became, as they do all over Africa, tangled together.

Three Gambian Fulas went over the border in search of illicit charcoal (charcoal is banned here to preserve forest cover). The entire story will probably never be told, but what is certain is that a bunch of angry Senegalese villagers ambushed them and chopped off their hands with cutlasses. To emphasise their rough justice, the Senegalese hammered nails into the Gambians' backs, and one Gambian died of his injuries.

As African countries go, the Gambia is a notably peaceful little place, but just once in a while individuals either Gambian or immigrant, can behave with terrifying rage. The most newsworthy event in the Nineties was the discovery of the body of a young Englishwoman near the Abuko Nature Reserve. Horror stories were passed from compound to compound, market-stall to market-stall. Her head was found some distance from her body and one hand was severed. Some said it was black magic, some said it was vile cult slaughter. Others said it was a protest at the Abuko conservation policy which condemned the hunting of chimpanzees, for — or so it was mooted — the manner of the killing parallelled the manner of the termination of chimps by poachers. Crime of passion? Racist revenge? In fact, although the murder has never been completely cleared up, the true story seems to be that someone tried to rob the girl and hit out wildly with a cutlass doing, perhaps, more damage than had ever been intended, spurred on by fear and panic, or quite possibly, drugs.

A Guinean immigrant spotted his wife strolling home in the moonlight hand in hand with her illicit lover. He lurked behind a wall, watching, seething, boiling over with jealousy, then leapt on the usurper and stabbed him to death. I have to admit that I felt a sneaking sympathy for the Guinean, a wood-cutter by profession. He spent long periods up-country, chopping wood, and it must have been a bit of a shock to see his missus making whoopee in his absence. But, interestingly enough, the local paper, reporting the whole sequence of events in flamboyantly purple prose, took a quite different view. It suggested that the Guinean should not have left his wife alone so often. 'Women,' they remarked in tolerant tones, 'can't be expected to control their sexual urges.'

The same could be said of some of the European women who came here on holiday. 'Ah think it's the sun melts the elastic in their drawers,' Big Mary observed one day in her dead-pan voice watching a middle-aged German woman in a skin-tight shiny scarlet cat-suit undulating provocatively and simpering behind pebble-lensed glasses at a well-known beach bumster. Later, we heard she paid for him to share her room in the large beach hotel nearby and, soon afterwards, was shown the door in Berlin by her disenchanted doctor husband, who had at last realised that his wife's holidays in Africa were for more than sunshine and surf. I suppose I sound like the pot calling the kettle black, except that when I met Ray I had no husband, no thoughts of romance whatsoever and (though hardly anyone believe me when I say this) lust was less important than laughing together and learning about each other's strengths and weaknesses and wishful thoughts. The fact that Ray had his own beach-bar and wasn't one of the strutting army of jolly jobless gigolos also counted in his favour. And I NEVER wore a red catsuit . . .

But if black-white relationships were, very often, ephemeral things, a week or a fortnight of heavy breathing, sweat, semen and sweet nothings that meant just that, nothing . . . what about black-black relationships? Gambian husbands seemed to me to show scathing disregard for the feelings of Gambian wives. Prominent figures could be seen sneaking off in their opulent cars with gilded girls while their wives stayed home. Village men spent long evenings chatting to tourists, drinking in the pub or visiting their mistresses while their wives and children dozed in the compound. And there were occasional sorrowful anonymous letters to local papers describing how young wives felt when, all of a sudden, a solemn uncle or brother came to say: 'Tomorrow your husband is taking another wife.'

In Muslim theory, subsequent wives should be acquired only with the approval and consent of the first wife (or so my English Muslim friend Iman assured me) and only when existing spouses were infertile or too frail to perform their marital and domestic duties. But all around me I could see men already financially burdened by one wife and numerous offspring who, nevertheless, married again for lust or money or status.

Some wives — perhaps those with the uncontrollable sexual urges mentioned in that newspaper — went to marabouts to buy jujus or potions to ensure that their husbands stayed put and stayed potent. Others would seek to get bad spells put on new rival wives or girl-friends. Some claimed that, in fact, they were relieved when their husbands brought home other wives because it gave them more leisure time and a 'sister' to gossip with. 'He is my husband still and I want him to be happy,' one saintly woman told me straight-faced. I just couldn't help wondering how the men would feel if the situations were reversed. As it was, many women led severely restricted lives, their worlds seldom extending outside the four walls of the family compound. Why? 'Their husbands want to protect them from other men,' a young male friend told me. 'They don't want their wives wandering about the town where they could be lured away by other men.' 'But surely?' I said, 'just because a woman goes shopping or visiting friends, it doesn't mean she's going to run off with the first guy who talks to her?' 'Ah,' said Lamin wisely. 'You don't know about these things. Some men would promise to give them presents if they left their husband. And women are very weak. They could be led astray very easily.'

I controlled an urge to argue this premise loudly and rudely because my informant was just 15 years of age, but he seemed sure of his ground. Could a Gambian woman be enticed by gold or silk dresses? Perhaps, perhaps. And, Lamin added, 'if a man has a car then he has no trouble winning ladies to him.' A school-girl wrote to the letters page of the paper complaining about 'these old daddies in Mercedes' who cruised past the school gates and invited nubile young students to 'come for a drive'. Leave us alone, she said. But some of her schoolmates were less virtuous, and teenage pregnancies were common. One baby was left in a bush-taxi by a presumably confused and guilt-torn young woman (the child has now been adopted). Another was dropped into a latrine by a girl with a low IQ but a high rate of sexual activity. The baby drowned or smothered to death. Shotgun weddings were common, often among perilously young and totally indigent couples. After the wedding, it often seemed to me, the couple hardly spoke to one another.

I saw distinguished old men striding along the road followed by two or three wives carrying bundles and cooking pots on their heads, and I wondered, were they all satisfied and contented? It was hard to believe, whatever the received thinking on the subject. Privately I heard of older wives and aunts and sisters making life hell for new young wives, and of new young wives of a steely and perfidious nature setting out to destroy the position and emotional security of older wives, even having them thrown out of the compound. But these were, perhaps, extreme cases. I dare say most merely jog along neither less nor more ecstatically than the average monogamous Western marriage.

One night we gave a lift to a friend from the village, who works evenings as a watchman. He would have been quicker to walk, for we stopped at Uncle Dembo's for 'a drink', met a bunch of celebrating Scots and the night rumbled along amiably till after 3am. 'Poor fellow,' I whispered tipsily to Ray. 'I bet his wife's sitting up waiting for him, absolutely furious.' 'His TWO wives, you mean,' Ray grinned wickedly. The lad is no more than 23. I imagined him taking off his flip-flops, trying to creep silently into his hut to be met by a scowling girl on either side of the door. Nagging in stereo.

The marabouts, or serangs as they are also called, probably profit most from other people's love tangles. But they also offer their services in all manner of other problem situations. Did I mention Farbakary, who used to spend all the money he made in his beach-bar on visits to marabouts? He went to the marabout to magic up better business. But had he saved the money he earned already, instead of spending it on the marabout, would he not have been as well off? The irony of the situation escaped him. There was also Ray's auntie who ought help from 'our' marabout to find out what happened to her stolen cow. And I have an English friend who went to a marabout when she felt her life was so troubled and crisis-ridden that someone else must have put a spell on her. 'What happened?' I asked breathlessly. 'He gave me some jujus which had to be hung in certain places, and he gave me some liquid and told me to go to the shower behind his compound and wash in it.'

'Did you?' 'In that shower, with all these people around? Certainly not.' (I've mentioned before that a Gambian shower is merely a patch of earth surrounded by a fence of palm-leaves or corrugated iron, where you sluice down with a jug and a bucket of water). But she confessed that later, in her tiled Western-style bathroom, she added the mystery liquid to her bath-water. Did it work? Well, to be sure, she won a court-case which had been threatening for many months to destroy her peace of mind . . . but might she not have won anyway, if right was on her side, which it was?

I am still an agnostic on these matters. But what to make of the case of — let's call him Helmut? A smooth, sharp character of some charm and a somewhat cavalier attitude to law and morality. He had survived other, far more menacing African countries before settling here to import cars and, in time, run a glitzy nightspot. Somewhere along the way, he made an enemy, a member of his staff whom he'd cheated in some way (or so the enemy claimed). 'You will be sorry,' said the injured party, who set off up-river to consult with a powerful marabout who was related to his family. We do not know what passed between them, but we know that Helmut wakened one morning to find himself paralysed

In a wheelchair, he boarded planes for England, then Germany, seeking treatment, but none could be found. The doctors could find nothing, physically, wrong. But Helmut could not walk. What was he to do? He decided to come back to the Gambia and seek to fight magic with magic. He had 'treatment' from several powerful practitioners submitting himself to all manner of local witchcraft and wisdom, surrounded by bones and leaves and various excretions. At first they said he was getting better, but lately I hear he still needs a wheelchair.

Of all the tribes, the Jolas seem to have the strongest reputation for supernatural abilities. Most people — even the Dakar militia and the Mandinka villagers in Southern Senegal — try not to tangle with the Jolas, as they believe that they are impervious to human weapons. 'Bullets cannot wound them,' Ray explained matter-of-factly. 'They have a magic which protects them from gun-shots and knife-stabs.' Why I wondered, if this were true, have the Caramance rebels' Jola members not defeated the entire Government movement? Surely with such powers they could walk through all opposition easily? No-one, including Ray, wanted to comment on this.

Up-river, every year, the Jolas hold a vast festival of music, food, dance and magic. They lash at themselves with knives and remain unscathed, fire bullets at each other and remain intact. I haven't seen this myself but Roel went to the festival once and all my Gambian relatives assure me these powers exist. Even Tom, our sonsy Scottish doctor friend, admits that there are more things in heaven and earth . . .

'I have a European colleague working in a clinic up there,' he told us. 'Sometimes she tries to give injections to Jola patients and the needle bends and refuses to puncture the skin. As a practising Christian, she has found that the only way to deal with these situation is to invoke her God, Whom even the Jolas admit may be more powerful than their animist spirits.' Animism, the worship of certain trees, plants stones, rivers, is more common in other part of West Africa but it does have its followers here. And the most devout Christian and Muslim Gambians are quite convinced the Jolas of the interior have special magic.

Many also believe in the African version of werewolves . . . that some families pass to certain members the ability to turn from men or women into hyenas. Joe, our Freetonian friend, uses his studies of tribal superstitions and traditions in many of his paintings and he explained, 'It is a gift which could be passed from a grandmother to a grandson. These hyenas stalk the land at night and are very strong. I have heard that people attacked by them have struck out with their cutlasses and, if they have managed to wound or kill one, the body that they find in the morning is the body of a human being, not a hyena . . .'

It is for protection against this and many other unseen but known dangers that almost every single new baby born in the country will be given jujus to wear round wrist, waist or ankle (or all three) to protect him. Recently we killed a puff adder in the forest and our watchman skinned it, dried it and made himself a handsome bracelet . . . not for adornment but for protection.

Mary and Hannah found a couple of smelly little leather pouches hanging from a nail on a tree behind Uncle Dembo's, containing slips of paper with (presumably) curses written in Arabic inside. Things had not been going well for them of late and their Gambian friends assured them it was because enemies had consulted a marabout to plot againt them. Mary, a staunch Roman Catholic (even if her colourful flow of obscene language doesn't sound very saintly) made a big show of wearing her silver crucifix outside her blouse and sat prominently at one of the tables with a pair of scissors, which she used to cut the offending article into small pieces. Around the same time she discovered a large snake in the kitchen cupboard and was convinced an ill-wisher had secreted it there, though I leaned toward the belief that it had probably slithered through the back-room window and sneaked in by itself.

Certainly the months that followed were to be nightmarish ones for Mary and Hannah, with a dramatic fall-off in business and a long acrimonious court battle with the bar owner. Their vehicles had already been sold off and gradually everything else went, leaving them virtually penniless. Was it all because of black magic? It's hard to be sure. Hannah had a tendency to get involved, loudly and self-righteously, in court battles, and neither of the two colourful and wise-cracking Scotswomen was known for being a shrinking violet or a placatory protagonist. They made enemies as vigorously as they made friends. But spells were certainly cast. After one legal tussle, relatives of the person who was attempting to sue hissed at her that she would be struck dumb (fat chance!), fall ill, even die. 'Aye? that's what the **** said,' she cackled at full volume, 'but ah'm a wee Glasgow Pape. It'll take mair than a ****ing marabout to keep me quiet!'

I had my own sinister symbol to deal with — a chain letter, post-marked Edinburgh, which arrived in the mail promising riches if I passed on twenty copies to friends, and doom and destruction if I didn't. I tore it up and burned it on our rubbish heap, while Ray shuddered and looked nervously over his shoulder. Naturally, I don't believe in all that nonsense.

But . . a night or so later, Ray drove a French traveller to a hotel in the small hours of the morning and, swerving to avoid a vehicle approaching on the centre of the road with full headlamps blazing, skidded and hit a eucalyptus tree. The Citroen and the tree embraced each other passionately and noisily and the Frenchman took a hard blow to the forehead which later needed stitches. The car needed more than stitches. Its front half was a mess and it took half-a-day to move it, finally plonking it on a friend's trailer and dragging it to his garage where it lay in confusion and embarrassment for many weeks. In time, it was attacked by panel-beaters, mechanics, welders and electricians and after many frustrating months it did manage to lumber back home, where it lay comatose acting as a bedroom for the cats. In time we would sell it and it would do sturdy, if erratic service as a local taxi, but right then, I wanted to weep every time I looked at it.

Was it because I had burned the chain letter?

Ray thought that was a possibility. Alternatively, he brooded, someone had put a hex on us. Virtually nothing that happens can be put down to sheer coincidence, bad luck, bad driving, bad management. My own feeling is that it's too easy to blame our own carelessness, laziness or stupidity on 'bad juju'. 'When something goes wrong, we have to look at our own contribution and try to avoid making the same mistake again,' I preached at Ray. I applied this philosophy to my own pressing problems of the moment which were as so often before, the infiltration into my kitchen by these pesky termites.

The whole world sometimes seemed to be crumbling around me, beneath my feet, around my ears and under the onion I was chopping for that night's stew. Not an emotional crisis, just an entomological one. And I doubt if it was a marabout who urged the termites to invade us. They were just following their natural instinct. But how I loathed them. When I write my block-buster Hollywood horror movie script, it won't feature dinosaurs and huge scaly things with fangs and tails; it will be about these little white-bellied ants taking over the world as we know it. Nibbling stools and chairs and the post that hold up the lights in the garden, the pretty woven beach-beds and even, from time to time, my venerable baobab tree itself.

I was crushing a garlic clove one morning when the pine planking work surface (made from the crates in which my worldly goods arrived from Scotland at the end of 1989) simply disintegrated in a spongy splintery heap. The nice hourglass-shaped wooden stools bought in Brufut were a throbbing mass of termites. I had wanted this place to have ethnic charm, all wood and bamboo and palm-leaves . . . but all I was doing was providing a high-fibre diet for Isoptera, as the entomologists would call it. Already we had gradually substituted a batch of bright red and yellow plastic chairs (bought from Mary and Hannah during their financial crises) for the wicker ones that had collapsed.

Later I was to throw out half-chewed cardboard boxes, in which I'd stored papers, photographs, envelopes and books, and replace them with plastic filing-trays bought in the supermarket. Would we end up bristling with polyurethane and stainless steel? I hoped not, but I couldn't guarantee it.

The only way to stop worrying about such things — and by now I was stoically accepting the fact that termites were as much a part of Africa as midges were part of Scotland — was to go and look at the sea, a constant source of joy and drama and spiritual refreshment. Once at midnight, we whirled along the beach in the second-hand Suzuki jeep we had acquired in exchange for the Land Rover (by then in a very wobbly condition) after the demise of the 2CV.

The tide was out and the water was black like coal but with silvery threads where the moon dabbled its finger-tips in the waves. The sand was a pale silvery grey and seemed to be moving, until I realised the effect was caused by thousands of crabs, skittering sideways, bobbing up and down from their holes, rushing about madly like Oxford Street commuters. Ray braked suddenly as we drove into the middle of a conference of plovers, which exploded into the air so that we were surrounded by ghostly black and white shapes. One smashed into the windscreen and fell dead to the beach. The crabs moved in.

I missed the rippling suspension of the 2CV. The jeep just battered over Gambian undulations, ruts, troughs, potholes, shaking the breath from our bodies. But it clambered up and down the beach like a goat and bucked boldly through bush that an ordinary car couldn't tackle and we were happy with it. By day we would go to Brufut and watch the mullet fishermen. They would stroll casually along the edge of the water, gazing calmly ahead as though merely out for a constitutional. Then some secret sign would alert them and they would spin their nets deftly into the shallows and haul them out shimmering and twitching with tiny grey mullet. Ray always bought a dozen or so then gathered palm fronds and twigs from the beach and lit a fire, while I practised my breast-stroke in the calm of the sea, for it is always flatter and stiller there than in Bijilo. He would lay the fish across the flames, turning them till they were charred blackish-bronze on the outside. He would rinse them in the sea and we would peel off the roasted skin and eat the pale, creamy flesh inside.

One day we were driving back from such a picnic when the heavens opened and the whole world was opaque. There was nothing to distinguish the swirling grey water of the ocean from the swirling grey rainwater on the beach and above and around us. We inched forward, plunging occasionally into great gouges cut into the beach by rushing rivers which poured down from the scrubland, rivers born that day from the rain. A geologist has lately commented ominously on how, in this very beautiful area between Bijilo and Brufut, seasonal lakes and channels have been created in a short space of time and the natural coastline is being destroyed. The sand-miners rushing to fill their trucks to satisfy the Gambian passion for building, have a lot to answer for. Partly the erosion of the Gambian coast is caused by the sea itself, by the failure to intensify tree-planting around the coast and by the fierce winds and tidal shifts. But also it is exacerbated by the convoys of trucks rumbling down on to the sand and disgorging teams of men with shovels. Every week they collected perhaps a thousand tons of sand from the beach ... how long could this go on before the land itself began to disappear? Already we saw palm and other trees toppled on to the shore where they had been dislodged by the greedy shovels and the whole coastal stretch looked like a chunk of green-brown bread with giant toothmarks bitten from it.

Even worse, at that time, many had no right to be there. One truck carried the motif of the National Aids Programme. One had UN number plates, and several had government plates. A nice little bit of moonlighting for the drivers and the total ruination of a magnificent beach frequented by tourists, local children and fishermen. Since the time of which I write, things have improved marginally. The government has wakened up to the disastrous consequence of indiscriminate looting of one small stretch of beach and the numbers of loads have been limited, with plans to move the whole operation down the coast (where, in time, there will inevitably be new damage and ugliness). It's a very difficult quandary to resolve, for people are entitled to build homes yet to import building materials from abroad would be beyond the average person's means. But is the building being done by 'average persons'? It seems to me that most is being done by wealthy Gambians and Lebanese who construct enormously ugly homes with dozens of rooms, far more than they really need; or elegant bungalows which they erect specifically to rent out at high rates to overseas residents.

Whatever the rights and wrongs (and surely the preservation of the very land we live on is more important than showing off to colleagues that your house is bigger than theirs?) the results are harrowing. The Muslim cemetery in Banjul is literally being washed into the sea. Granny's bones could be cruising towards the Canaries.

Something else was being eaten away, apart from the wood munched by my termites and the land guzzled by the Atlantic and the sand-trucks. For in Banjul dock in the summer of '92, some mysterious creature seemed to be swallowing up whole containers of corned-beef, milk and other comestibles sent out as 'food aid' for hungry Gambians, by nations in the west. One 17-tonne consignment of corned beef from Scandinavia marked 'a gift to the people of the Gambia', and 'not to be sold', turned up in a multitude of local shops, selling for about £1 a tin. The meat which survived the docks was mostly sent to schools and day centres. It was a rather dreadful pinkish luncheon meat, most of it, but nourishing enough and school lunches played a vital role in maintaining the nutritional levels of children. Rice, peanut soup and pink luncheon meat may not be everyone's idea of a succulent lunch but for most of these children it was the mainstay of their diet and an alternative to hunger. Sad, therefore, that when it reached the schools it was depleted yet again by teachers and kitchen helpers who either took it for their own families or hawked it to the villagers. Private enterprise flourished; it was just a shame that it often did so at the expense of the very poorest and least able citizens

We ourselves had proved to be utterly inept at business. A Ghanaian woman in Manchester had promised to import natty batik shirts and shorts from us, made by the inestimable Modou the tailor, as well as patchwork bedcovers stitched by Choam in the village and carved wooden drums made by old craftsmen at Brikama. But she had had cashflow problems, not to mention problems with the customs people at Manchester airport and needed nothing more from us. Our last planned consignment now sat in a wicker basket (as yet uneaten by termites) in our hallway. Would we sell them to tourists during the season? Or just save them and send them to family and friends as Christmas presents? I visualised chums in Glasgow shivering in December temperatures, rain and sleet knocking against their windows, opening up tie-dye bikinis and rainbow-hued shorts, then going back to their burst pipes and chilblains.

Not that we didn't have burst pipes right here in the sweltering heat. The two current watchmen were digging a trench for the foundations of a new ornamental wall we were planning in the garden when they chopped one of the water-pipes in half. Our precious water for washing clothes, flushing the toilets and moistening the soil round the banana trees, gushed uselessly in the trench and it took us three days to find a plumber to come and mend it. It was at times like this that it was almost medically obligatory for us to jump into the jeep and head for the beach. A swim in the sea was my Mogadon.

The Leaning Tower of Bijilo

Try to picture our water-tower. A structure like a miniature pylon some five metres tall, made from sturdy angle-iron, topped by a 1,000 litre tub of sky-blue glass fibre, with a saucer-shaped lid. All of this poised astride the top of our 27-metre-deep well, in which the pump ingests the water and belches it up a grey plastic pipe into the tank.

Today, we have water from the public supply, but in the summer of '92 we relied on the natural waters under the earth. The system worked reasonably well, until one day . . .

I was carrying a box of rubbish towards the inexorably growing heap of tin-cans, charred papers, orange-juice cartons, vegetable peelings, plastic bottles and nameless gunge which is still our only means of waste disposal. Every day I poked pieces of newspaper and dry twigs and weeds into it and tried my best to burn everything degradable. It was, fortunately, tucked into a corner at the rear of the compound, and some kind of crawling weed with pretty white flowers had encircled it, while a rogue papaya tree had grown up from a seed and inexplicably flourished, spreading concealing shadows over the mess. Carol's compost heap was a dim memory.

Suddenly I heard Ray's voice screeching 'Help!' I looked over towards the water-tower and there was my beloved husband clinging to the top of it as it listed slowly towards a forty-five degree angle. I had a fleeting, irreverent image of King Kong clinging to the top of the Empire State Building, then shuddered in horror at the thought of his falling, falling, and being crushed under the heavy angle-iron.

'Lamin!' I roared to our young watchman of the moment, 'Come! Quickly!' We both clung to the other side of the structure, which, fortunately decided to jam without tilting any more. Ray clambered down, shaking, and I hugged him, not quite sure whether to laugh or cry. He had been doing what he had done many times before—climbing up to check the water-level.

We discovered that one leg of the tower had not been securely included when the other three were being covered by the cement base around the mouth of the well. Not only that, but the summer rains had caused the earth to shift.

The tank itself seemed to be sitting just a few centimetres off centre, and all of these factors had converged so that Ray's puny weight had caused the whole thing to shudder and tilt.

Ray tied some rope to the opposite iron legs and towed the thing upright with the jeep. He and Lamin dug around the errant leg and packed it with stones and concrete. After much banging and clanging and thudding, he announced: 'That's it fixed now. It will be fine.'

Two nights later we came home late after having had supper on the beach with Tom and Joan. It was our regular Friday date at a charming beach bar perched on a headland at Fajara, where the four of us, and a succession of itinerant friends, would meet to eat, drink, gossip and tell each other our problems. We had told Tom about the dramatic doings around the well, and he, like me, had to stifle a giggle at the thought of Ray hanging like an abseiler on a mountain peak. But he added: 'I hope it's OK now, Ray. You be careful, old chap.' 'Oh, don't worry,' said Ray airily. 'It's all mended.'

As we drove into the compound, our jeep headlights picked out a squeegee silhouette behind the black tracery of the tree where the weaver birds hold their noisy conferences at dawn. The tower had tilted again. Ray cursed in wonderfully onomatopoeic Wollof. I felt like crying. Next day it was hauled upright once again. The iron legs, now slightly buckled, were hammered straight and solid concrete was poured all around them. The tank, which looks like a giant honey-pot, was shoogled around until I decreed that it was poised absolutely dead centre. As I write, it is still solidly in position.

But during all the excitement, we realised, the lid of the tank had disappeared. How can a two-metre wide glass fibre disc simply vanish? We hunted high and low, exploring the bush around the compound, even the forest.

'It must have blown away,' suggested Carol. We imagined it whirling through the air, alighting in Brufut or Tanji, like a giant blue butterfly. 'Hummm. I think someone's stolen it,' growled Ray, ever suspicious of his fellow-man. What would a thief do with a blue glass fibre lid two metres wide? We all speculated but couldn't think of anything. 'Let's just watch out for anyone playing with a very large frisbee,' chuckled Rab wittily, and we scowled at him. 'Maybe the airport will receive reports of an unidentified flying object passing over Yundum,' chortled someone else, and Ray stomped into the house in a huff. It's not that he doesn't have a sense of humour; we laugh together a lot. It's just that domestic crises like these upset him far more seriously than they upset me.

Many, many days later we found the flying-saucer-cum-frisbee. It had been carried by the wind and dropped into a neglected corner of the compound, behind some dilapidated kirinting, on top of the hole in the ground, which used to be an African toilet before we got real plumbing. That Friday we joined Tom and Joan, and Caroline and Julius, for our sociable supper on the beach and told them all about the leaning tower of Bijilo, the flying blue saucer and other trivial but entertaining chitchat. Tom told us about his latest frustrations and triumphs in the children's hospital and Caroline told us about the latest convoluted memos and feasibility studies to issue from the U.N., for whose operations, it often seemed to me, whole forests of trees must be chopped down to provide enough paper.

One of the assets of the beach-bar was its dinky little toilets, for as I have said so often, a good toilet is a jewel to be treasured in the Gambia. These were crisply white-painted circular edifices containing clean water, a towel and meticulously maintained Elsan loos. The place also boasted wooden beach-beds, chairs and hammocks and an unparalleled view over the beach. We would all watch the sun plop into the gleaming pewter ocean like a ripe mango, sending its golden juices trickling over the waves. Mullet often glittered and skipped in the shallows, stirring the water till it frothed like champagne.

As the sky grew black, the owner, a Gambian, and his Swedish wife would put hurricane lamps on the tables and we would talk in flickering light like the members of a seance group. The atmosphere was comforting and even romantic, though the actual meal could be something of a gamble. Not that the food wasn't good and cheap, but sometimes it just wasn't there .

'We'd like three steak and chips, one fish and chips and one chicken and chips,' we announced confidently one night. 'And a bottle of red wine.'

'Er . . . em . . . sorry. But the steak's finished .'

'Oh. Well, make it three fish and chips and two chicken and chips,'' we said cheerfully.

'Well . . . er . . . actually there isn't any fish. And there's only one piece of chicken left,' mumbled the embarrassed proprietor. 'Would, umm, er, would anyone like an omelette?'

Worse still, there was no wine. This was serious. Tom and I traditionally shared a bottle of wine while the others drank beer or Coke. Ray volunteered to go and find someone who could sell him a bottle of plonk. He disappeared for over an hour. 'Probably having a beer in every pub on Kairaba Avenue,' smiled Tom tolerantly, while I fumed like a typical wife (which I am, after all). In fact, he came back looking fed-up and furious. Pub number one had no wine. Pub number two had some but wouldn't sell a bottle. In the end he'd found a cafe which would sell him wine but only by the glass. The waiter slowly and painstakingly measured glasses from one bottle and poured them into another, counting ponderously. Seven very small glasses at ten dalasis each failed even to fill the litre bottle. Especially infuriating because the wine in question cost 19 dalasis a litre in the supermarket. Never mind, 'Let's eat,' said Ray, getting over his chagrin, 'Did they find us some steak?' We all laughed grimly and asked him how he felt about an omelette.

But no-one was downcast. The setting as so beautiful, and now the grass umbrellas over the hammocks and tables were like big black flowers against a starry purple sky.

Ray and Tom planned a fishing trip with Rory, architect and bagpipe player, who had bought himself a jaunty little glass fibre boat with an outboard engine. On the appointed day, Joan and I drove them to Denton Bridge, a fine structure financed in the 1980s by the Overseas Development Agency to the tune of almost £3 million, carrying on its shoulders the 'M1' as the dual carriageway to Banjul is known to locals and holiday makers. It, like its century-old predecessor, spanned the murky, mangrove-fringed Oyster Creek, where old boats rotted away picturesquely and new ex-patriates' pleasure-boats bobbed and awaited their owners' Sunday afternoon pleasure, be it fishing or water-skiing.

Equipped with rods, beer, and boundless enthusiasm, the three bold fishermen set off into the secret world of the creeks, where African darters with slim, sinuous necks, anvil-headed hammerkops and green-backed herons plunged and strolled and trembled in the shadows. Later they circled back and entered the sea itself, the yellow tourist beaches stretching south, the Atlantic tossing and twitching ahead. We left them to it and headed for that same beach-bar on the headland, ate chips and soaked up the sun and exchanged female confidences. When we went to collect the men, their faces were solemn and sorrowful and their hands were empty. 'Oh dear, no luck?'' we murmured not very sympathetically. Then they all grinned and snorted and Ray produced a long silver barracuda from behind his back, big enough to have provided some twenty or thirty portions at around £6 or £7 a head in any of the smarter hotels. They were all bursting with boyish pride.

Often on a Sunday, Ray drove Cameron and me to Brufut beach. He would take his fishing-rod and stand like a slender black statue staring out to sea, willing a butterfish or a tuna to scoff his bait. Cameron and I would go treasure-hunting. We would find big pink crabs with Prussian blue claws which glowed in the light; jelly-fish with frilly edges, translucent mauve and cerise and blue, cuttlefish bulging unpleasantly from their budgie-food shells, their jelly-like bodies trailing tendrils so that all Gambians know them as 'octopus'. Pied kingfisher fell like stones into the water to pop up again triumphantly with fish

Ray and Cameron scanning the Atlantic and hoping for a bite at beautiful Brufut beach.

sparkling in their heavy beaks. The resident reef heron would pace daintily through a miniature inland lake of shallow, warm water behind the rough sandy beach, its voice a short self-conscious croak as it soared like a kite and scanned the sea's edge for fish.

When Cameron swam, as he did, in his fashion, totally without fear, it was with his head submerged, hands flapping at his sides, feet kicking, so that he looked like a little frog. Sometimes we would go in convoy to Brufut, with Tom and Joan, or Joe and Andrea, or anyone else who wanted to bring a sandwich and a towel. It beats Ayr beach by a wide margin!

But let me tell you more about Joe and Andrea. Once, when I had met Andrea at a supper-party at Tom's house, and warmed to her quirky sense of humour and frank, open manner, I invited her to a barbecue, thinking she would enjoy meeting Joe. She was an artist from Boise, Idaho, who had lived for two years in a tiny room in a compound in Bakau, drawing and painting delicate little pieces based on ancient African geometry and culture. Joe was a Freetonian, who had arrived in Banjul a few years earlier with a few dollars and some paint-brushes and tubes in his bag. At first he lived with a family there, who regarded him suspiciously because he was a foreigner, and only opened up their hearts and their food-bowl to him when they realised his talent (initially for painting shop-signs for local traders) could bring in some money.

Eventually he ended up in Kololi village, where he painted fragile little water-colours of pale African landscapes dotted with baobab trees, round huts and mysterious old men, who he said were marabouts, or scary symbolic scenes incorporating mythical figures and magic. Like any good hostess, I liked to see my guests having someone to talk to with a common interest. But I was as surprised — and delighted — as they when the meeting led to a warm friendship and then to love and — although this comes later in my narrative — a promise of marriage. Ray was thrilled. He is a vigorous believer in marriage. I remember when I first met him and fell in love with him, I said: 'Couldn't we just live together?' and he was appalled. 'That is not respectable. We should be married,'he insisted, and of course he was right. 'Even when you have problems, you two are an example of how mixed marriages can work,' Andrea used to say to us in her slow mid-West drawl.

What an embarrassing responsibility! But we were touched by the fact that our marriage, turbulent and eventful as it certainly was, was nevertheless an inspiration to dear friends like these. And Andrea also gave me inspiration, for it was around then that I began to dig out the paints and brushes that had been gathering dust at the bottom of a straw basket in the hall, and play about with shapes and colours, not very skillfully but with great enthusiasm. The first paints had been given to me by Scottish actress-comedienne Dorothy Paul as a wedding present at a farewell lunch in Glasgow in 1989, but never opened. The others had been left by Glasgow art teacher Callum when he and Betty came for the first of many holidays in the Gambia and I confided in him that I had 'done' Higher art at school and once even won a medal for a painting of a stuffed seagull at Glasgow Art Galleries at the age of 13 or so!

But now I took pencils and paper when we went to the beach and tried to reproduce the sinewy lines of Ray's back as he cast his line far out to sea, the flapping baggy trousers of the mullet-fishermen as they waded along the shallows ready to throw their nets, or little brother Eliman's concave back and jutting stomach as he studied Cameron's futile attempts to lure a landcrab out of its hole with a piece of his cheese sandwich.

For a while, it became a gentle obsession, not to mention excellent therapy, as I sat at the living-room table and painted, from memory and photographs, women in the market with bowls of vegetables and peanuts on their heads, women with babies clasped like limpets to their backs, children grinning under the green canopy of a mango tree. Looking at them now, these awkward water-colours, they are pretty feeble. Callum, on one of his trips, glanced at them bleakly and said, in his Scottish art teacher's voice, 'Och hen, you're just colouring in.' But all the same, I sold quite a few of them to our guests, who, perhaps, didn't know much about art but knew what they liked, and I am rather proud of the fact that my wee pictures are hanging on walls in Bremen, Aberdeen, Perth and Paris. So there!

The one painting I did purely for myself, and from life not photographs or mental images, was of Ray. (I should say that my reason for not painting Gambian women and children from life was that they would never have stayed still long enough, and anyway, would have been suspicious and shy at being thus depicted.) Ray wouldn't have sat still either, but it so happened he was stretched out on the sofa, sound asleep, an empty beer-can and a glass in front of him on a small table, violet shadows cutting across his cheeks, hands in repose, long, bare bony feet full of interesting paintable angles and lights and shades. I've seen better pictures executed by 12-year-olds in school, but I like it, and it does have an element of the tenderness I feel for this touchy, vain, vulnerable, impetuous African man.

Magali, my French healer, would have approved of the painting therapy. Hadn't she, after all, insisted that I had to allow my creative side, such as it is, to develop uninhibited by domestic frustrations? All very well, but occasionally these domestic frustrations were enough to make a saint spit.

The jeep had developed some very nasty ailments and was spending longer and longer in dusty repair yards, cheek by jowl with obsolete Renaults, disjointed Datsuns, crippled Peugeots and asthmatic Ladas, having bits put in and taken out, welded, adjusted, taken out again, put in again . . . Ray stayed with it and supervised its painful surgical procedures, lying in the dust beside the mechanics, watching their every move. There were two reasons for this. One was that he wanted to learn from them, so that, in time, he could do more of our repairs to save money. The other was that he was convinced, possibly correctly, that if he left the car alone it would have what few new and efficient parts it contained whipped off and replaced by old ones. This does happen, I'm told, and Ray has, as I've indicated before, a very suspicious nature

In these dust-filled yards, with no pits, ramps, electronic equipment or college-trained staff, people relied almost entirely on gut instinct, borrowed tools, long intervals of shaking of heads, banging recalcitrant protuberances with a hammer, and generally taking an unconscionably long time to do the simplest of jobs. But that's not really fair. They really didn't have the equipment or the tools they needed, and yet they could improvise and make do and mend in a manner which would horrify, yet gain the envy of, a European mechanic. Components that would have been condemned in Britain and replaced by expensive new ones, could be salvaged, welded, bolted or taped together to serve another few months or even years. When a particular size of spanner was not available, an 'apprentice' — often a boy barely as high as the bonnet of the car — would be sent to search for one in another yard, and pay five or ten dalasis to borrow it. Old oil drums were cut down and hammered and used as patches for floors and wings, and the welding was remarkably good. Indeed, our exhaust system soon became more patches than original material, it was worked on so many times. The roads around Bijilo, many of them merely tracks and trenches through the bush, are not designed to preserve the lower regions of cars.

While all these repairs were going on, and I was stuck at home fuming impatiently, our water-pump grunted, sneezed, wheezed and finally refused to pull up one more drop of water from our well. The pale blue honey-pot with its frisbee lid was empty, and a batch of tourists were due to arrive in a few days. We diagnosed that the pump had pulled up some mud and fallen leaves during the turbulent rainy season, when the winds throw debris and greenery around indiscriminately. We looked at each other sorrowfully. What were we to do? I had become used to water flowing from the taps and gurgling through the lavatory cistern, and so had our guests. Now we were back to hauling buckets nearly thirty metres from the bottom of the well, or trudging round to the ITC standpipe, a long way off past the cattle and the clumps of eucalyptus.

The plumber said he knew a man in Bakau who knew all about pumps. Ray rushed to see him. The man who knew all about pumps said he knew all about lots of pumps, but not ours. 'You'd better take it to Dakar,' he said helpfully. The makers of our model had, according to the hand-book, an agent in Dakar.

The capital of Senegal is about five hours drive away. They spoke French there, for heaven's sake. What was the French for: 'Can you examine our water-pump and do a quick repair?' We sighed in unison. It so happened that Nadhia, our French friend from Casamance, was visiting us at the time. *'C'est pas problème,'* she said brightly. 'I'll come with you.'

We packed enough clothes for two overnights in Dakar, reckoning that would be the minimum time we would need, and worrying in case the small amount of money we had would be less than the price demanded. We prayed that the jeep, back from its latest spell with the mechanic, would not let us down. We put a jerry-can of petrol on the roof-rack, filled bottles with drinking water, sprayed everything in the house with insecticide so that we didn't come back to find a host of squatting cockroaches and ants, locked everything up and set off.

We got as far as Serrekunda when Nadhia, the efficient Parisienne, said: 'Don't you think we should phone the agent in Dakar first?' 'What a good idea,' we said.

We rang the number listed in the hand-book for African agents for our pump's manufacturer. It made a sound like a tortured tomcat. We tried again. 'That will be four dalasis fifty,' said the girl in Gamtel helpfully. 'But we didn't speak to anyone yet,' we yelled. 'It's registered on the computer that you made a connection,' said the girl implacably. We paid up our four dalasis fifty for listening to the tortured tomcat and checked the Dakar phone book. It was dated 1988. Another Gamtel girl agreed grudgingly to consult with the Senegalese operator. She did so, and revealed that all Senegal numbers had been changed.

'Why, then, don't you throw this old book away?' I asked crisply, flapping the obsolescent directory under her nose. She looked offended, and surprised and put the book back on a table for other users.

In the end, a real voice came on the line and Nadhia talked to it. She talked in flowing, cajoling, confident tones, but the voice said, *'Mais non, c'est pas possible de promêttre . . .'*

It was not remotely possible to guarantee how long it would take to repair the pump, if indeed it could be repaired at all, and it certainly wasn't possible to do anything to it under the terms of the manufacturer's guarantee. 'But how long do you think it might take?' pleaded Nadhia. *'Peut-être deux semaines, peut-être deux mois . .'*

We all experienced severe withdrawal symptoms and decided not to go to Dakar after all. Ray looked almost jubilant. He hates Dakar. We drove home and unlocked all the doors and breathed in poisonous insecticide fumes. Later we bought new buckets for the well and began pulling up water by hand. It seemed harder now than it used to. We had been spoiled. Never mind that a large proportion of the population gets its water this way, I thought uncharitably. I want running water again. Picnics on the beach and painting palm trees and plump mangoes dangling from branches of leafy green against transparent azure skies did little to relieve my frustration this time.

'Someone must have put a spell on the compound to bring us bad luck,' muttered Ray. This was his usual line of justification for any ills that befell us. When I snapped that he should have considered putting a net over the well-top during the rains to prevent windblown debris being swept into the funnel and down to the water below, he sulked. We sat at opposite ends of the sofa, glaring at the wall, then looked at each other and smiled. What was all the fuss about? We had survived our first two years in this house without any fancy plumbing, and most of our previous tourists had been mercifully good-natured about it, and had even joined in the water-pulling with gusto, considering it part of their African adventure. Anyway, to be honest, it was mostly young Lamin the watchman who had the drudgery to put up with, as this was considered to be a watchman's job, not just by us, but by Gambians in general. That's if they were lucky enough to HAVE a watchman. Otherwise, of course, it was women's work!

'She Showed Me
Her Bottom'

It was at times like this we realised, that we needed friends. 'Let's go and see Roderick,' we told each other. Yes, our big pal from Perth was back, with a tongue like lemon zest and a heart of gold. You may recall that on his previous visit, he brought us clootie dumpling. This time he came brandishing tinned black pudding, Scotch broth mix and shortbread. He is determined I won't lose touch with my Scottish origins

We went to his hotel and plied him with flattery and alcohol, and I pretended to sob bravely as we described our adventures with the water system and the terrible implication of a pump on the blink. 'Och, aye,' he drawled sardonically. 'And what do you want ME to do about it?' But within minutes he had, of course, agreed to carry the offending appliance back to Britain and try to have it mended there by the firm that manufactured it in the first place. Next morning he went off to the airport, listing to one side under the weight of the pump, grinning bleakly through gritted teeth.

That night, we ate fried eggs and black pudding and drank a toast to old friends like him. We did it by candlelight because, the night before as we were preparing to go and sweet-talk Roderick, the generator newly returned from 'a complete servicing', made noises like a jet plane and all the lights in the compound blew up. Were we never to have a trouble-free day?

No, it seemed we weren't. The back axle of the jeep set up a kind of whining noise and Ray took it and the generator to the workshop in Bakau muttering as he went about bad luck and bad spells and bad bloody mechanics. I typed my stories in a spirit of apprehension. Maybe the typewriter would spontaneously ignite? Perhaps the roof would fall in on me. Or the baobab tree would uproot itself. Quite possibly the dog would be sick on a tourist's bed. In fact nothing really awful happened . . . unless you count the plastic water-container unaccountably springing a leak and dribbling all over the kitchen floor, and the murder of a magnificent Red Bishop (breeding plumage vivid scarlet and black, with a short tail and a black crown) by one of the cats, who then chewed it up on the verandah leaving a dusting of vermilion feathers fluttering on the breeze.

There were at that time, still six cats. The foster daddy of them all, Penny, the lovable hermaphrodite, had simply disappeared and never come back. Perhaps he (she?) couldn't stand all these squawling moggies around the place. I knew the feeling. One of Awa-dingding's litter of black and white boys had fallen sick and died. The two babies skipped around eating black pudding and birds, bread and milk, with utter lack of discrimination, and every time I put one foot outside our front door, six feline voices set up a plaintive miaowing which could be heard in Guinea Conakry.

Tom and Joan were leaving soon to go back to Scotland and suggested it would be a good idea if they left us their pet cock and hen. Eeeek! I imagined Spotty (the kitten that looks as though someone had dropped black puddings and oranges on a field of white) racing after the chickens in a multi-coloured flurry. Do cats eat cockerels? Then Ray's mum said she'd like to give us some ducks. Mmm. 'I quite like duck,' I pondered. 'I could make some orange sauce . . .'

'Mariama,' gasped Ray, horrified. 'I couldn't eat duck! Nasty dirty things. We would have to keep them as pets.' Do cats eat ducks? They would probably wander into the tourists' rooms and leave their trade-mark on the floors. And I would get fond of them and wouldn't want to cook them, even if Ray wanted to eat them. We fobbed Ray's Mum off politely, and told Tom and Joan we appreciated their offer but couldn't guarantee their chickens' safety among our cat population. We waited expectantly for news about the pump, and we bought new light bulbs and ran the generator and the jeep for quite some time without anything awful happening. We began to breathe more slowly and I stopped clenching all my muscles and curving my back and went back to walking tall and slow and easy, the way I'd done when Magali urged me to relax for the sake of my womb and my nerves.

And we were delighted to welcome Nadhia and Diack, back from Senegal just a week or so after Nadhia's efforts to persuade Dakar to solve our pump problem. Diack was looking as handsome and cheerful as ever and Nadhia was as sleek and Parisienne as ever. Her fair hair is always swept straight back from a high forehead in a crisp band of blue fabric, and she wears her indigo tie-dyes with aplomb.

She and Diack looked happy and kept holding hands and sneaking kisses, though Nadhia still worried about Diack's faithfulness, for his charm was the kind that somehow almost involuntarily spreads itself around. He said he had to go back to Kafountine to tend the business, and I knew Nadhia would worry that his old girlfriend from the village would insinuate herself into his company, but, she confided later, 'Diack, 'e 'as to make up hees mind. I love him and I sink he loves me, but he must give up other women.' We were to have lots of long intimate chats about her problems and other feminine topics, but first we had an unexpected crisis to deal with . . . the secret lusts of our watchman.

Diack had gone home the day before and Nadhia was tucked up in hut B, having decided to trust him, and enjoy a few days relaxation in the Gambia, which, as I have explained, is regarded by the people of Casamance as positively sophisticated, with its supermarkets and hotels and electric lighting. Next morning, though, she came over from her room to have coffee with us, looking hollow-eyed and bashful. 'I am, I don't know 'ow to say, but I 'ave to tell you, Mariama . . .' I looked at her expectantly. What catastrophe could have happened alone in a little hut? 'Eet is ze boy, ze watchman . . . 'E ave come to my room at five o'clock zis morning and I was very frightened. He said he loved me. I shouted at him to go. . .'

Oh, no. It was bad enough having to deal with recalcitrant back axles and seditious generators. But a lecherous watchman? Young L—, bright-eyed and bushy-tailed, whom we'd hoped was going to prove industrious, reliable, honest; whose private passions, to be frank, we hadn't even considered. There was only one thing to do. 'Pack up your things and GO!' I thundered at him, pointing a quivering finger towards the gate. 'But, I, er, I wasn't . . . ' 'GO! OUT! LEAVE!' 'But I was, er, I only wanted to tell her her door wasn't locked,' he snuffled unconvincingly. 'How did you know it wasn't locked unless you turned the handle and opened it?' I snapped. 'You were inside her room. In the middle of the night! Go.'

He trudged off, mumbling to himself and Nadhia gulped down several coffees and half a packet of cigarettes.

That evening, he came to the gate, looking pleased with himself, and handed Ray a letter, which, we discovered later, had not been written by himself but by a friend whose literary effluences were so remarkable that he should probably have been writing for the big screen — making blue movies.

It was a very long letter, and the English was, to put it mildly, erratic as well as erotic. It was intended as a justification for L—'s behaviour. It contained such gems as: 'She looked at me and I could tell that she loved me passionately. I went to have a shower and she came and jumped on me and pleaded with me to rape her. She showed me her bottom . . .' And much more in the same vain. Since Nadhia was in the house with me during all the periods when these titillating incidents were alleged to have happened, we decided that L— and his friend were strong contenders for the romantic fiction award of the year.

We sat in the living-room, well out of earshot of the Gambia's answer to Jackie Collins, and screeched with laughter. Nadhia coughed on her cigarette smoke. 'Aha, my bottom!' she spluttered. 'Eet ees my bottom which has driven him wild with longing!' We tried to visualise her leaping lewdly on L—, throwing aside her long wrap-around indigo skirt of heavy woven cotton, and we fell about sniggering. Then we straightened our faces and advanced on the hapless youth. 'You fool! You criminal! You liar!' roared Ray, who was enjoying himself immensely. 'You have slandered our friend and she is terribly distressed and angry. Do you not know,' he improvised brilliantly, 'that she herself is a friend of the Minister of Justice and the head of the Gendarmerie and also of President Diouf of Senegal, and she is going to see them all. They will all be looking for you and they will take you to court and you will go to prison for forty years!'

L— crumpled like a falling leaf from the baobab tree, and shook in his shoes. 'I am sorry. I beg her forgiveness. I made it all up. It was my friend. He invented these things to save me. I'm sorry, I'm sorry.' He squeaked like a mouse and ran off into the bush and was not seen again for many months. We all felt secretly sorry for him, but Nadhia kept the letter to show Diack. 'Oh, eet ees so funny. Diack will laugh.' We still make remarks about Nadhia's bottom every time we see her. 'Not been showing it to anyone lately, I hope?' I'll say casually, and she'll explode into indignant cachinnation.

It all helped to take our mind off our mechanical mishaps.

Ray's young brother Modou and his friend, another Modou, were pressed into service as acting temporary watchmen. Modou the friend was addressed as Tom by Modou the brother. 'Tom' is the term Gambians use for other people with the same name as them. He was from Guinea Bissau, which gave us a slight communication problem, as he spoke only Portuguese and a little Wollof. Nadhia had lived in Brazil for a long time, so she could talk to him, but was reluctant to do so in case he too developed signs of desire.

When I called 'Modou' they both came running. As the days passed, though, most of the running was done by Portuguese Modou, as we privately called him, since Bijilo Modou considered himself, as a member of the family, the senior employee and therefore entitled to boss 'Tom' around and leave most of the work to him.

Nadhia went off on one of her Gambian shopping sprees buying cheap red Spanish wine which she could sell to Kafountine campement at a profit, a frying pan, curtain fabric, curry powder and enamel basins for rice. Thus laden, she decided to make her way south by the coastal route, to avoid the Customs post at Seleti, in case they confiscated her wine, or even her curry-powder. It is a constant source of irritation between the Gambia and Senegal that many items are much cheaper here than there. This results not just in people like Nadhia and Diack buying items of shopping to take home, but in Gambian merchants re-exporting truckloads of goods, not just to Senegal but through Senegal to Mali, Mauritania and Guinea Bissau. Every so often Senegal closes or tightens its borders, and indeed, as I write, the situation has become tense.

The virtual collapse of the Maastricht Treaty and the monetary upheavals in Europe, specifically of the French franc, had played havoc with the Senegalese CFA franc, and this, combined with many complex homegrown Senegalese economic problems (the President even calling for all civil servants to accept a cut in salary) has resulted in a complete closure of trade borders, urgent talks between the two ECOWAS nations, and our own President urging traders to make use of air and sea freight as an alternative to road transport.

But in 1992, as we were to see for ourselves, Senegal's problems were of a different nature. We drove Nadhia to Kartong, the last outpost on the coast before the mangrove-dense creek which marks the border. We bounced through fishing villages past dusty fields of millet, past the pretty mosque of Tujereng, with its spiral staircase inside a little tower, along the narrow empty lanes of the far south, where the beach becomes enormously wide and empty except for an occasional fisherman working on his net. The creeks beyond Kartong, you will remember, are where some of our guests found themselves stuck in the mud during their pirogue trip into the silent green channels.

The journey took us two hours, and was extremely bumpy and dusty. At the tiny police post before the border, our friend the border policeman, wearing old jeans and a tee-shirt, came out sighing. He saw us looking inquisitively at a cluster of women and children huddled on a bench outside his tiny headquarters. 'Ah, these poor people,' he said. 'They have come here from Casamance this morning. Some of their husbands and fathers have been killed.' Once again the Casamance rebels were creating havoc and refugees were fleeing to the haven of the Gambia.

We helped Nadhia clamber into a skinny dug-out canoe with her bags of wine and enamel basins, and watched as she was paddled across the dense olive water to the far side of the creek where a Senegalese bush-taxi was waiting for passengers. 'Take care!' we called after her anxiously.

We drove back homewards stopping at Brufut for a swim to wash off some of the dust and soothe our jeep-jolted bodies. Our mullet-fisherman friend approached us, looking sad. His baggy pantaloons flared like sails in the breeze and his craggy dark face was puckered and pensive. ``You see these boats over there,'' he nodded towards the place where the Brufut fishing pirogues normally moored between catches. We realised that there were many extra craft there, packed with people, huddled under makeshift canopies and sails. On board, women wept and children chattered. Cooking-pots simmered over little gas-rings and washing flapped in the sea-wind. They were, said the mullet-man, more refugees.

At one point in 1992 there were over 2000 refugees from Senegal in the Gambia. The authorities, and the Gambian Red Cross often aided by both Muslim and Christian organisations, did sterling work in housing them in makeshift quarters and finding rice and cassava for them to eat. In Brufut, many had relatives and continued with their traditional occupation of fishing while waiting for their country to come to its senses. Many returned home when peace agreements were signed and conciliatory noises made, only to find that the factionalism re-surfaced and they were once more afraid of having their houses burned, their rice stolen or their lives threatened.

It was a small and perhaps insignificant struggle compared with, say, the carnage happening further south in Liberia, but it was still a sorrowful state of affairs.

We forgot about the real violence across the frontier when we watched the satisfying fictional fighting of Schwarzenegger, Van Damm, and Clint Eastwood on our new acquisition . . . a combined TV and VCR. We have no television station in the Gambia, and Senegalese television, which we could pick up, is reputedly incredibly boring. But we have many, many video shops. Indeed, if you drive around the exclusive areas of Fajara and Cape Point you will also see enormous mesh saucers . . . the satellite dishes of rich Gambians and immigrants.

We had just bought our set, and were like children with a new toy. My sister, in Scotland, was shocked when I wrote and told her about it. 'You're supposed to be sitting under the stars watching the palm trees nodding and listening to the crickets and frogs,' she wrote to me indignantly. 'I thought you'd given up Western playthings for the simple life?'

'Look, you,' I wrote back. 'I do lead a simple life. I listen to the frogs and the crickets. I get my water from the well' (the pump was still in England, never to return). 'I have spent the last three years making my own amusements, playing cards by candlelight, drinking attaya under the stars, reading and writing and planning next day's menus for the tourists. But allow me a couple of hours each evening to watch a movie. We love it!'

And indeed we did. The quality of the videos from the particular shop we patronised was less than perfect. They flickered a lot, and they often had messages flashed across them that said: 'This video is for demonstration purposes only. If you have paid money to watch it, please phone this number immediately . . .' I don't think the laws of video piracy have reached the Gambia. In any case the owners of certain shops brazenly hire out tapes which are obviously copies. We watched, as I hinted before, a patchy, mostly black-and-white pirate copy of *Home Alone 2* long before the official video was available in Britain.

And we had other sources. Friends like Roderick would bring us out tapes of *The Beechgrove Garden* and *The Antiques Roadshow*, *Rab C Nesbitt* and *Birds of a Feather*, *Newsnight* and *Panorama*. There isn't much chance of our becoming square-eyed as we could only watch after we had made and served supper to our guests and cleared away their plates, and before we switched the generator off, which was seldom later than 11 pm.

Films cost fifteen dalasis to rent, which is just over £1, an expensive luxury in Gambian terms (which were the terms I now thought in). But we rationalised that for two of us to go to the cinema in Serrekunda would cost 20 dalasis plus petrol, and involve late hours, sweaty clammy air, mosquitoes and an over-rich diet of kung-fu films. Another reckless purchase we could ill afford, and one which really was stupid, I now realise in retrospect, was Mary and Hannah's washing-machine which they had to sell when their feud with the owner of Uncle Dembo's was boiling up to an explosion.

They needed the money; we persuaded ourselves that the machine would be a boon. Haddy, who cleaned the tourists' huts, coped magnificently with sheets and towels and even, on occasion, blankets, dunking them in a tub of water pulled from the well, rubbing them furiously, wringing them by hand and hanging them out to dry in the hot hard sun of early winter, when the nights can be sharp and cold and the days like a furnace. But when I washed our shirts and shorts and trousers, I developed a sore back, raw hands from trying to screw out the moisture, and bad temper because I felt there were other, more creative things I could be doing.

'We'll just pop in the clothes, switch on, spin-dry, and save Haddy and ourselves such a lot of effort,' we told ourselves, barely remembering that we would have to do this in the evening hours of darkness these being the only times when there was electricity to switch anything on at all. The twin-tub was bright apple green, the colour of British kitchen fittings in the 1950s, and it was made in China. Its maker's name and control instruction were all written in Chinese calligraphy. The hose for emptying it was broken, which we didn't discover until we flooded the kitchen floor. That had been immediately before the water-pump croaked and died. Thereafter, we tried filling the machine with buckets and found that it used so much water, most of which escaped and flowed over the floor, that we became exhausted and fractious and had to put the bundles of sodden soapy clothes outside for Haddy to wash properly next morning. To this day, the green machine stands unused in the bathroom taking up space and developing crumbling rust patches around its bottom.

I began to realise that mechanical possessions merely complicated our existence. I began to remember, with sentimental affection, the days when we didn't have a generator, therefore didn't get upset at reading and eating by kerosene lamps or candles. I recalled the period before we had any water-pump, when we just took it for granted that water came in buckets and not out of taps. I even looked back warmly to the time when we had no car and used the crowded, clattering, always entertaining local bush-taxis to get us from place to place, or walked long healthy distances along the beach carrying our shopping bags.

The simple life was better, I would say wisely to Ray. He looked doubtful. He'd had 26 years of the simple life before he met me and he had been happy to leave it behind him. Not that our present mode of existence was exactly luxurious or gadget-packed, but compared to life in a cramped village compound, where food was eaten with the hands, squatting on the floor, and books, pictures, kettles, forks, floor-tiles, proper sheets, flush toilets and gas cookers were unknown, he reckoned he liked things better as they were. And as for me, well, I admit it, I *would* miss the video.

Nevertheless, the human dramas would invariably out-class the screen dramas for pathos, humour, horror or high excitement. And there was something happening almost every day to make my heart beat faster or my hair stand on end.

One calm Sunday afternoon, when Ray was in South Gambia showing the sights to some visitors and I was peacefully chopping vegetables for soup, there came a volley of bangs and rattles at the door. I opened up and found Modou, Ray's brother, gabbling in a mixture of Wollof and English. 'One of your tubabs . . . *da nga dem gaiche* . . . is drown . . .'

At first I thought he said 'is drunk' and imagined some sunburnt Brit staggering along the sand singing bawdy songs after a surfeit of Julbrew beer. But right behind Modou was John, who had arrived the week before with Scott, our sweet gay friend from Soho, and he was sweating and gasping and covered with sand and dried salt. He was more coherent than Modou and snapped out: 'It's Fred. He almost drowned.'

Fred was an amiable round-faced Celtic enthusiast who owned the flower shop round the corner from the *Evening Times* and *Glasgow Herald* printing press where I had worked for so many years. During these years I had often bought from him bunches of tulips for my Mum, clumps of daffodils for myself and fussy bouquets for *Evening Times* fashion shows and formal lunches. His arrival out of the blue had been a surprise that triggered off many happy memories and a lot of Glasgow gossip and laughter. And now, dear God, he was lying on the beach gulping and retching and lapsing into unconsciousness.

I could cope with voracious termites, tetchy cars, even lust-crazed watchmen. But this? I was in danger of gibbering and falling apart. I gawked at John and he gawked at me. Since Ray was away with the jeep we had no transport. There were no phones within a couple of miles of the village and no village doctor. Should I go to the beach or should I prepare a hut for Fred if the others could carry him back up the path? Should I try to jog to the hotel area and get help? Should I sit down and suck my thumb?

John left me dithering and galloped back to the beach, where he found Fred till lying, dazed and spewing up salt water, surrounded by our other guests, Julie and Doug from Pennicuik, Scott and of course Margaret, Fred's companion, who was almost in hysterics. Julie was a nurse by profession, which added a calm and comforting note to incipient chaos. By sheer chance, a hotel manager with a large four-wheel-drive vehicle caught sight of the distraught knot of people and swiftly offered to run Fred to the clinic. He was kept in overnight while at home we tried to piece together what had happened, and discovered that big, gentle Scott, the emotional bit-actor and part-time waiter, was the hero of the day.

Fred and the others had been larking about in the breakers when a treacherous wave, abetted by a sneaky cross-current, tugged him out of his depth and pulled him down, while also hurling him farther away from the shore. Scott, a bald-pated giant of a man for all his soft-voiced Soho-swinger style, was a strong swimmer and without thinking he plunged towards Fred, ignoring spontaneously the knowledge that he too could be tugged by the current and drowned. He grasped hold of Fred and, helped by the others, drew him towards the safety of the shore. By this time Fred was purple and spluttering feebly: 'Leave me to die. Don't risk your own life. Leave me . . .'

All of this came out piecemeal while we sat around, speaking in dull low voices, waiting to hear if Fred was all right. Julie dosed Margaret with sleeping pills and put her to bed, for she was physically and emotionally exhausted. Next day, Fred came home, a bit shaky but fine, and we all made feeble jokes and patted his shoulder. Ray had come home shortly after Fred had been admitted to hospital and had been volubly horrified, rushing about in all directions at once. I had, in fact, been fairly calm and businesslike most of the time, but it was that afternoon, when Fred was beginning to enjoy the drama of it all and wallow in the attention, while making everyone chuckle at his description of his adventures, that I broke down and sobbed on Ray's shoulder, finally admitting to myself the absolute horror of what might have happened. It provided Fred with a grand story to tell in the pubs near my old newspaper office, when he went back to Glasgow to dispense romance, remembrance and recognition in the form of roses, freesias, lilies and carnations just as he'd always done. He also, I heard, sent a handsome arrangement of dried flowers to Scott, and they all kept in touch long after the holiday was over, linked inextricably by the experience.

It certainly made the news from England, that our water-pump was permanently *hors de combat* and our attempts to mend it had broken the terms of the guarantee so that we had no chance of a free replacement, seem trivial and unimportant. The guests were all remarkably tolerant about washing from jugs and buckets, and the Gambia Utilities Company were rumoured to be connecting our area to the new mains water system which had arrived in the village itself a few months before. Needless to say, the actual connection took many weeks, as GUC employees came, then disappeared for days, came again, and went off again. To be fair, they had other priorities.

The village of Kololi, where my daughter lived and where there was, in theory, a piped water-supply, fed into the standpipes where the women filled their basins and buckets, had been almost dry for months. The women, including Carol, would trudge around at dawn, looking for a tap that would produce even a tiny trickle and squabbling over each small pailful. Inspired by Carol, they decided to stage a peaceful but plaintive demonstration, with posters saying 'women need water', and 'water is a human right.' One local councillor was shocked when he heard their plans. 'You'll embarrass the government!' he expostulated. Oh dearie me, we couldn't have that, could we? Someone eventually persuaded the GUC to truck in some water every day, but it could only be dispensed at the rate of one large bowl per woman per day. Since each woman invariably had a husband and up to eight or nine kids to look after the situation was intolerable.

Neither was it unique. Many areas had, and still have, these periods of unhygienic and uncomfortable frustration, and on one occasion a furious group of women in the Cape Point area blocked the road in a less peaceful demonstration than that of the Kololi women, resulting in nasty scenes when the gun-wielding Tactical Support Group of the police were called out to restore order. On the other hand the Government has, through a new utilities organisation now responsible for power and water, guaranteed potable water for all within a few years, and the situation is slowly but steadily improving.

We were lucky. We had our well. Many people in areas where standpipes had been introduced, foolishly allowed their wells to become blocked with rubbish and bricks and dead cats. The anomaly, as one newspaper pointed out, was that this country had no drought situation like that in Southern Africa. It had, in fact, a very high water table, and Banjul itself suffers flooding during the summer rains which drop millions of gallons of water on to us between July and October. It was the storage and distribution of water that was a inadequate or non-existent.

We were sympathetic but not, I confess, overwhelmed by other people's water problems. The sun was stroking the carmine petals of the hibiscus blossoms as we sat under the baobab tree mulling over Fred's

Great Adventure. We all agreed languorously that life wasn't so bad, sipping cold beer and eating grilled tuna-fish. We were having yet another of our self-indulgent barbecues. Tom and Joan came, as did the editor of the local daily newspaper, a Liberian refugee, followed by Joe the artist (we call him Joe the artist to distinguish him from Joe the plumber). Norman the chef from Stirling was back and so was Marilyn our Manchester travel agent.

While other establishments along the coast were playing bingo or watching Fula acrobats or dancing to scratchy reggae music, what were we doing? We were having a poetry reading. Scott's poems, now published (by Scott himself) in a slender volume called *Our Best Dressed Crooks*, range through the sorrowful to the bawdy to the bitterly cynical. They are not comfortable, easy listening, although they can be savagely funny.

Introducing Scott at the beginning of his reading, I wondered nervously how the audience would respond. How would an Edinburgh taxi-driver, a Christian evangelist (the Liberian), a sonsy doctor and a football-daft florist deal with poems about homosexuality, incest, lager louts, homelessness and a man dressing up in:

> A Dorothy Squires wig, peach lip gloss
> Jewels and pearls all bought from Argos
> Now they introduce me as glorious Sam
> Watch my lips I am what I am.

I needn't have worried. Scott is a nice guy and the niceness came seeping through the poems along with many moments of pathos and many gusts of laughter. When he was finished, I made a little speech, with a lump in my throat, about his heroic action a few days before, and everyone cheered and clapped and thumped the table. Frogs hopped about under our seats and the kittens rubbed against our legs. I served a home-made vegetable soup for twenty-one people and hoped the buckets in the loo would last the evening.

Marilyn, with the Coronation Street accent, had been less than ecstatic when I had invited her to a poetry reading. But when it was over, she was beaming and cuddling Scott and saying: 'Eee, luv, that were grand!'

A Black Imp on My Shoulder

A few days before my birthday in November 1992, which was also our third wedding anniversary, I began to sweat and shiver. People had always said to me: 'Don't you take pills for malaria?' I had always said: 'Oh no, I don't bother. Everyone here gets malaria eventually so I suppose it will happen to me one day. But this is West Africa. It's just one of those things.' So casual, so naive.

I was as hot and dry as a burnt steak, and then moisture poured off me in rivers, soaking the sheets and seeping into the mattress. Then I felt cold again and shook like a eucalyptus in the wind. I moved on to the day-bed in the living-room so that Ray could get some sleep. I halluci-nated for hours in the lonely darkness. The entire population of Hieronymus Bosch's tortured imagination entered my aching head and skipped about in front of my red-rimmed, bleary eyes. People I didn't know floated about beside the television and the typing table. A small black imp sat on my shoulder, whispering: 'You won't sleep. You won't get better.' He came with me to the toilet and watched as I vomited, for I couldn't hold down even a sip of water. 'You'll never be able to eat again,' he confided happily.

Caroline came with cold drinks and mineral water and forgave me when I cried and snapped at her unreasonably for no reason. Some English friends came and all I could do was huddle under a blanket, shivering and gaze vaguely at them with one rheumy eye, wishing they would go away. The blessed Tom and Joan came with ice and more cool drinks and medication. Tom took a blood sample and told me what I had was malignant tertian malaria, which was the nastiest one to have, and without treatment was occasionally fatal but with treatment could be cured completely and for ever. Ray's mum and dad and brothers all came to wish me better and I just wanted them to vanish and leave me to sweat and shake and retch alone. When I began to feel better, my legs moved like weighted bags of rice. I shuffled slowly like a very old lady for the first few days. My mouth tasted like a badger's bum.

My 53rd birthday, and Joan and Tom McKay produced a surprise meal complete with cake. Left to right — handsome Julius, me, Tom, Joan, beautiful Caroline, and Ray. It was a day or two before I succumbed to malaria and had a black imp on my shoulder ...!

'I'm going to take you to the Hotel Kalissai in Casamance to convalesce,' Ray announced. We had heard from Nadhia that things were now fairly quiet there and Ray had quizzed bush-taxi drivers and tour-guides who had been down recently and found the situation calm. Carol said she would house-sit for us. We packed our very few 'good' clothes, some books and swimming things, and set off singing, feeling like kids playing hookey from school. We stopped at the Post Office to check our mail box, and I sat back and shut my eyes and thought of the dense woodland and lush fields around our hotel destination, the superb food, the blissfully deserted beach. Ray bawled through the window. 'Mariama,' his face was twisted into a scowl. 'Where is our suitcase?'

I sat up blearily and goggled at him. 'What do you mean? You put it on the roof-rack.' 'Well, it's not there now. Someone must have stolen it. Why didn't you watch out for thieves?' We frowned at each other and I felt post-malarial tears welling up. 'Don't blame me! You should have tied the case on securely.' We were oblivious to the fact that the thief would have had to be eight feet tall with extremely strong shoulders and amazingly light fingers to whisk a suitcase from the roof of a jeep while I was sitting right underneath. We drove towards home. 'We'll find some more clothes and start out again,' said Ray miserably, thinking of his nice trousers and tee-shirts in the disappearing case while I brooded over the expensive shampoo and conditioner and the nice fat best-seller I'd looked forward to reading.

At home we threw some faded clothes into another bag and I sulked and snivelled at Carol, who had been astonished to see us returning when she thought we were well on our way to Senegal. 'Well, one thing's for sure,' I insisted. 'I can't go to the beach at Abène without a swimsuit.' I demanded a stop at the Senegambia Hotel to buy another bikini. And guess what? Ray met his brother Lamin who began to relate the remarkable tale of how a friend of his who was a coach driver had seen a suitcase flying off the top of a jeep just like ours bouncing to a stop at the roadside. 'He picked it up and brought it back to the hotel. There he is now; he's just going in with the case . . .,' said Lamin, at which Ray ran across the forecourt leaving his brother open-mouthed and grabbed our case from the bemused bus-driver, shaking his hand warmly and thrusting 100 dalasis into it to express his gratitude.

I already had my new swimwear and now we both had a feeling of euphoria. Sometimes it's easy to forget, among our foolish little crises and catastrophes, that good things happen in the Gambia all the time and there are lots of nice honest folk around.

We started singing again, and spun merrily along the quiet roads of the south, where rice-paddies splashed the fields with emerald green and the coconut palms threw delicate shadows over golden clearings. As we entered Abène, the village nearest to the hotel, we saw armoured cars dozing like dinosaurs in the darker shadows. Scruffy soldiers from Dakar re-routed from the southern town of Diouloulou, toted guns and grunted at us from under the mango trees. The rebels, it was at first claimed, had raided the village the previous night. Later it emerged that what had happened was a petty dispute between neighbours of different tribes, far removed from politics.

We didn't care. I have rhapsodised before about the hotel's bungalow-style rooms, under low thatched roofs snuggled into copses of flowering shrubs and trees, with air-conditioning and luxurious bathrooms, and the terraces smothered in bougainvillaea and oleander peppered profusely with butterflies. Ray drove off to Kafountine to say hullo to Diack and Nadhia, while I lay on the beach, miles of golden emptiness stretching to either side of me, reading my book. Later I strolled up to the terrace bar and asked for a glass of cold white wine. 'Uggh!' I whined after one sip. 'It tastes foul.' Michel, the owner of the hotel (the one who has his own little aeroplane with which he flits like another butterfly between Ziguinchor and the airstrip tucked out of sight behind the garden) was courteously concerned and had another bottle of good French wine opened for me. It tasted awful too, and I belatedly realised that I was experiencing the after-effects of the Cloroquine with which Tom had dosed me to defeat the malaria. It was several weeks before wine, or cigarettes for that matter, tasted in any way pleasurable to me. I resigned myself to tonic water and Coke and went back to stretch my feeble bones in the caressing warmth of the sun.

When Ray came back we strolled slowly along the beach for miles, finding little petrified forests of bleached mangrove stumps protruding from the sand in some places, exotic shells of creamy pink, and placid water where I could swim slowly and feel my body gradually returning to normal.

We were the only guests. All the French tourists who would once have been strolling around in expensive beachwear had rung up to cancel 'because of the rebels'. French television had shown shots of some of the fighting far south in the Ziguinchor area which had greatly exaggerated the situation and had resulted in a complete collapse of Casamance's holiday industry. The big hotels, including Club Med at Cap Skirring, had all closed down already. Michel hung on grimly, loathe to lock up and leave his staff jobless and his beautiful gardens running wild.

We were sorry for him, as we sat listening to his woes in the dining-room, alone except for the apprehensive-looking waiters. 'Why doesn't President Diouf DO something?' we all asked each other. 'He says all his best troops are in Liberia with the ECOMOG forces, fighting Charles Taylor,' sighed Michel. 'Also, he has an election coming up in February 1993 and he's trying to keep the lid on things until then.' Someone came in to tell us that two rebels had been caught and killed in Bignonia, an hour or so's drive away. I abandoned my usually pacifist stance and wished they'd catch the whole damn lot of them and let this beautiful region's economy struggle back to normal, while the locals got on with their lives in peace.

After two days of swimming and walking and drinking orange juice by the litre, I began to feel like a new person. As the solitary guests we ate crab and lamb kebabs and huge prawns and coffee ice-cream and felt like millionaires. My legs worked properly and my head didn't ache any more. It was a blissful break from routine. Ironically, it was on the elegant terrace there at dusk, while the sun melted like golden syrup into the sea, that a very large mosquito settled on my ankle and drew blood before Ray slapped it away. In the months to come I was to have malaria again. It wasn't to be nearly as unpleasant as the first bout, though nasty enough in its way, but it was the variety which wanders back into your life at regular intervals and I didn't become free of it until the summer of 1993. But I didn't know about it then, and we drove home buoyantly.

Back in Bijilo, two German travellers had arrived, Peter and Linda from Hamburg. He was a big, hairy, ambling young man with a severe stutter, and she was a painfully shy red-headed vegetarian, which gave me a chance to show off my quiches which contain courgettes and okra and bitter tomatoes and all manner of things you don't find in a flaccid frozen tart from your local supermarket. One night, as Ray cooked ladyfish over the wood fire under the stars, Peter said: 'Y-y-y-you've built a little p-p-p-paradise here, Mariama,' and I felt inordinately pleased.

I also felt very slim and fit. The malaria slashed half-a-stone from my weight in a few days, though it's not a method of dieting I would recommend. And we had bought yet another new toy, but this one was less self-indulgent than the video and infinitely more useful than the washing-machine. It was a proper gas-cooker, worked by butane, with four rings and a tiny oven. After several years of cooking frantically for up to eight or ten people on a two-ring burner, this was sheer luxury — as well as being the reason I was able to make quiches for Linda, not to mention pies and bread-puddings, biscuits and fruit tarts. They were all intended for the tourists but naturally I nibbled, and so replaced the missing half-stone.

Very soon afterwards, we headed south again, this time with Mandy Rhodes, a Scottish TV reporter, and her husband, who had asked us to show them the real West Africa. We went to a campement this time, which is more financially accessible than the hotel. Mandy came back from a stroll looking rather shaken. 'There was a man along at the fish-packing plant carrying a big gun and a load of cartridges,' she whispered, looking over her shoulder for guerrillas hiding in the bushes.

We told Alieu, one of the members of the cooperative which runs Situkoto campement. 'No no! I don't think it was a soldier,' he told us easily, 'It would be a devil. There are twenty-eight devils along this stretch of the coast.'

'Ah, of course,' said Mandy. 'I knew there would be a perfectly logical explanation.'

In the Gambia too, devils were perfectly acceptable, though unwelcome, denizens of the everyday world. Remember the watchman in the beach-bar who'd gibbered to us in the morning that a devil had come in during the night and floated about near the palm ceiling? And unexplained bush fires, bad crops and dry wells were often the fault of devils. As for me, having had several conversations with that little black imp that attended me during my malaria, I was hardly in a position to pooh-pooh anything. Delirium it may have been, but who knew what inspired other people's devils?

Mandy's trip wasn't an unqualified success. After the elaborate facilities of the large Gambian hotel she'd been occupying, she found camp life hard going. I have to admit it was an acquired taste. The rooms were simple to the point of cell-like austerity with unglazed windows, concrete floors and tree-twigs, hanging from the ceiling as clothes-hooks. There were no showers, just hairy blankets and no maid-service, not even a daily flick of the floors with a broom. The loos suffered from a severe lack of ever having had contact with a handful of Vim or Domestos.

Mandy steadfastly refused to have a shower, for fear of spiders, cockroaches or frogs and splashed about in the sea instead. Later I tactfully pointed out some of these shortcomings to Nadhia, for I'd noticed that our own guests, if they came down here for a short visit, always returned extolling the beauties of Casamance but saying how wonderful it was to back 'home' in our clean, bright little huts with their pillows and pictures on the walls and a daily clean-out.

On another trip, we discovered Jeanette's place, Le Kossey, just along the beach from the luxury hotel where I had convalesced. It was a cluster of huts right on the soft yellow beach, surrounded by an incredible profusion of flowers. Jeanette, a sturdy Senegalese married to a Belgian, is addicted to gardening. She has her own nursery bed, and she is almost always to be found in boots and old trousers, digging and mulching, transplanting and pruning, raking and watering. Ranks of hibiscus vie for space with clusters of scented jasmine and crescents of oleander . . . every conceivable flower of the tropics. She was justifiably proud of her little empire.

'I quite agree with you. It's much nicer than here,' a local said. 'But you see, that's because Jeanette and her husband own it. Here, we have a cooperative, so no-one owns anything. A boss cannot shout at the girls to clean the loo, or buy pillows or sheets, or insist that someone brushes the rooms, because that wouldn't be part of the cooperative principle. Everything has to be done by committee, when the villagers sit round a table for hours discussing minute details but seldom making any decisions.'

Perhaps benign dictatorship was more satisfactory. Back home, I was able to nag as much as I liked without causing a revolution. 'Haddy, please lift the boxes up instead of just brushing around them. Do you know it's five days since the sheets in hut B were changed?' In fact, Haddy was a gem of the highest order. Massively pregnant she turned up early every morning and worked furiously so that by noon she could go home and feed her two-year-old son. She did more in four hours that the other girls used to do between them in eight hours last season. She was introduced to us by Ray's cousin Pa Jobe and I loved her dearly, for she had a sensible, open personality and always wanted to do more than I asked her, instead of less, which was an unusual characteristic, I'd cynically decided. What on earth would I do when the baby arrived, I wondered selfishly?

Inside the house, I battled, as ever, with dust and grime. Haddy cleaned the tourist huts but I would have felt guilty about asking her to do my own cleaning. Joan and I had often discussed this. As well as working as a volunteer at the hospital, she resolutely scrubbed, polished and dusted their large bungalow in Fajara, knowing that she was exceptional among ex-pat wives, who tended to have maids and cooks. 'I'm quite capable of doing my own ironing and washing my own windows,' she would say uncompromisingly. The boredom and lethargy that infected a few of the white wives in the area never had a chance with Joan! Or me.

I crawled on my hands and knees extracting thick cushions of dust and cobwebs from the bottom of the clothes-rack and under the bed. 'Where does it all come from?' I wailed at Ray. The wind, of course, puffed it through the louvred windows, dust from the Sahara stirred and thickened to a nice consistency by the Harmattan. I would have feverish spells of being houseproud, sneezing as the dust crept up my nose, and pulling cobwebs from my hair, then I would give up and ignore it, and go and blether to the guests, which was much more entertaining.

Colin and Cathie had descended upon us from Dakar. Colin Wallis had spent five weeks in a camp on the edge of the desert, ringing rare birds. The most triumphant achievement for a bird-ringer, who is quite different to a twitcher, or bird-watcher, he explained, was when a bird that he had ringed in some distant country was spotted and identified in England. The camp provided accommodation and food of a basic African kind, and the volunteers provided the eyes and ears and energy to ring the many exotic species that proliferate in West Africa. 'You'd be surprised. It was quite hard work,' he asserted and flopped down in the sun to relax with Cathie, who'd flown out to join him. While he was here, he drew superbly detailed black and white pictures of birds, a collection of which were going to be exhibited in the UK on his return.

Two South Africans and a Zimbabwean were next to arrive. They'd come via London, bringing bicycles on which they made hot and uncomfortable trips into the hinterland. One of them was a literacy teacher in a black township and the other two were, they said, 'plant doctors'. No-one could say we didn't have a varied bunch of people passing through our gates.

Each of them had absorbing stories to tell and most of them had been to many foreign lands, from which they had brought colourful recollections. Portuguese Modou benefited from this cosmopolitan atmosphere. Peter and Linda were teaching him to play cards in German, while Cathie and Colin encouraged him to count in English and my daughter Carol brought him learn-to-read cards from school. He sat for hours outside the watchman's hut reading and writing, and when it was time for his wages, he would keep a few dalasis and ask us to save the rest for him. 'I am saving so that one day I can travel, when I learn to speak many languages.'

'Where will you go?' I asked. 'Oh, England and Germany . . . and, er, Scotland,' he added tactfully. I suggested to Ray that he teach him to say 'Here's tae us, wha's like us? Gey few and they're a' deid!' This was one of his favourite sayings, and he was apt to spout it loudly in the middle of genteel dinner-parties and smoky barbecues. The guests came and went and enriched our lives in their various small ways. But we had our permanent residents to think of. The cats.

The situation was becoming insupportable. I remembered how I used to sit stroking Oliver, Rusty and Chou-chou in my Glasgow flat, spoiling them with Whiskas and cleaning out their litter trays and wishing I lived in a wide open space where I could have lots of cats running free, climbing trees and chasing butterflies. Well, now I had it.

Awa-dingding was pregnant yet again. This was entirely our fault as we kept promising ourselves and her that we'd take her to Abuko Nature Reserve, where there is some kind of animal clinic, and have her spayed. But we were always too busy, or the clinic was shut or the car had broken down. The current count was three randy black and white boys, born in March, strutting their stuff and trying to gang-bang the two little girl kittens who were most certainly under-age. They were, nevertheless, promiscuous little sluts, given to fluttering their eyelashes and wiggling their tails provocatively. The nights were filled with yowls and screeches and throaty sighs.

Meanwhile, Awadingding hauled her vast belly around stoically, and I dreaded the arrival of new kittens as much as she probably did. I have to confess, and it makes me feel ill to write it, that when the last litter was born, I drowned two of the infants minutes after the birth. It was a gruesome experience; something I remember my mother doing when I was young and our cats gave birth, but I had never had to do it myself. I had nightmares in which small pink creatures with closed eyes and paws like tiny spiders twitched and wriggled for ever.

I was talking to someone about cats in general when I looked across at the South African literacy teacher and saw that she had a stripey grey kitten on her lap which she was stroking absent-mindedly as she sipped her coffee. 'Where did THAT come from?' I hooted. 'That's not one of ours!' 'Oh, I'm sorry, I thought it was,' she shrugged, 'There are so many kittens it's hard to tell the diference.'

A Dutch newspaper reporter and his wife and daughter were in residence and the date was just a few days before Christmas, so it was Joop from the Rotterdam Daily who named the newcomer 'Christmas'. It did not deserve such a cute, happy, holy, significant name. It was smaller than any of them but it terrorised the other cats, and it tried to do the same with the guests and us, snaking across the tables grabbing fish and meat in its sharp little teeth as it fled, and snarling and scratching anyone daft enough to go near it to try to remonstrate with it. In between bouts of thieving, mugging and vandalising, it would curl up on someone's knee looking sweet and vulnerable and purring prettily. I hated it.

My mind, though was on special menus, festive barbecues and peeling and grating kilos and kilos of carrots for carrot and orange soup on Christmas Eve. We were about to become full to the brim of our little holiday hideaway, and it was at times like this that I needed the indispensable Haddy more than ever. As luck would have it, it was also at a time like this that her baby decided it would make its appearance. One day, she was slogging away over buckets of washing and trays of dishes. Next day, she was in labour.

Largely pregnant as she had been, I hadn't realised quite how close she was to D-day. Her sister-in-law came along to break the news, while I was flapping about trying to clean the rooms, swill out the loos and clear the breakfasts, assuming that Haddy had merely taken the morning off to go to the clinic. When I heard that the baby had arrived I was consumed with guilt. Was it premature? Had I inadvertently hastened things on by giving Haddy too much work? 'No no,' said the sister-in-law. 'It was her time. No problem.' I thought of British mothers, 'taking things easy' during the final weeks, putting their feet up and being careful not to lift heavy weights.

The sister-in-law, a slow-moving dumpy girl, in contrast to Haddy's tall, lanky, bustling figure, declared that she was my temporary assistant. She left smudges on the windows, dust on the floors and crumbs on the tables. I followed her around with a wet cloth and a brush, and wished Haddy would come back. But life had its little compensations. The GUC had hooked us in to the local supply. They had installed a meter, dug trenches, laid pipes, and after a week there was a gurgling and spluttering noise and a few drops of water squirted from a tap, then stopped. This went on for several weeks: roar, splutter, dribble, stop. Then, one memorable morning, at 5 a.m. to be precise, I was wakened by a sound like Victoria Falls. Had the rains started six months early? I shook Ray and he rushed outside to find water swirling over the edge of our 1000-litre tank, gushing over the dry earth around the well and soaking away while the meter whirled merrily round. Ray galloped across the compound and turned off the stop-valve. Wonderful, wonderful. We had water.

But inside the house things weren't so wonderful. The much-coveted liquid splashed from a leak under the sink and flowed freely acros the bathroom and the hall, gaining force with each minute. Ray drove at high speed to Kololi village and importuned Joe the plumber just as his eyes were opening slowly to greet the dawn. We realised that when the house was built, the plumber who had installed all the fittings had omitted to insert a second stop valve behind the house, hence the overflow. He had also heat-treated a piece of ordinary lead piping behind the sink and bent it into an L-shape, instead of installing an elbow joint. Through several harsh hot seasons and several moist wet seaons and occasional splurges of heavy use when the water-pump was functioning and our taps were running, the pipe had finally worn through at its weakest point.

Joe looked at it glumly as water spurted merrily like a Tivoli fountain. He twisted the end with a monkey-wrench to stop the flow then he and Ray went to the market to buy new bits and pieces. I meanwhile mopped and wrung out old towels and mopped again until the lake which had formed in the middle of the house was reduced to some moist patches. At least in Africa the depredations of burst pipes dry up very quickly! For the moment, we had generous supplies of tap water. Would it last? The protest action of the women of Kololi, including my daughter, seemed to have sparked off a reaction in high places, and improvements in the public supply were being promised daily.

This would have been the time for me to enjoy some refreshing cool showers. But the malaria would not leave me alone, and for a few days at a time, every few weeks, I had an aching head and aching bones and alternate fevers and shivers. A splash of cold water made me flinch. One day we went for lunch with Roderick (his third visit to the Gambia in less than a year). This time he brought us that traditional Scottish New Year treat, Black Bun, a dense mass of rich fruits, spices and sugar pressed into a thin pastry shell. I exchanged a few bright sociable phrases with him then lapsed into a malarial mood, dizzy and shaking and unable even to look at the hamburger and chips I'd so optimistically ordered. Ray had to take me home and tuck me up in bed, and I slept the evening through, barely aware of his dashing about barbecueing fish, making up salad, setting tables. In a couple of days, the attack vanished, but I never knew quite when it might sneak up on me from behind and lay me low.

Now Ray had to go to a funeral. It was only eight months since we had gone to the naming ceremony of cousin Hassan's baby son, and now we'd been told that the child had died in hospital. The naming christening and the wedding to Hassan's' mother had taken place on the same day. This was a fairly usual occurrence, the Gambian version of the shotgun wedding. I have photographs still of the bride-mother, shyly sitting with her baby tucked into her arms. She is wearing a dress of vivid grass green, and her eyes are large and slightly startled, as though to become a wife and a parent on the same day was all a little frightening. The baby was very tiny. Many, many babies are born underweight. Haddy's baby, for instance, although very beautiful and alert, was far tinier than I would have expected. There are many reasons.

Some valuable foods are 'taboo' in some more primitive parts of the country, which inhibits a woman's diet at an important time. She may need extra protein and calories, but she doesn't have the purchasing power to buy them. In a big family — and almost all Gambian families are big — everyone dips into the evening bowl of benachin, domada or mbahal. It is not always a foregone conclusion that the rest of the group will hold back to allow the pregnant woman a larger share. There is also the matter of the heavy work pregnant women carry out as a matter of course (hence my still-present feeling of guilt about Haddy), which, according to doctors, can cause lower birth-weights.

In the developing countries, women take an active — indeed a dominant — role in agriculture and animal husbandry, as well as looking after other children, preparing food, gathering fuel and drawing water. The miracle is that so many do, in fact, produce such bonny babies. Having too many children too fast also causes small birth-weights, a predictable result of what is called 'maternal exhaustion syndrome'.

Perhaps the cause of Hassan's son's death had nothing to do with its tiny size at birth. But no-one could tell me, for when a baby dies, 'it is God's will', and few parents will pester the doctor for a cause of death. This doesn't mean that the causes are unrecorded. When Tom was consultant paediatrician at the Banjul children's hospital, he spent long hours in the evenings annotating the manner and reason of child deaths. Many agencies, including the World Health Organisation, the Family Planning Association and the Government itself, have a vital interest in acquiring and assessing these facts and figures, because only by collating them and holding them up to the concerned eye of the people will any improvements be wrought. Persuading fathers to pull up the water from the well instead of their wives, preventing grandmothers from passing on, literally, old wives' tales of a damaging nature, ensuring that women understand exactly what pregnancy and childbirth are all about and how their own health and strength influence the health and strength of their babies . . . all of these are tasks that take decades, if not generations, but they are tasks that must be undertaken in the name of common sense if not of humanity.

Tragically, the biggest enemy is ignorance. A girl in Carol's compound had a baby, and it cried and cried during the first couple of days. Carol discovered that the women — not just the young mother herself, but the grandmother and married sisters — believed that colostrum, the watery liquid produced from the breasts in the first couple of days, was not good for the baby. They fed it, therefore, on bottled water and sugar, while the mother's breasts, as it were, lay idle. This baby died within a couple of weeks. Who knows if it was this early starvation which killed it, but a combination of factors like this can surely culminate in crisis.

People didn't brood too long on death, even of babies, perhaps because it was so easy to have another, and another, and another. Toddlers tumbled around everywhere we went, huge-eyed, their hair sometimes twisted into tiny topknots, wearing tatty tee-shirts or miniature cotton kaftans, staring silently sometimes, but more often grinning and giggling and calling 'Mariama! Mariama! Any sweets?'

I sometimes grew broody and wondered if we should try to adopt a baby. I dreamed of telling stories and teaching ABCs to some beautiful tot, who would grow up safe and well-fed and educated . . . then I realised that by the time he or she was 20, I would be in my seventies, and who wants a mother who is also a grandmother? I pushed the idea aside.

Friends and Neighbours

Around us, an orgy of building was taking place. Our 'road' is a network of deeply-rutted, thickly-sanded paths through the bush towards the hotel area. Thorn bushes and monkey-apple trees and eucalyptus protrude from the scratchy weeds and bushes. On our left, as we drive the two miles or so to the telephone and the bank, the ground is always empty and open, for it fringes the fences of the International Trypanotolerance Centre and building is prohibited. On the right, however, parcels of land have gradually been sold, and the skeletons of houses in a variety of strange, ambitious shapes and sizes grow a little larger every month, waiting for the flesh of roofs and windows, paint and tiles to make them into homes. This process can take years and sometimes it is never completed and the skeletons loom, embarrassed, until the bush grows around them and softens their angular nakedness.

The owners are Lebanese, American, European, but mostly Gambian people, who have made some money and want to display it in the most solid way possible, in land and building. For land is the greatest status symbol of the African, even if it lies empty for many generations. Unfortunately, many have dreams beyond their resources, and the shells of huge elaborate edifices are begun, never to be finished. 'I wish they'd build nice little houses like ours, and finish them,' I'd say to Ray.

I secretly wished that our nice little house wasn't so little, as we stored boxes of sugar and coffee and toilet rolls in the bathroom and I tripped over bags of onions and rice in the hall. For what had been planned as our sweet little love-nest had become perforce, the office, storeroom, reception area and general gloryhole for our tiny but some-how all-pervading holiday business. I still loved it though. Its rough plaster walls painted in cream, its smooth golden-brown floor-tiles, my Glasgow pictures on the walls, with snaps of my mum and my grand-children tucked into their frames, the bowl of dried baobab calyxes like petrified brown velvet flowers, the vase my son gave me fifteen years ago, the 'wally dugs' I bought in an antique shop a lifetime ago, the varnished golden table made by the carpenter in the village, the straw baskets full of things we 'might need one day' but never used. It was my haven, my patchwork covering of old and new, Gambian and Scottish; the crumbling door-frames turned to desiccated sponge by the termites didn't really matter at all.

Neighbours — not permanent fixtures, but people who were building their future homes, or second homes, nearby, or simply walling off their land to stake out their territory — came to call. M— was one. He was in advertising and he drove a flashy four-wheel drive car. He was an elegant, educated, entertainingly opinionated Gambian yuppie, or at least that was my private assessment of him, especially when, one late afternoon when the sky was turning softly yellow and the heat had retreated leaving a pleasant mild breeze, he came in and had a beer and produced, from his smartly tailored jacket, his new cell-phone. Between sips of beer he telephoned friends and associates, enjoying our wide-eyed appreciation of his new toy.

If there is one thing above — or it sometimes seems, alone among — all the other institutional services in the Gambia which works superbly and is the envy of all Africa, it is our telecommunication network, Gamtel. We have no phone line in Bijilo; if there is an accident or a fire, people have to run or drive to a telephone several miles away. But I can go into the local Gamtel office near the hotels and make superbly clear telephone calls to the other side of the world.

I can send faxes far and wide, cheaply and easily, and receive messages from the office staff, who now know us well enough to realise that I am 'Rosemary Long', 'Mariama Faal', 'Rosie', 'Ray and Rosie', 'Mr and Mrs Faal' or just 'Montrose Holidays'. (All of these nomenclatures have been used by correspondents sending faxes). But I still long for the day when the telephone lines which snake above the fan-palms and mango trees as far as Ker Serigne village will extend their magic to our little neck of the woods.

Sometimes Ray went for fish or ice or petrol and was gone for hours. I would sulk. Had he gone for a drink and forgotten all about me? Then I would panic. Had he been stopped by the police because of some footling matter of a faulty side light or a broken indicator and had the car impounded (as happens to many drivers)? Had he had an accident? Was he lying bruised and bleeding on a sheetless bed in the city hospital? Had the car broken down? Was he lying underneath it on some deserted road trying to change a tyre or mend a shattered axle? Invariably he arrived safe and well but irritable and dusty and indignant at me for being indignant at HIM. 'There was no butterfish in Tanji, so I had to drive to Sanyang and they only had barracuda which was very expensive, so in the end I met a man from Gunjur and he was selling two very nice tuna, and here they are!' He would hold up two shimmering blue-silver tuna and I would congratulate him, thinking to myself that it would have been easier to nip into the supermarket for some sausages.

Or he would say: 'There was a very long queue in the petrol station and while I was waiting — because there is a big petrol shortage just now — I met my uncle and he begged me to take him to the clinic because he had bad pains in his stomach. When we got there, there was a power failure and we had to wait a long time in the dark until the light came on and the doctor came.' Or: 'I ran out of petrol and I didn't have a 'gallon'' — the Gambian name for a five-litre plastic container — 'so I waited till a friend of mine who was a taxi-driver came past and he borrowed me' — the Gambian word for loaned — 'his gallon and took me to Bakau and I got some petrol and came back but while I was coming, another friend of the taxi-driver's needed a lift to Manjai Kunda, so that made the journey longer . . . '

The petrol tank on the jeep was a home-made effort and full of rust, which, no matter how often it was cleaned out, eventually caused the arteries of the car to become blocked, and could only be cleared by Ray sucking an obnoxious pipe and spitting the dirt into the earth. He sometimes had to do this four or five times on one short journey . . . another time-waster. (I used to shudder at the fact that the first thing he did after the unpleasantness of this little task was to light a cigarette to calm his temper. I always waited for a belch of flame to gush from his lips).

None of these delays would have been at all bothersome if I hadn't felt so remote and uninformed. With a telephone (assuming that the diversion had occurred somewhere near a phone-box) he could buzz me and tell me 'Uncle Alieu needs a lift to Brikama to buy a sheep for the end of Ramadan . . .' or 'The boy who was putting air into the tyre was so busy talking to a friend that one tyre exploded and now I have to go and find another tyre . . . ' (This did actually happen, I assure you).

Gamtel offered portable phones for sale but their price — about £500 at that time — discouraged us. We contented ourselves with watching M— in action. One day he brought another neighbour along, an affable prominent person, who was building a house not for himself but in the hope of renting it out, preferably to a rich 'tubab'. He kept looking lasciviously at M—'s state-of-the-art phone. 'I would really like one of these. If I was up-river in my other office I could keep in touch with headquarters,' he explained reasonably. There are phone-boxes up-river, but I could understand how desirable a portable phone would be for his image. 'Tell the Chairman,' I joked helpfully, 'that he should really consider issuing cell-phones to all his managers.' He looked thoughtful, then wistful. He could probably afford to buy one himself. Not that top people's salaries are especially generous, but, one way or another, the people at the top in the Gambia did seem invariably to have spare parcels of ground, orchards, grandiose cars and, as often as not, the corpulent girth that is the African indication of prosperity. I suppose the same could be said about many European politicians.

M—had ideas befitting his station, and his education in the United States, about how his house was going to look when it was finished. A steep gabled roof reaching almost to the ground, special slate brought in from Guinea Bissau . . . 'And a swimming-pool?' I asked lightly. 'Yes, I was thinking about that,' he replied solemnly. As it is, after the first few enthusiastic months of foundation-laying, he disappeared from sight and his house, like so many others, grew no further. Cows graze among the concrete blocks and stone partridges scuttle in the concealing waist-high weeds. Perhaps by the time you read this he will have come back and the house will have been built.

Another neighbour for a time was a highly-placed person in the utilities company, which was very useful when our water was spluttering and stopping at vital moments. Very gradually the spurts became a steady trickle and the trickle became a steady flow. It was inevitable that this would happen, we reasoned, given all these high-powered neighbours, even if we seldom actually saw anything of them, just heaps of sand being delivered and the occasional bunch of labourers shovelling cement.

There were two reasons for this obsession with building. One was that all the earlier 'desirable areas' along the coast were already full of intricate villas, sprawling bungalows, art deco mansions, and even a number of structures which looked like a cross between Provençale farmhouses and Chinese tea-pavilions. The only way to develop was south. This doesn't mean for a moment that we stepped from our gateway into anything remotely resembling a suburban English avenue. We stepped still into a corrugation of sand or mud, depending on the season, watched over by willowy eucalyptus, jagged palms, browsing cows and acres of dusty weeds which scratched our elbows and embroidered our clothes with dozens of tiny prickly burrs. Monkeys occasionally loped from bush to bush as we approached, sniggering at us over their shoulders. The violet plantain eater, still stunningly clad in purple and scarlet and glossy green with a sunshine yellow beak, spent many weeks in a tree some twenty yards from the compound, and once a host of small green parrots exploded into the air like new green leaves. A scrawny shrub with dazzling vermilion flowers punctured the golden-brown landscape at intervals like traffic lights set at red. This was how I liked it. The unfinished buildings irritated me, but in a way I was glad they grew no higher, and relieved when the undergrowth steadily obscured them from view.

Another reason for the building boom was the cement war, as it came to be known. Our lawyer Amadou, a large, hugely intelligent and much respected Gambian, always caused us much puzzlement when we went to see him in his small, fairly unprepossessing office overlooking the docks and we found him speaking busily on ship-to-shore radio. Later it transpired that he had gone into the cement business in a big way, shipping in boatloads of raw cement, which he had processed and bagged in his own large modern factory. He slashed the price of cement from D52 to D37 and enraged the main competitor, whose owner also happened to be a lawyer. He was obliged to cut his prices too, but the battle was waged in the local press and in the halls of government. It simmered down eventually, and the prices rose again but never as high as they had been before. Amadou became an unofficial patron saint of potential house-builders.

Business was what everyone wanted to succeed in. Amadou was, I suspect, even more admired for his cement trading than for his impressive legal qualifications, gathered in Russia and England and elsewhere. Boys did not dream of writing books, discovering new planets or becoming brain surgeons, mostly because anything remotely resembling these things was virtually impossible for ninety-nine per cent of Gambians. But anyone could be lucky enough to buy something for ten dalasis and sell it for twenty, and that was business. This spirit of entrepreneurism even affected the tourists. Werner and Marianne, German guests who were addicted to the Gambia, bought a piece of land in Bijilo for, we suspected, a very shrewd price. But it swallowed up a sizable chunk of their holiday money, which meant they didn't have enough cash to pay their food bills. Somehow we were talked into accepting thirty-two cassettes of Cream, Bowie, Bob Marley, Eric Burden and Janis Joplin as settlement of their beer bill, and now they were trying to offer a radio cassette player in compensation for their meals and cigarettes.

Ray, who has a passion for cassette players, stereos, walkmans and anything with buttons that makes a loud noise, was looking interested. I was looking exasperated. 'We don't NEED another cassette player!' I fumed. Already we had the one I brought from Scotland, one we bought from Mary and Hannah, and one that Roel and Helma gave in settlement of THEIR food bill two years earlier. One was broken, since another German had tried to put in his tapes upside down while he was drunk. But we still had plenty of musical capability.

'We can sell it at a profit,' predicted Ray. Hah! Wollofs may be the wheeler-dealers of tribal lore, the sharp negotiators and hard bargainers, but this Wollof had never yet pulled off a canny deal, and I knew that we would be stuck with the cassettes and the cassette player for as long as they functioned. Still, it was better than nothing. I shrugged, and cleared another space in the living-room, which was beginning to look like a branch of Dixon's.

Marianne and Werner were a dreamy, gentle pair, middle-aged hippies with long dun-coloured hair and placid expressions, who smoked and drank the weeks away and played loud sounds which boomed into the night air until they handed the cassette-player over to us, and were rendered mercifully silent. This time they'd brought their friend Thomas with them, a dozy sort of chap who kept forgetting to turn up for meals, and on occasion brought home a young lady with damson skin, a page three figure wrapped in shiny fabric, and a faint air of professionalism about her. 'I hope you're going to pay the double room rate,' I told Thomas prissily.

The Germans and the English tended to move into separate camps, no matter how we tried to integrate them. Gary and Liz were there trying to mend their broken marriage. Derek and Daphne kept saying, 'It's paradise! It's paradise!' which was very good for my self-esteem. I don't know if it's the African setting, but somehow the English seemed more quintessentially English and the Germans seemed more quintessentially German. The invisible wall between them worried me, but it didn't worry them, so I left them to it. And they were all very tolerant of our ever-erratic service.

One night the beef sauce for the pasta bolognese was bubbling aromatically, the table was set and the salad was made, when the gas faded and died. It was too late to buy a refill canister. 'Don't worry,' said the guests in their two languages and mopped up the sauce with chunks of bread. They didn't even moan about having no tea or coffee afterwards. When the water ran out, as it still did from time to time, they would wander to the well and try to pull up buckets themselves until Ray came to their rescue. When the cats jumped on the table and shared their dinner, they just laughed.

The warmth of the sun, the slow loping walk of the Gambians, the rich hot colours of the clothes, the dusty perfumed air around the lush flowers and brittle grasses, the profusion of night stars and the remorseless roar of the ocean . . . all of these pleasantly soothed the senses of visitors so that nervous hyperactive workaholics found themselves dozing in hammocks day after day or staring enchanted at some exotic bird for hours at a time.

Perfectionists who, at home, would complain to the *maitre d'* if their napkin was crumpled or their carrots julienne weren't the right length, munched happily on the Gambian bread and chunky platters of local rice and fish, with frogs playing hide and seek under the tables and the fruits of the baobab tree plopping down on the grass roof over their heads.

Being, for the most part, experienced travellers, many had eaten far worse food in far worse places! Alan and Susan from Edinburgh were a case in point. As we drove them from the airport, wending our way through the crazed drivers, creaking lorries, wandering sheep and dreamy boys pushing loaded barrows, I said to them: 'Sorry the jeep's not very comfortable and our roads are so bumpy.'

'Huh, don't worry about us,' drawled Susan, who was in her sixties and had an artificial hip. 'We were once in a bus in Zimbabwe for 48 hours on roads far worse than this.' She and Alan, who was much younger than she and absolutely devoted to her, had met in Madagascar. Since then they had set out to collect countries, trekking casually through Burkino Faso, up the Andes or in the hill villages of Bali. Susan was planning on going to Greenland, vaguely wondering if the sledges would be a slight problem, but prepared to try them anyway.

She was a big, brisk woman with hair escaping wildly from its pins, sensible walking boots and a hearty laugh. 'We don't hold Christmas,' she said brusquely at the beginning of their stay and they went off up-river to sleep in remote huts in the bush over the festive season, far away from tinsel garlands and paper crackers. That was the time when Joop the Rotterdam journalist was there, and he parried their reminiscences with his own anecdotes of Cuba and Kenya and other places. Colin, the bird-ringer, revealed that he had ringed rare species all over the world. It made me feel ever so provincial, such a stay-at-home. Even when I was living and working in Glasgow, my travels were tame compared with these people's. I had been in New York and Hollywood, Trinidad and Thailand, all over Europe, but never with walking boots and a rucksack. I had done it in the course of being a journalist, or as a holidaymaker, but always the safe, easy way, with room-service. And in the Gambia, I seldom went further than Casamance, and more often stayed home and considered a trip to the ice factory as a big outing! But that didn't stop me wanting to strike young Geische, a ingenuous German student working as a volunteer in a Sukuta school. She came to book a room for her mother. 'I am bringing my mudder here for a holiday,' she said earnestly. 'I sink she is zo brave to come all the way to Africa to see me at her age. You know, she is 52!' I smiled through my teeth at her and metaphorically adjusted my hearing aid and colostomy bag and hobbled off on my zimmer. Ageism!

During the time I have lived here, I have only once experienced ageism from a Gambian. Most of the time Ray's friends greeted me warmly and were thrilled at his marriage. Just once, a half-uncle in the village, meeting him on the road, said 'How's that old woman then?' in a sneering kind of voice. Ray hasn't spoken to him since. Most of the time neither of us thinks about the gap in our ages. But there are moments when I catch sight of myself in a mirror and notice the lines fanning out from my eyes and the looseness under my chin, and feel panicky. Or Ray will say, innocently, 'Oh, I met that woman today, you know the old one who drives the Peugeot . . .' and I know 'that woman' is younger than I. Gambians will automatically refer (in the kindliest and best-meant manner) to 'that old pa' or 'the old mother', if they see a white man who is bald or has a beard, or a woman with grey hair.

They do this affectionately and respectfully. Gambian men and women appreciate age and demand and expect respect when they have it, unlike Westerners who strive always to look younger, dieting, tinting, pummelling and plucking in a perpetual attempt to create false youth. If I stopped bleaching my hair, would Ray still love me? If I developed cataracts, like my mother, or went deaf, like my grandfather, would he still want me? I seldom worry about such things, but I admit that they hover like butterflies in the corners of my mind.

I smile kindly at Gambian acquaintances who say: 'Ah, Mariama, you are Ray's wife, so you are my sister.' I snarl inwardly at a policeman who calls me mother. I am a mother. I am a grandmother. But I dye my hair and wear leggings and shorts and hold my stomach muscles in when I'm on the beach. If I wasn't married to Ray, would I let it all go? I hope not. If Susan can cross Greenland on a sledge, I can wear a mini-dress and no bra.

Geische's dear old mother was in fact slim and charming and better company, I felt, than Geische herself, who was young enough to assume that she knew everything, including everything the Gambians were doing wrong . . . 'Zey should do this . . . Why do they keep doing zat . . . ?' she lectured. I was suffering, perhaps, from a surfeit of Germans, Angles, Saxons and even Joop. For I grew a mite maudlin when I spent too long without talking to another Scot. It was nice to talk, just once in a while, to people who knew what a jeely-piece was, or a wee hauf, or a right guddle. The first few weeks of the season had been unashamedly tartan, what with Fred the florist, Dougie the taxi-driver, and a batch of other people from North of the Border. After they left, my jokes fell flat on teutonic ears and only Ray understood me when I said 'Och, I'm fair scunnered!'

The weather decided to play the fool. Several times it rained, only a drizzle, but bewilderingly unseasonally. One night there was thunder and lightning. For several weeks the skies where overcast and tourists were snuggling into sweaters and tracksuit trousers, looking startled, as furious chill winds belched through the trees and puffed the blue smoke from Ray's barbecue fire in all directions. The Hamattan winds can sting the eyes and irritate the nasal passages and those of us who live in its path have spells of spitting and sneezing and wishing we could pick our noses in public. On the other hand, we welcome the cool freshness of morningtime in November and December, and the fact that we can sleep without the clammy heat of summer stifling our dreams and making our bodies too hot and itchy for real repose.

One festive day S— our Senegalese drummer friend, who had moved in as watchman in place of Portuguese Modou (who just vanished one day . . . perhaps to Germany or England or Scotland?) played his marvellous music on the djembe while the youngsters from the village danced like dervishes, foot-stamping, bottom-waggling, arm windmilling, tooth-flashing. The guests joined in, even Geische's aged mother and Ray's venerable wife. Geische, needless to say, demonstrated some Gambian dancing she'd been learning at a nearby music-and-dance school, but complained that the music S—played was Wollof not Mandinka.

The dull weather failed to dampen spirits. I, in fact, was ebullient because hardy, helpful, humorous, resourceful Haddy was back, a mere ten days after the birth of her daughter, hair intricately braided, waist as slender as a willow, ready and willing to change the beds and clear the tables. One day she brought the baby along and Cathie and Colin took photographs of it and her, both beaming and wearing their best frocks.

Photographs were also taken of Awa-dingding with her new offspring (her third litter in her short, scrawny life). Yes, I did drown two again, and I know it's awful, but I felt three more babies was quite enough for her to handle, and I could tell by the look in her slanty yellow eyes that she quite agreed with me. I don't actually think Awa-dingding ever really felt cut out for motherhood. She weaned her children far faster than any feline baby book would have recommended, although they still clung to her teats between meals of rice and bread and milk.

In the new litter she was left with two silver and white stripey tots and one ginger and white, all, mercifully, boys. They were born in a corner of one of the tourist toilets, where Graham from Wembley found them when he went for an early morning widdle. German Marianne scooped them all up and settled them into a large travel-bag in her room, lined with an old sweater, and later they were moved into the hut we used as a storeroom-cum-library, beside the battered paperbacks and three-year-old magazines. The guests all sneaked in with saucers of milk and pieces of fish and chicken and Awa-dingding lay like a queen, purring at all the attention and pretending she'd planned this family all along. Since Christmas had installed itself in the compound and refused to leave, that meant we had ten cats. What on earth would I do if we ever had people in who were allergic to them? So far it hasn't happened.

Fussing over the new babies helped to take everyone's mind off the fact that the water system, about which, you'll recall, I had so recently dared to be complacent, had gone peculiar again. It roared and spluttered somewhere in the pipes outside in the lane but there seemed to be a gremlin in the works, and S— once more hauled up supplies the old-fashioned way, for twelve people's ablutions and for Haddy's washing. I watched in despair as the Hamattan dust settled again on my shelves, ornaments and picture-frames. Just as a bonus one of our neighbours decided to clear the scrub and bush and palm stumps from his building lot by burning it. The wind was blowing right in our direction and malodorous ash dropped thickly on to the verandah and filtered into the house. I yelled at the neighbour in an un-ladylike fashion and he apologised profusely so that I felt guilty for being so crabbit (another Scottish expression, but you must know what I mean!).

I was feeling, I think, slightly claustrophobic. Ray had taken some of the guests to Casamance for two days and I stayed home and tended the others. Another day, he took some of them to South Gambia, and various family responsibilities called him away from time to time. An uncle, for instance, had a car-crash in which several people were injured and Ray spent hours with him in the police station trying to persuade the forces of law and order not to lock his uncle up. There was, at that time, a tendency to lock drivers up regardless of who was to blame. Like all Gambian crises it could be solved only by endless hours of talking, arm-waving, negotiating and cajoling. I am used to it now, or tell myself I am, but occasionally I lose patience when I hear something take an hour to settle which I feel could be straightened out in five minutes. 'You don't know the Gambian way,' Ray would say. I did know it; it just exasperated me sometimes. Yet these long debates and circumlocuitous explanations and expostulations were in their way, a lesson for those of us from Europe who thought time spent talking was time wasted. From them, paradoxically, lasting solutions were often found, friendships formed, understandings established and bruised feelings smoothed over.

I resented, I suppose, time without Ray. A good friend of mine in Glasgow lives separately from her husband with no very harsh emotions on either side. 'I need my own space,' she had said when she moved into her bijou apartment. 'I can't be bothered having him around. In fact, I don't really believe in marriage.' Well, I believed in mine. Not that I didn't appreciate spells alone to read and write and bake and clear out cupboards without interruption, but only for limited periods. After that, I pined. We compensated when we could by skulking off with sandwiches and beer or flasks of coffee, driving along the beach to some empty stretch of sand backed by a straggly forest of nodding grasses, two-metres tall with lacy heads of rippled bristles that whispered in the wind.

I had mixed feelings about being a seaside landlady. Was this really what I wanted to do? Cooking beef stews in three-kilo quantities, counting knives and forks, listening to endless travellers's tales, smiling politely even when my back was sore or my head hurt? Yes, I guess it was, for if it wasn't for all these gregarious, good-natured gallivanting folk, what would I have to write about? I would mutter that I wanted peace to type or paint or plan another book, but a part of my mind was still concocting salads, making shopping lists and wondering if I should put the kettle on for the afternoon coffees. I think it was a continuation of an earlier life as a mother-and-journalist.

In that earlier life — how distant it seems now — I would change nappies and regulate the washing machine, make cakes and iron skirts, kiss sore knees and recite nursery rhymes while typing features about Glasgow's single parents, homeless youths, education crises, cultural achievements and medical advances. I held a telephone in one hand and a bottle of gripe water in the other. I burned soup while I became engrossed in statistics about Scottish heart disease. I rushed off to interview important people with Gerber's baby spinach stains on my skirt. I suspect if you put me in a luxurious empty room with a sophisticated word processor, an ice-box full of cool drinks, a comprehensive library, utter silence and no interruptions at all, I would stare blankly at the wall and wonder if I should wash the windows.

I probably fussed over the tourists too much, when I could perfectly well have been writing. Maybe I was like C.S. Lewis's 'sort of woman who lives for others. You can tell the others by their hunted expressions.'

Och, enough of this introspection!

Wild Things

Say 'Africa' to, anyone in a European city and chances are he'll say: 'Ah, snakes!' As you've seen, a couple of snakes had slithered into the perimeter of my life in the Gambia, but none had done me any personal harm and they were as much part of the natural state of things as squirrels in Hampstead Heath or wolves in Yellowstone Park.

We were on the beach fishing when Ray said: 'Mariama, look at that snake coming out of the water.' I looked in the direction of his pointing finger and saw a long thin black stick in the frothy garland that separates sea from sand. 'It's just a stick,' I said. 'Watch it,' said Ray. I watched and witnessed an autocratic raising of a tiny head, a swift stylish wiggle, and then it was a stick again.

We walked towards it and Ray threw handfuls of sand to encourage it to slide across the sand and up into the bush. This was because, in the distance, we saw a bevy of small boys squabbling and tumbling on the beach, kicking imaginary footballs, pushing one another into the surf. We knew that if they saw the snake they would come to batter it to death. This, as I have written, is the almost invariable response to reptiles of whatever kind. Panic, jump up and down, howl and start lobbing stones and sticks at them. The terror is perfectly understandable because in myth and in fact many people must, in many places and at many times, have been brought into their villages suffering from snake bite during the long and exotic history of West Africa. In Scotland, people don't exactly jump for joy at the prospect of walking through the gorse and heather without sturdy boots, in the knowledge that venomous adders could well be lurking there.

Nevertheless, I have it on reasonably good authority that there are but four poisonous species among the several dozen kinds of snakes found in this part of the Sahel and they prefer, on the whole, to live in secluded spots where they won't be disturbed by human-beings, as much an anathema to them as they are to us. In case you want to make a note of it, the fatal four are the black cobra, the spitting cobra (the type that did for Maradonna, amiable yellow-furred uncle of our dog Stanley), the green mamba and the puff adder. I turned to the pages of my *Naturalist's Guide to the Gambia* by Etienne Edberg (now sadly out of print) and discovered the following advice: 'Don't panic and wave your arms or make any sudden movements that might frighten it. Stand still. If it doesn't move off, back away and make a detour round it. Even if it happens to move in your direction, don't worry. A few quick strides are sufficient to outdistance any snake. No snake will attack you unprovoked.' There was, I found out, a teensy little exception to this rule but more of that anon. For the moment, I believed it all implicitly, although I preferred not ever to have to test the theory for myself. It is true that the spitting cobra only went for Maradonna because its leisurely private passage down a tree branch and over the roof of the watchman's hut was fractured by Mr M (the wanjho-growing watchman) screeching and bawling as though all the hounds of hell were after him, which excited the dogs and made them yap at the snake which predictably became flustered and bad-tempered and lunged at both dogs. Stanley suffered only from temporary blindness, caused by the expectoration, but Maradonna bore the marks of its fangs, and died.

The snake on the beach, which I looked up in Mr Edberg's book, was almost certainly a Smyth's water snake, and perfectly harmless. But it was spotted by the little boys, who came charging along the beach like gladiators, waving their sticks, and ended its little holiday at the seaside in a swift and brutal manner. Many Gambians, like many Westerners, respect the bird, beast and reptile life of their environment. Many, like many Westerners, do not. We were driving towards the suburb of Bakoteh one day when we witnessed a Renault Four driver deliberately swerving across the road in order to try and crush to death a large monitor lizard which was peacefully pottering to the other side. Fortunately he missed.

The monitor lizard can be up to five feet long, and although it is meant (again according to Mr Edberg's book!) to hang around rivers and mangrove swamps, it has become quite urbanised and can often be seen swaggering across wide tarmac roads. One has taken up residence by the Senegambia Hotel swimming-pool, where it toddles comfortably under sun-beds and around the heaps of beach towels, sun-oil and canned drinks. It is photographed almost as often as the crocodiles in the sacred pool in Bakau. One came into our garden once. The watchmen and Ray's young brothers pursued it and beat it to death before I could stop them. 'It eats the water-melons,' I was told.

Turtles were victimised by fishermen, either because they dragged their nets or because customers wanted them for their shells and flesh. More often they just rotted on the beach. Baboons were beaten back by farmers who objected to their despoliation of crops. Small beautiful birds were shot by 'sportsmen'. I wanted to weep at these things but no more than I wanted to weep at fox-hunters in Surrey, badger-baiters, otter-coursers, and little boys in Glasgow who pumped air into kittens until they burst. People, anywhere, can be cruel to other creatures. In the Gambia I found impetuous acts of violence prompted by fear or poverty, but seldom the slow calculated sadism of the West.

Often, people were immensely proud of their wild life and anxious to show it off to tourists. We would see boys earnestly pointing out rare birds and plants and many became very competent amateur ornithologists.

Talking of ornithologists, the bird-watcher was back. He assured us bashfully that this time he would avoid black pelicans — though he wondered wistfully how the sensuous little Senegalese lady of the night was faring. I changed the subject to bulbuls and buzzards. His travel club at home was waiting breathlessly for him to return and give them a talk, with slides, on the wild life of West Africa. He was determined therefore to set aside manly pleasures and concentrate on taking pictures of hippopotamus and crocodiles and red-throated bee-eaters. The place to find hippos, antelopes, and even lions, is across the border in Senegal.

Follow the river far inland to Basse, then to Fatoto, the last outpost of the Gambia, then further still and across the Senegalese line into Nyokolokoba National Park and (I am told, for I have never done it) you will find all of these, and more, in hundreds of rolling acres of dense forest and thick bush protected by the Senegalese government. This was where Bill planned to go, but something kept going wrong. On the first morning, as dawn was breathing pink puffs of air into the slate-dark sky, Ray ran him to Kanefing bus depot. The up-river express bus was full. 'I'm not standing all the way to Basse!' declared Bill, for he had done that once before, seven hours of bone-shaking discomfort pressed against many hot and sweating bodies. Today they have a modern air-conditioned coach, for seated passenger only, on some of the Basse runs. But not in early '93. Bill came back to Bijilo and went for a swim. Next day he rose at five, to the distant chant of the first call to prayers, and shuffled through the darkness to the village to catch a bush-taxi which he had been told went to town early. It never came so he returned to his hut and fell asleep till noon. I think Abuko nature reserve was as far as he got. There were no hippos but he caught a glimpse of the crocodile and lots of impressive birds. The travel club would just have to make do.

But he was a little miffed by the chatter over breakfast of Claire and Larry. As if in answer to my yearning to hear Scottish voices again, this art student-and-doctor couple from Edinburgh came to stay. They were followed a few days later by Callum and Betty from Glasgow. The Scots were back in position! Bill's chagrin was caused by the fact that the laid-back Edinburgh couple, who didn't know the difference between a fulvous tree-duck and a bar-tailed godwit not only reached Nyokolokoba, but saw all manner of photogenic subjects. 'Oh, gosh, it was great!' enthused Claire. 'We actually came face to face with some lions in a clearing in the forest as we were driving through with a group of other travellers. They were amazing! and hippos . . . there were so many of them!' Bill smiled gamely and pretended he didn't care.

'Wouldn't you think?' I asked Ray later, 'that they would have been afraid of the lions?' 'Oh, I don't think so,' said Ray casually. 'Lions are OK. They wouldn't hurt them.' Since there are no lions in the Gambia I'm not sure on what he bases this assumption. His *bête noire* (or rather a kind of dirty yellow) is of course the hyena. Mr Edberg reports that hyenas had been seen in the outskirts of Banjul, the capital city, and that 'in the mornings you might be able to find its tracks on the beach outside your hotel.' But his book was published eleven years earlier and I suspect that the growth in numbers of beach-bars, roads, hotel complexes and motor-cars had obliged the hyena to seek shelter far inland. The book also mentioned aardvarks, warthogs, manatees and jackals and although I'm sure they all had their moments, I doubt if any of them have been seen for more than a decade. All the more reason to preserve what wildlife is left — even the snakes.

As for our own wildlife, it was getting wilder by the minute. The two big boy cats, Patch and Nyet Kunyul ('Blackie' in English) were still determined to rape the girl kittens and the shrieks in the night were disturbing the tourists. They had to have their manhood removed, I told Ray, who winced. The only 'small animal' vet I could trace worked at the MRC (The Medical Research Centre). Our friend Derek at the ITC and his colleagues there were 'large animal' men — donkeys, cows, goats, horses, maybe, but cats? Pshaw! I kept trying to ring Abuko Nature Reserve. First time, I got Ghana Airways who were understandably bewildered when I launched into a diatribe on how urgently I needed two cats neutered. The girl in Gamtel tried the number, as listed for Abuko, and she got Ghana Airways too. She checked with the operator and we tried another number. I was connected to Dr Somebody, whose name sounded just the same as the name of a vet I'd been given. 'Aha,' I babbled. 'you'll be able to help me. You see, I have these two male cats and I really have to have something done about them . . .' 'Yes, yes, I quite understand,' he said pleasantly, 'But I'm a doctor of human resources . . .' That was when I decided to go to the MRC.

I mentioned Gary and Liz before, didn't I? Gary was a manufacturer of trendy clothes in London, and Liz used to be a landscape gardener who worked for Bill Wyman of the Stones. She recalled that it was around the time of the Bill-and-Mandy story and she spent much of her time brandishing her secateurs at sweaty sleuths from the *Sun* and the *News of the World*, who offered her mouth-watering sums of money to reveal anything new about her employer. 'I don't know ANYTHING,' she told them flatly, slicing heads off roses in a threatening manner. She and Gary loved cats and had quantities of them at home. She said she would come with me and hold the cats while I drove. Ray said he couldn't possibly cope with such a grisly mission.

She stroked the cats tenderly as they writhed about in an old shopping bag and we bumped along the road to Fajara. We watched the preparations in the vet's living-room, while he jabbed anaesthetic into both indignant back-ends, and laid one of his wife's tablecloth on an occasional table near the TV. He wandered into the kitchen muttering that he couldn't find his instruments; his wife kept tidying them away. We left, promising to return next day and collect the patients.

When we did, we realised that blood was seeping through the shopping bag all over Liz's knees. At home, Nyet Kunyul was fine, if somewhat smelly and matted with excrement and blood, and highly aggrieved at what he'd had to submit to. But Patch was in great distress and hid among the banana plants, leaving clots of blood everywhere, while we tried to coax him to come to us and show us the damage. We tracked him down gasping in a large sanguineous puddle, and wrapped him gently in a cloth. Liz cradled him in her arms and we went back to the vet. 'Oh dear!' he said and laid Patch on an embroidered tea-cloth. We sat and tried not to watch as he did unmentionable things with shiny steel gadgets. To relieve the tension we whispered to each other about hamsters we'd had which had fallen into buckets of wallpaper paste and atrophied, cats that had become stuck up chimneys, parrots that had perished, all in a desperate attempt to take our minds off the matter in hand. The vet ignored us, probably finding our humour in the worst possible taste. Patch recovered magnificently, and took to cuddling up platonically with Snowball the white kitten, in a box on the verandah, an amiable eunuch.

I was immensely grateful to Liz. She is one of a succession of guests we have had who have helped us in ways far removed from the normal expectations between hosts and customers. I think of Regina the Swiss girl who sent the dog flea-collars, another Swiss who crawled under our car to drain off the engine oil, emerging black and greasy and smiling happily, Norman who assembled the food mixer, Scott who saved Fred's life, and many others who have joined in our agonising over the generator, nursed our kittens, pulled up water, given medicine to sick watchmen and cleared away the dishes when I had malaria.

I was in fact having malaria again, a day or so after the bloody business at the vet's. And Ray was shuffling around looking resentful with a black eye. Well, perhaps purple, against his skin. He also had a sore throat. The reason for this was that a Lebanese driver who made an illegal right turn which almost dented the Suzuki and almost gave Ray a heart-attack, had not only failed to apologise but had blamed Ray and called him a stupid black bastard. Ray got predictably cross at this and lunged at the Lebanese, who summoned one of his Gambian heavies to thump Ray on the eye and grab his throat as though to strangle him. Just another jolly little evening in this polyglot paradise. Witnesses came forward in droves to offer to back Ray up if he wanted to take the matter further, but there wouldn't have been much point. Next day his eye ached and the tear-duct was blocked so that moisture streamed pathetically down one side of his face. Poor wee soul.

We were, thankfully, sustained and soothed during these minor tribulations by Callum and Betty, who made kindly clucking noises over us, told us funny stories and plied me with wine. 'Don't you bother your heads about cooking for us,' they would say. 'Leave these dishes where they are and we'll sort them all out.' There is always something very comforting about having Glaswegians around in times of misfortune.

It was, in any case, a mere matter of days until my malaria had faded yet again and Ray had stopped crying. The cats were leaping around like healthy kangaroos, and we were planning to have a wee African-Scottish ceilidh. That afternoon, there was a practice session, when Callum began recording S—playing his drums. M—the portable-phone-owner joined in with surprising skill and vigour. Callum put down his tape recorder and picked up his guitar and sang some raw, raunchy blues.

S— the drummer, with his thick crinkly beard and gap teeth, was living on site now, with N—his wife. We hadn't planned it that way but when he worked for us days only, N—complained of being left alone so long. Their village, she said, was full of wicked characters and she was afraid. Sometimes she stopped S— coming to work at all because she was nervous or sick or lonely. Or there would be other reasons for his absenteeism. Once a fellow-musician bit his finger during an argument. Another time, he said, his clothes went on fire. Once he saw a devil at the roadside. He also, I have to say, delayed his home-going a little by stopping off at the pub for a beer or three or four, which made N—more tetchy than ever.

All in all, it seemed a good idea to install the two of them in the watchman's hut and at first it worked admirably. N—, who used to be the dancer in S—'s band and who is his second wife (there's another, and a son, in Senegal), seemed happy and sang to herself as she brushed the paths around the hut and cooked S—'s supper over an African wood stove. It was February, the month of St Valentine, lovers, romance. Later events were to modify my view of the success of the arrangement, as you will see. But for now, peace. S— 'picked up' a parrot. I don't know where, but he offered it to me as a present. I suspect N— didn't want it fouling her new little home. I said, thank you very much, but, er, no. It huddled outside their room looking as sick, as, well, as a parrot, I suppose. One day it disappeared. I wondered what was in their rice that evening.

A drummer with tall friend helps Andrea from Ayrshire celebrate her 21st birthday under the baobab tree. Ray's brother Lamin is second right.

Around New Year time, Ray's jaunty handsome 18-year-old brother Modou developed a crush on Geische. She would cycle back from her voluntary teaching in Sukuta and the two of them would disappear to the beach. Sometimes we would pass them tucked into a concealed nook. Geische's mother had gone home and so would she, soon, so the romance was bound to be ephemeral but Modou took it very seriously.

So seriously that he told Geische he was 22, which was her own age. I let slip the truth one day (not entirely accidentally) and she was furious. One of the reasons we hired S— round the clock was that Modou's tour of duty with us was so often interrupted by his deep and meaningful conversations with the ineffably earnest Geische, or by their long cycle rides. When it was time for her to return to University I suspect she rather enjoyed the feeling that Modou would be heart-broken. In fact, a few months later, he announced his engagement to a pretty girl he'd known since schooldays. A Gambian girl, unlikely to lecture him about how his country should be run.

Modou had probably disapproved of Geische's determination to enjoy just a holiday romance. Gambian young men, for all their willingness to chat up European girls, secretly disapproved of the Western custom of having several, or many, lovers before actually choosing to marry. In their own culture, ideally — and in reality, when you enter the less exposed areas of the country — a girl should be a virgin when she marries. In the coastal areas, I doubt if this qualification is often demanded. And yet this is presumptuous of me. In villages like Bijilo, families keep a firm eye on their girls, who are in any case too busy helping with the cooking, husking the peanuts, gathering okra, fetching water and washing clothes to have much time or energy for promiscuity. Lust, of course, will always find a way.

I suppose it was lust that had brought S— and N— together. They were an odd couple, he amiable and vague, she brisk and bird-like, with sharp eyes that watched everything. I began to be aware of a certain tension in the area in and around their hut, and it came to a head one night late, when Ray was taking some Germans to the airport. A rat-a-tat at the door and there was N—, pecking the air and hopping about, her feathers ruffled. 'Mariama! That man he is killing me. He is a wicked man. I am going to my family. He is beating me. Look at my body. It is in a very bad condition. This man, he has been drinking canna. He is crazy.'

Her body looked OK to me, but I put away the airmail *Guardian* crossword, found my flipflops and went out to investigate. S— saw me coming and slipped out of the gate to shuffle in the shadows, while N— continued to berate him, her eyes like sparks, her voice tremulous but fierce. She was, as our friend Callum had remarked a day or two earlier, what a Glasgow man calls 'a right nippie sweetie.' All the same, S— did indeed look like a man who had been drinking African gin, vacant-eyed and yet ready to erupt. N— said he had hit her with a bottle, a claim that could not lightly be ignored. I commanded S— to emerge from the shadows and delivered a stern lecture, a cross between Claire Raynor and Margaret Thatcher, on the principles of marital tolerance, give-and-take, restraint, understanding and so on (all the things I usually disregard myself), delivered in a whispered shout, as I tried to be awe-inspiring without waking the tourists. Then I realised that, cringing round a corner, one guest was already there, a frail, intense young German who had, though it was hard to believe, travelled through Europe and North Africa, being robbed at gunpoint in Mali and having other spine-chilling adventures. He looked, now, as though he would prefer the Malian brigands to this domestic affray. He looked like he wanted to cry. 'I was here, about to share their rice,' he quavered. He was almost destitute and saved money on meals by dipping into Gambian rice-bowls whenever possible. 'They began to argue. I tried to talk to them, but . . .' he gulped and went silent.

'You see,' I thundered (whisperingly). 'You are disturbing our guests. Now you, N—, get inside that hut and lie down and keep quiet and go to sleep. You, S—, stay out here where you are supposed to be, and look after the compound. And LEAVE HER ALONE.' N— stopped chirruping and fluttering and retreated sulkily into their hut, making noises in her throat like a pigeon, and puffing out her little chest. S— shot her a venomous look and grinned sloppily at me. I went back to the house and my candlelight crossword.

Five minutes later there were squawks and moans and rumbles from the direction of their hut. I stomped across the compound again and found them circling each other like angry hyenas. 'He beat me again,' whimpered N—. 'He is crazy. I hate him. Look, look at my body.' S— mumbled and made vague threatening gestures towards her. I went between them and pushed him so hard he nearly fell over.

'You! Get out of this compound! A man who beats his wife is a bad man. Go!' I pointed towards the gate with a haughty flourish and he trudged off, though not without another slanging match when he tried to take their radio and N— hurled herself at him, clawing it back. 'It is mine! You see, Mariama, he steals my things!'

'N—, shut up! I'm sick of your noise. I'm sick of you both. Go and lie down. S— is gone. He won't disturb you any more. We'll sort all this out in the morning. PLEASE keep quiet.' Lights were flickering at the windows of the tourist rooms and I could see Callum's angular figure outlined in the doorway, his beard twitching inquisitively. I watched as S— began to skulk along the lane, towards the silver and black patchwork of the bush. Suddenly a spiky hand grabbed my arm. It was N— . 'Mariama. Oh, Mariama! Please, let him stay here. Don't send him away. He won't do anything else to disturb you. I will look after him. Please let him in!' She snatched off her cotton head-cloth and threw it down on the ground in a gesture of sacrifice, then stooped over my hands, clutching, crying, begging. I pulled away and felt like slapping her silly face. Ten minutes ago she'd been telling me he was a devil and she never wanted to see him again. I shrugged and stamped crossly back to the house. Silence filled the compound like featherdown.

In the morning, Ray spoke to them both, wagging his finger a lot and shaking his head. 'They've promised to behave. They say there will be no more trouble,' he said doubtfully. S— slept till late afternoon, his head, I hoped, throbbing through his dreams as a result of too much canna. A teaspoonful of canna is too much.

For a few days things remained calm. I was sniffy at S—, refusing to greet him in the accustomed manner, sighing and shaking my head as he passed.

Actually, I liked S—. Drink and perhaps his wife's demands had unveiled a side of him I'd never seen before in two years of knowing him, during which time he had delighted us with his drumming, entertained us with his stories and always shown good temper and kindness to us and our visitors. He wasn't a very good watchman-cum-gardener, to be sure. Marigolds shrivelled and vanished, the bananas seemed to be retreating backwards into the earth and the guests kept mentioning shyly that there was no water in the toilets. But this was not unprecedented. It was personality that mattered more, and S—'s personality seemed to have soured and warped temporarily. I suppose our employing someone who had been our friend was misguided. And why should a brilliant drummer be a wonderful watchman? Or even a satisfactory husband?

N— sometimes clucked about cooking and brushing the paths, but mostly she was just sitting, watching. If S— spoke to any of the guests, particularly the women, she scowled and called him to her. There was a certain brooding instability in the air. One afternoon, she came to my door again, waving two pieces of paper in her hands. 'Mariama, who made these things?' she asked ominously, her face puckered in anger. She held the papers as though they were unexploded bombs. What were they? Well, that day Callum, who you'll recall is an artist, had been encouraging our little brother Eliman and his friend Momodou to draw pictures of one another. Childish scrawls, with sausage-like fingers, dots for eyes, corkscrew hair. On one was written, in pencil, 'My name is Eliman Faal. This is my friend Momodou.' On the other was written: 'My name is Momodou Tambedou. This is my friend Eliman.' Pretty harmless, you might have thought. But not to N—.

'S—, he no like this at all.' She shook the papers in my face. 'These things are very bad. Aieee!' she went off, haranguing the hibiscus and hissing at the cats. Ray came back from the village while I still stood there, scratching my head and wondering what on earth was going on. N— rushed to him with the drawings and confided: 'This is bad magic.

I no like.' It emerged that S—, urged no doubt by his wife, had taken the pictures to be representations of him. I couldn't see why, as they had no gaps between their front teeth, no beard, no djembe drum in the forefront. The implications were far-reaching. I painted my little water-colours of women and babies and cheeky wee boys. Many of our friends were artists. Was every sketch of a human figure to bring on a crisis? Was drawing people an un-Gambian activity? The problem was surely a combination of N—'s animism and S—'s general credulity. There are a fair number of animist enclaves in the Gambia, worshipping stones and trees and stuff like that, and perhaps drawings and photographs were frightening because they stole a part of the soul. S—, too, quite often reported seeing devils and other unconventional creatures. But it was all too much for me .

If Callum took out a notebook and pencil or a camera, N—shivered and pierced him with her flashing black eyes. We felt uneasy, and so did they, to be fair. We talked about whether we should ask them to leave. Yet S— was a friend and N— was just an impressionable neurotic woman. We had to make allowances . . .

In the end, we didn't have to, because they themselves suddenly packed all their things and left. S— looked embarrassed as he collected the balance of his wages. N—looked stormy as she strode along the lane with her basins and bundles on her head. It was I felt, a relief to have them gone . Our painterly friends Joe and Andrea, now firmly estab-lished as a couple, were coming to live in one of our rooms any day. It would have been disconcerting if N—had seen their pictures and begun to hiss and fizz, especially as both of them tend to incorporate the odd demon or strange beast into their work.

Andrea had been living for over two years in the compound in Baku and it was becoming oppressive. She had come to the Gambia after having a love affair, which later proved disastrous, with a Gambian student in the US. Although they had parted, the country fascinated her, and his family were kind to her. She had a small room, in which a row of straw baskets with lids comprised her furniture. In one basket were all her clothes. In another were her cup, plate, spoon, candles, tin opener and saucepan. That was her kitchen. Another — the most important — sheltered her paintings and brushes and sketches. We would visit her and she'd be squatting on a low stool, snipping paper and pasting it in complex patterns, painting and shading with delicate pastels. Her art is hard to describe, but beautiful. She was distracted often, not just by our occasional visits, but by people from the compound coming to borrow or beg, American volunteers popping by to chat, and by other more personal tensions. She felt she had to leave, and we had a room spare, far away from our house, tucked in a corner; the house Carol and Rab once occupied. At first it had been she alone who was to move in, but Joe, somehow, became a permanent fixture too.

In practical terms her flitting was swift and easy. A matter of packing the baskets into a friend's car, with a few rolled-up rugs and tools and low tables, and she was installed. But in emotional terms it was an experience loaded with sorrow and confusion. 'I can't stop crying,' Andrea sobbed. 'I'm so happy to be leaving Bakau and coming here, yet I am torn up by so many conflicting feelings. That little room was part of my life for two years, and so were the people around me. I feel strange, but I'll be fine soon.' She was. She simmered water for tea on a tiny camping stove, and lizards danced up the white wall of her room.

Straggly bougainvillaea had gained a toehold and were now creeping up the gable end. Weeds and palm trees pushed each other about in a green and guileless muddle behind the building and when the wind pushed its fingers through the palm leaves it made a sound like chattering teeth. The weaver-birds jabbered and the sea roared in the distance, but all the sounds merged into a melodious, comforting lullaby and Andrea was ecstatic. 'It's so peaceful! So cute. I'm so happy.' Then she began to cry again. It took a couple of days for the happiness to soak up the tears.

Through Andrea, I met new people. One was an incredibly volatile, funny, witty Gambian woman who owned her own batik factory. She had lived many years abroad and was savagely funny when she denounced the little pecadilloes and peculiarities of people she knew. Rugged Canadian girls working for a volunteer organisation came by to have their hair cut. Did I tell you that Andrea, as well as being an artist, had her own cutting salon in America? Here the women would sit on wobbly chairs among the weeds, while Andrea snipped and the strands of hair blew away and merged with the seed-heads and crunchy leaves. She cut my hair too, not in the presumptuous, proprietary way of most hairdressers, who work on the hair and forget the head beneath it, the face beyond it. Hers was the way of a sculptor, making a satisfying shape, following the spontaneous curve of the material with which she was working, never going against its grain, always cutting dry. Other hairdressers cut the hair wet, so that it is lifeless, malleable clay that they can shape the way they want it. Andrea liked it dry so that she could see the way it wanted to go, let it develop its character. People used to fly hundreds of miles to her salon back home to have her cut their hair. I could understand why.

Another friend was Lola, a Spanish college lecturer from Canada, large and sweet-natured, loved by her students. She's building a house quite near to where we live. Friends told her: 'Oh, you can't live there. It's too remote. It's wild. You won't be safe.' She was sixty-six and they worried about her, but they shouldn't have. Bijilo isn't all that remote. We would be near by. And the villagers, though spread out over a large area, were solicitous of incomers. The only thing that might ever land Lola in trouble was her immense generosity.

Take for example the house she was building, a stylish little chalet with a verandah, cupboards, proper plumbing and tiled floors, set among a profusion of young mango trees, lemon trees, papayas and grapefruit which she had had planted. The house wasn't for her. Her home would be built later, when she retired and moved from her apartment in town. No, this house was for the watchman. It is, it must be, the most luxurious watchman's home in the Gambia. We would joke with her about it. 'Is it going to have a jacuzzi? What about the TV room?' She would answer succinctly. 'When my house is built, which will be a very nice house, designed by my daughter who is an architect, I would be ashamed and embarrassed to have another human-being living in the same compound in a house like a dog-kennel.'

Like a dog-kennel? You should see the actual dog-kennel she's building now for the dogs she is bringing to help guard the compound in its 'remote, wild' location. It's a proper cement structure, airy and spacious. I don't want Stanley to see it in case he feels deprived. Stanley sleeps on the verandah, or curled up on one of our beach-beds so that his hairs form a fine mesh over the surface of the mattresses. The cats too sleep where they can curl up, usually inside the boxes of books or magazines, or inside the car if we forget to roll up the windows. Sometimes I find one curled up in a wicker bread-basket, looking like a nesting hen. My mother was appalled that we kept our animals outside. 'Poor wee things,' she sniffled. Poor wee things? It is warmer out there than in a Glasgow flat with the central heating turned on full. There are butterflies and lizards to pursue and if you work them the right way, the tourists will feed you on biscuits and potato crisps and cheese. That's what I reckon our four-legged team would say. They have a pretty cushy life, compared with their spindly, obsequious brothers and sisters living on sufferance on the fringes of village compounds or in the bush or in the shelter of the beach-bars, thin as whippets, with pleading eyes.

Andrea didn't share my fondness for cats and dogs, she admitted, bawling: 'Goddammit!' as Awa-dingding poked her sharp nose into a bowl of beans. But on most other things we concurred. We shared tales of magic and mystery. I wrote a short story about a completely black cat which was coveted by everyone for its powerful pelt, and which withstood all attempts to capture it, in smugly sinister ways. I wrote another about a watchman and his wife; the wife was a pecking, fluttering creature who finally disappeared into the forest, where only the shadows of swooping wings could later be seen. Joe and Andrea read my stories and relished them, adding their own suggestions, their own little touches of the uncanny, the spooky.

We talked about having a Friday afternoon discussion session with a few other women friends, reading stories aloud and looking at pictures and listening to tapes. We never did though. There was always something else to do, and the weeks edged through their allotted span so smoothly that we hardly noticed time passing. Africa does that to you. It blurs your sense of time, makes minutes into hours or even days, yet sometimes steals away whole days and nights in the twinkling of an eye. Sometimes, when I look at those low-lying over-bright stars, the horizontal curve of the crescent moon, the cerise dawn that can suddenly become dusk and you feel the day has blown away on the hot wind . . . . I feel we are tilted a little more on the earth's axis than other places. Things are slightly askew. The trivial becomes vital, the important becomes insignificant, the nonsensical becomes believable and the factual becomes incredible.

Goodbye, Nyet Kunyul, Goodbye Andrea

Perhaps having Andrea and Joe around made me more fascinated (still retaining a certain scepticism) by the supernatural aspect of Gambian belief. But even if they hadn't been there I couldn't have avoided the sense that among Ray's fellow country-men and women, there was a conviction that, no matter how devoutly you said your prayers, studied the Koran and went to the mosque, there were nevertheless other influences lurking in the unseen places which must be given respect for they were older than Mohammed, older than Christ, as old as the earth on which we walked. Superstitious drivel, I might have said, but couldn't.

Ray's brother Lamin had a job driving a mini-bus and a bush-taxi to Farafenni, several bumpy hours' drive away. One Sunday morning as we were strolling round the garden looking for secret clusters of beans or chilli-pepper plants, finding a mottled green globular water-melon hidden under a cascade of Japanese hibiscus, Ray's mother hurried into the compound, her beautiful fine-boned face stamped all over with fear and worry. Moisture trembled on the long lashes under eloquent almond shaped eyes. She twisted the old cotton wrap that was wound hastily around her hips, long fingers darting nervously into the fabric.

She broke into a flood of Wollof, tripping over the words. Ray listened then snapped out a couple of questions. She went off weeping and Ray walked towards the jeep. 'I have to go,' he said. 'Lamin's bush-taxi has had an accident.' Before he left he burst into tears. 'I - I thought she was going to say Lamin was dead,' he choked out. 'Stupid woman. Why did she give me a shock like that?' He drove off. It was twelve hours before he returned, tired and aching all over from steering the Suzuki around craters and gashes in the roads. Lamin, he explained, had been driving with a full load of passengers when a woman suddenly stepped out right in front of him. He yanked the steering wheel sharply to one side, not realising there was a vast deep pothole beside him. At the same time before he could right the vehicle, the steering column snapped and he had no way to control it. It lurched and, with a noise of grinding metal and frightened exclamations from the passengers, fell over on its side.

Amongst the old men and women, farmers and fruit-sellers, youths and pretty girls, there was confusion but no major injury, just scrapes and bruises and cuts. Lamin was dazed and sore but safe. There was just one fatality, a two-month old baby girl, which had been clutched in its mother's arms when the crash happened. Ray's father and the Imam went to Farafenni too to see the relatives of the dead baby and offer their prayers and condolences. The police muttered and looked stern but in the end it was obvious it wasn't Lamin's fault.

According to the people who lived in the area, it was the fault of something far beyond Lamin's powers to avoid, and I don't mean the pothole or the steering. 'They explained it to me,' said Ray matter-of-factly. 'The woman who walked in front of the vehicle, she wasn't a real woman. She was a devil. She has been seen before doing the same thing, and several accidents have happened in exactly the same place.' A ghost of a traffic victim gaining her revenge, morbidly set on taking others to join her on the other side? Or just a load of hokum?

That happened quite recently. Let me go back to the early spring of 1993 and happier events. I had known for some time that our beautiful friend Caroline was expecting a visit from an old college friend called Glen. 'He's a reporter with ITN,' she'd informed us. When he arrived, she brought him to see us and I bustled about in the kitchen making coffee. He sprawled on the living-room sofa, tall, tanned, handsome and called after me casually: 'Do you remember Thailand, Rosemary?'

'Good lord!' I stared at him and remembered . . . 'You were the young radio reporter!' Yes, indeed. Nine years ago I had gone on a trip to Thailand with a small group of journalists. They were, for the most part, an odd lot. There was an elderly Irish lady who looked halfway between Mary Poppins and Old Mother Riley, in long black dresses and white hair in a bun, always fingering her rosary and going to mass in Bangkok and Phuket. There was an editor from a newspaper in England which I shall not name, who overdosed on cigarettes, alcohol and Thai body massages and almost died on the bus to Chiang Mai, wheezing and gasping and going purple in the face.

That was my principal impression from the 'educational' trip organised by a travel company in conjunction with the Thai tourist industry: the women sitting demurely in the marble halls of enormous luxury hotels sipping jasmine tea and iced water while the men scuttled off to experience the body massages and the exotic night-life. One night we rebelled — even the Irish lady — and demanded to be taken with them, all piling into trishaws and trying to look worldly-wise. After an hour or so of watching appallingly young girls with fat sweaty American oil workers, lissome dancers doing unmentionable things with bottles and cigarettes, and almost invisible boys in the shadows of Pat Pong, Bangkok's notorious red light district, asking 'You wanty fucky,' we asked to be taken home.

Glen had been the most congenial of the group, though I wondered how he reconciled his own visits to the massage joints with the fiancée he had told me all about on the flight out. Later he said: 'It's Thailand. It's part of the experience.' He was so young, so excited by it all, and now here he was on my sofa, a tough experienced man-of-the-world, covering stories in Moscow, Israel and all over. I produced (yawn, yawn) my photo album, with pictures of me feeding elephants with bananas at the elephant training camp and staring at innumerable golden buddhas. How strange to meet again like this I thought. He looked so much more grown-up, assured, filled-out and I don't think the fiancée ever became his wife. I suppose he looked at me and thought: so much older, greyer, more lived-in. Oh, it's a small world, we clichéed, laughing. But coincidences like this are part and parcel of the magic of the Gambia. Never have I been in a place where you are so likely to meet someone who lived next door to your mother, or someone who used to be married to your boss, or someone who knew your best friend at school.

The next afternoon Ray and I took Caroline and Julius and their visitor to the balmy beach of Brufut for a picnic. We also took John and Catherine from Perth, tootling along the sand, stopping from time to time while the fishermen lowered their lines to allow us to pass. 'Our' fisherman showed us a clutch of fat butterfish he'd just snared, and promised to keep them for us on our way home.

We passed, on our left, hidden high on a wooden promontory, the holy place of Sanimentering, where there is a prayer-hut made of mud-blocks, an ancient baobab and a sacred pool. Locals place gifts on an altar, mingling the religion of their ancestors easily with the religion of the Koran.

On our left the colourful fishing boats of the Ghanaians bobbed like toys on the hazy jade of the sea, and in Brufut itself, in the bay, pirogues belonging to Senegalese refugees nudged the local boats. The refugees stayed on in a kind of limbo, losing their haunted look and becoming almost integrated into village life. Ray bought a bucketful of grey mullet, newly scooped from the shallows, and built a fire on the beach roasting the fish so that they were black and sooty on the outside, creamy white inside. We ate them from the top on the jeep-bonnet, with a couple of plastic bags spread out as a tablecloth. Caroline produced some long golden bread sticks.

John eyed up the fishing-boats, hewn skillfully from tree-trunks. His gaze was not that of an idle tourist, but of a true professional, for John's trade — craft, I should say — in Scotland was making cobles, the small, smoothly polished circular wooden boats which are used for salmon fishing in the cold sparkling waters of Scottish rivers, where they bounce easily over the rocky dips and falls. Like the Gambians and Senegalese, John began with the raw tree, slicing and trimming and stroking it into a thing of efficiency and elegance. His boats were much sought after by Scottish lairds. He worked alone in his workshop near Perth, like an artist in a studio, and I suspected this is what he would do until some distant day when his hands were too old to hold a plane or a chisel.

I think this is why he was so at home in the Gambia, where mechanisation and high tech are still on the fringes of industry. Most carpenters and boat-builders work with the same tools that have been used since men began making things from wood, their hands sensitive to the grain and the finish, just as the village bakers created their chewy but delicious bread in clay ovens and the tailors made clothes on ancient sewing-machines and stitched buttons and trimmings by hand. The satisfaction of making something from start to finish is something Europeans in large computerised production centres don't experience. I enjoyed watching the drum-makers transforming a chunk of tree-trunk into a narrow-waisted instrument, covered with carefully beaten and stretched goat or sheep hide (the male skin, I understand, is better) and held firm with intricately cross-crossed cords. Or the balafon-makers, arranging calabashes in graduated sizes so that each tap on the wooden 'keys' produced it own hollow, haunting sound. The men and women in Musu Kebba's factory, sitting over their vats of natural dyes, tying and soaking and drying until their designs materialised without benefit of any machine. Pa Corr, our silversmith friend, huddled in his tiny shop melting chunks of silver bought in Senegal and working them into delicate filigrees, chains, carved bracelets. Ali, one-time lounge lizard, with the ability to charm women of all ages, shapes and nationalities, now carves wood into hotel key-tags, turtles and lighter-cases.

The women gather and winnow their peanuts and roast them to sell, sometimes sprinkling them with salt, sometimes with sugar. Or they excoriate each nut's silky brown skin and pound with their wooden pestles until they have produced thick, oily, gamboge-coloured peanut paste to sell in the market. How strange that some American and British residents will go to the supermarket and buy imported peanut butter that costs about ten times the price!

Village soap was made from groundnut oil, fencing was made from elephant grass, brooms from twigs, ladles from hammered tomato tins, and tooth-cleaning sticks from a particular kind of twig. Children tied sticks to tin-cans to make push-about toys. I was a technocrat. I bought sweeping brushes with handles and string-mops with handles to save back-ache; but it was hard to persuade Haddy at first to use them, she was so used to stooping with her little bundle of twigs. Maybe that's why she had a strong healthy back and I had intermittent aches and pains?

Things are changing, maybe too fast. At Christmas, the supermarkets which have sprung up in the last few years, rival those in the UK. The carols blare out on the tannoy and the shelves bulge with computer games and stereos, electric coffee grinders and tins of imported lychees and raspberries. They are bought by ex-pats and Lebanese, and more and more by the Gambian bourgeoisie at prices which reflect the tough import and sales taxes. I buy my cheese and soap powder and coffee there, but I still prefer the little hole-in-the-wall shops for tomato paste, bread, sugar, candles and kerosene. In the market the rows of women with their tiny hillocks of pale green fluted bitter tomatoes, ladies' fingers, purple egg-plants and monster-shaped sweet potatoes will go on trading, for few village women have ever been inside a supermarket. One day I suppose they will venture inside, prompted perhaps by their daughters. For now the buxom schoolgirls in their crisp white blouses and blue skirts flock into supermarkets to goggle at the goods and splurge on an ice-cream or a can of fizzy drink.

We came back from a shopping trip to find one of our German guests jumping up and down excitedly at the gate. 'Hey, you know what?' he called as we switched off the engine. 'Modou caught a snake.' 'Oh no! Where was it?'

'In the forest there. Modou has killed it.'

Another poor wee snake whacked to death, I thought, just for the sake of it. 'Let me see it,' I sighed, and pushed my way into the woods across from our compound past scratchy bushes and trees that linked arms as though to stop intruders. And there it was. Not just dead but already skinned, and instantly recognisable. I felt a queasy sensation in my stomach. 'Where did you put the skin?' I asked Modou in a small voice. 'It's here,' he replied proudly and exhibited a long wide skin with arc-shaped grey-brown patterns on an off-white background attached to a little wide-jawed head. Oh, oh! The puff adder was the most dangerous snake in the Gambia, very slow and sluggish to move, unnaturally thick in the body, a highly venomous species of viper. If you see it first you're quite safe, as it's too turgid to chase you. But mostly it just curls up among the grass and fallen leaves and waits for you to step on it. Then it strikes. 'Eeek!' I said. I consoled myself a little with the thought that they are very rare.

On only one other occasion did I see one and then the watchman made its skin into an amulet, which he said was a powerful talisman against danger.

Over in their small corner, Joe and Andrea painted on, unaware of any excitement. Their two dark heads twitched a little as they eyed their work and adjusted a line or an angle. Pots and brushes and crayons were ranged around them. Andrea painted squatting low on a tiny stool. She said this was the most comfortable position. I tried it once for typing, but it didn't work. I felt like a garden gnome.

We enjoyed having them around. They brought their own tranquillity and a sense of patient, inevitable purpose. My soups and stews, however imaginative, would disappear down many gullets. Even my regular features for the *Herald* newspaper would soon wrap potato peelings for dustbins or be crunched up to kindle old-fashioned fires. But what Joe and Andrea made would develop very slowly and tenderly and then hang on someone's wall, perhaps through generations. Or lie on a table, in the case of one of Andrea's productions, which was a full set of 78 tarots, every one a detailed and exquisite piece on its own, but meant to be looked at and handled and moved about in conjunction with its fellows, the Knight of Swords, the Empress, the Tower . . . I dreaded that one day Cameron would wander in and draw a moustache on the Priestess.

When they stopped working at dusk, Joe was the cook. Often now we took turns at entertaining each other to meals. Joe made a Nigerian supper dish which was so good we persuaded him to make it for our tourists many times. He fried slices of sweet potato, cut lengthwise in golden-red palm oil, topped them with lengthwise slices of fried banana, and spooned over them black-eyed beans cooked till tender then fried with onion, pepper, ginger, garlic and tomato paste, also in palm oil, which has a unique rich flavour quite different to the pale inoffensive oils of corn, groundnut or vegetable. I don't know about its cholesterol count, but the Gambians eat it a lot, and you don't often see obesity here or talk of heart attacks. Or, rather, not in the villages and in the hinterland. Surprisingly enough there was recently delivered a stern warning by the Gambia Food and Nutrition Association about the perils of urban living. Town Gambians, the kind who drove there in cars or bush-taxis, worked in offices and rushed out for fast food at lunchtime, were in danger, said GAFNA. Prosperity was bringing its own dangers. A rural dweller in a mudblock house, earning tiny sums from his arduous labours in the fields, and eating rice and grain and vegetables with occasional fish was in fact potentially a healthier person than the corpulent businessman and the amply-padded secretary in their sedentary positions in Banjul. It made me feel quite nostalgic for Glasgow, where I used regularly to write features warning folk about the deadly properties of mutton pies and bridies, chocolate biscuits and beer. Here the fast food delicacies — which would feed a rural family for a week — are afra which is slices of goat, mutton or beef highly seasoned and grilled over a wood fire, hard-boiled eggs, little meat and onion pies rather like samosa, chawarma (kebabs) and chicken roasted with blindingly hot chilli peppers.

Inevitably, the diseases of the affluent West, diabetes, strokes and high blood pressure, were filtering into the cities. The women in *Bonfire of the Vanities*, expensively dressed skeletons, would turn no-one on here. Thin means poor. I didn't care. I preferred thin.

Larry, the doctor who'd seen hippos and lions at Nyokolokoba Park, diagnosed my malaria problem as arising from the fact that cloroquine and other prophylactics merely blotted it out of my blood-stream, but didn't reach my liver or spleen where the pesky protozoan parasite was now evidently lurking. I needed Primaquine, he told me, and true enough a course supplied by another doctor friend in Glasgow did the trick. Touch wood. It had certainly helped me keep my weight down a little, but as my sister wrote from Rutherglen, 'There must be better ways of dieting.'

Andrea and Joe, left to their own devices and their own drastically minimal budget, would have pretty well lived on beans. But I enjoyed making them cakes and jam and puddings. Andrea was an ample person, always swathed in flowing kaftans and baggy tops and trousers she made herself from authentic local materials. Joe was thin as a bamboo pole. We fed them on fish as often as we could, for if Ray caught it himself it saved money, something we were constantly obliged to do for sometimes I felt that dalasis must have a special property which caused them to melt in the heat. 'We had three hundred and fifty yesterday. What happened to it?' I would moan. 'We gave the old man who looks after the garden twenty-five, and you gave that lady with the baby who was begging outside the post office twenty, and the kerosene was finished, so that cost fifteen, and we put some petrol in the car and bought some tomatoes and aubergines,' Ray would point out patiently.

Fishing was a way of combining frugality with fun. I would swim throwing myself under the waves and feeling instantly refreshed as the water whirled away any tiredness, worry, tension or temper. I would sometimes, not very vigorously, do a few exercise, so long as no-one but Ray was near. I would lie in the sun reading Margaret Attwood or Iris Murdoch or even Stephen King. Ray would cast the line (from a rod we bought in Glasgow — another modern accoutrement; once he used a simple hand-line) and stand up to the waist in water for hours on end, his own kind of therapy. Sometimes he would catch a whole series of plump butterfish, hideous-looking fish with ugly faces and fat bodies like urban fast food-eaters, and thick coarse skin which peeled off like a rabbit's to reveal firm white flesh of almost chicken-like texture.

He didn't know when to stop. After two or three fish I would call: 'That's enough! That's plenty for you and me and Joe and Andrea and the watchman and anyone else who turns up.' But the bug would get him. He would stand there with the waves punching him, a predatory gleam in his eyes, while I began to burn and long for a cup of tea. 'I'm going up to the house,' I said sometimes, and left him staring towards America. Once, two hours later, he arrived looking like someone who had fought a lion. He was holding a huge ray with wide triangular wings and a long snakey tail which I think has a poisonous sting at the end. We all gathered round and made admiring noises, but no-one wanted to eat it, even the dog.

It lay on the grass while the cats eyed it nervously and black and white pied crows dive-bombed it then soared off, stymied. I think Joe buried it eventually.

Next door to Joe and Andrea's room for a couple of weeks, we had Butterfly David. We called him that because, although he had short Marine-style hair and a fund of tough stories about guns and battles and other macho subjects, he was an ardent butterfly collector, a noted expert in the field and arrived carrying a large net, big enough for Ray to have scooped up his giant ray, and trays for the samples he hoped to collect. The idea of butterflies being scooped out of the leafy air and pinned down in neat little rows upset me more than killing fish, but David made it seem acceptable, he was so fanatically absorbed in his hobby. He came to the Gambia with all the enthusiasm I had earlier seen in bird-watchers, but he was less successful than they, partly because they didn't have to catch and pinion their quarries, only to record them in their little notebooks, and partly because it was March. The best time I told him (having hurriedly looked it up in the invaluable Mr Edberg's book) to spot African Monarchs and Cirus Swallowtails and Blue Pansies is at the end of the rainy season. Indeed, in November, there are clouds of little white and yellow butterflies filling the air like rose petals thrown at a wedding. I have no idea if they are rare or not, but they are multitudinous, obliterating hotel signs, polka-dotting the wall of the house, cascading over the long grasses.

David did see quite a few, but it was the period of high, dry wind, which persuades the butterflies to fly high to avoid being blown violently against the ground or the tree-trunks.

Later he asked me to mail his box of specimens to him, saying it saved having to explain to the people in Customs exactly what a lepidopterist was and why the labels said Papilio Demodocus and Precis Clelia. A friend told me, after I'd obligingly labelled, stamped and posted the box, that exporting butterflies was illegal. For many months I waited for Interpol to close in on me, but they never came.

David arrived with another big tough ex-army chap called Malcolm whom he'd met on the plane. They hit it off and discussed all the rough tough places they'd visited and fights they'd participated in. It sat oddly with David's meticulous handling of the tiny triangular pochettes made from blue paper in which he packed his specimens and the dreamy tone in which he described the collection of over 200 rare moth species which he himself had bred at home. He was a Lancashire lad with a lusty laugh. He told us once a TV crew came to film one of his exceptionally rare moths, a very large and luscious-looking creature, when it hatched out of its chrysalis. Unfortunately it died just before the crew arrived so David pinned it quickly to a wall. 'Oh, it's magnificent,' gushed the director. 'But is it all right? It's very still. 'Yes, yes, it's fine,' said David smoothly. 'It always sleeps by day.'

David and Malcolm, who was from Liverpool but lived in Glasgow and had a cottage in Ballachulish near Glencoe, decided to go to Nyokolokoba Park, where Malcolm wanted to take shots of the hippos and lions. They hitched a lift to Basse on a lorry carrying a three-piece suite on the back. They sat on the sofa, high in the air, surveying the passing rice paddies and cashew-forests, nabobs on their palanquin. They brought me back a bag of cashew fruits, a yellowish rose colour, shaped like small apples with the boomerang-shaped nuts embedded in the top. I chopped up the fleshy fruit with papaya and orange juice and made jam. My jam-making still had its good days and its bad days. There were two jars of dark brown grapefruit toffee sitting on top of a cupboard. The taste was rather good, but the consistency was that of wood-glue. On the other hand, I had serried ranks of papaya jam the colour of a golden sunset.

Another tangled romance was complicating the slow sunny vibrations in the compound. Ursula was here from Switzerland, an earnest, sweet, kind woman in her thirties who was emotionally torn over her feelings for a young Gambian man called Mamadi. 'I am very fond of him, and I love the Gambia, but I have my job and my responsibilities at home. I am not brave like you, Rosemary. I don't think I have the confidence to give everything up and come here to be married. And now he is hurt and thinks I am cruel . . .'

They would sit under the big tree talking solemnly, sighing often, and as the afternoon grew softer and darker, she would send him away and gaze after his sulky retreating figure looking desolate. They reached a kind of understanding. Ursula bought a car for Mamadi to run as a taxi, and said she would come back, and that she would think long and hard about their relationship. She wrote to me that a fortune-teller told her she would go and live abroad, so perhaps there's hope for Mamadi yet. You don't have to be brave, I wanted to tell her, just daft enough, like me, and enough in love.

Another forlorn resident among the little thatched roofs and wilting banana trees was our dear little 2CV. After its accident, when we bought the jeep, we spent many months trying to make the 2CV into a viable, mobile, left-hand-drive little asset, but we didn't have much luck. Every time the supposedly well-equipped, well-staffed garage in Bakau sent it back to us, something else went wrong. It was home again allegedly 'running like a wee bird.' A phoenix perhaps? A crow with a broken wing? Still, we believed them, and contacted two Swedish people who had been wanting to buy a sturdy economical little car — as this one ought to be, and once was — for their charitable work in the Gambia. They were saintly people, who gave immense quantities of time and money and affection to this country and had adopted or fostered several Gambian children, including a little handicapped girl who was having therapy in Sweden.

They took the car out for a test drive, leaving the children with us and were gone for two hours. When they came back they were sticky, dusty and definitely fed-up. They had had to walk back, they panted, from the point where the car had got stuck and refused to move. Smoke, they added, had been billowing through the floor, and when you changed gear from third to fourth, it went slower instead of faster. Then it stopped completely. And had we noticed it didn't have a driving mirror? They were too nice to curse us, but we felt very embarrassed. Even if they'd been crazy enough to want to buy the car, I wouldn't have allowed it. They deserved better, especially since one of the tasks it was wanted for was carrying old sick ladies and young sick children to hospital.

Ray telephoned the garage *again* and shouted at them *again* and they expressed surprise *again* and said we should bring it in and they would look into it. Meanwhile the jeep needed new piston rings. The bike was broken. Butterfly David was grumbling about the scarcity of little gossamer wings, and only Malcolm was truly happy, since he had met a vivacious blonde (you see how these journalistic phrases keep entering my vocabulary?) Swedish girl and fallen madly in love. He swaggered about looking pleased with himself and had long showers from which he emerged smelling of manly perfume and toothpaste.

We smiled at such uncomplicated, anxious-to-please demonstrations of romantic intentions, carnal as these intentions undoubtedly were, and shrugged off our worries and went to bed.

At midnight, I heard a cawing sound, as though a giant bird was trapped in the thorn bushes. I went outside with a torch and peered into the inky blackness, in which tiny shards of starlight scraped strange white patterns on the swaying blacker-than-black shapes of trees and bushes. The beam from the torch found Nyet Kunyul, who had been so hale and happy after his nasty experience at the vet's, my dearest and most doting big black and white boy-cat, lying at the rear of the house, writhing, bucking, mouth stretched in a horrific rictal grin, sinewy close-furred body as stretched and taut as a bowstring.

I stroked him and he looked at me pleadingly, then gave one last agonised cry, and died. He had been my pet, following me around like a dog as I hung out washing and cleared tables, staring at me inquisitively when I read a newspaper or drew pencil sketches of flowers and birds, chasing the crumpled papers when I threw them away. I didn't waken Ray, who sleeps like someone in a coma. I sat on the sofa and drank wine without tasting it, and cried. So silly, really. Babies died every day in Tom's hospital. Mothers died in labour. He was only a cat, not important.

But I cried.

At six o'clock, when dawn was still hiding in dark robes, I heard the same cawing sound and for a moment I thought I had imagined Nyet Kunyul's death, or it was being re-run for me again, a black comedy on video. I went out on to the verandah and there was Snowball, one of the girl-cats, the one that cuddled up to Patch after his little operation, and she was throwing herself across the tiles, crowing in fear and pain, with that same terrible dying smile. I tried to touch her and she bit my hand and her fur turned pink with my blood. Then she died.

Ray was awake now and patted me ineffectually as I cried and shouted in frustration. Patch, the other black-and-white boy was lying under a copse of giant sun-flowers, looking poorly. 'What *is* this?' said Ray. 'What is wrong here?' We drove round to the ITC and spoke to two hardened Scottish vets, the 'Big animal' men, and they thought it was probably poison, insecticide, not ours because we've never used it, but maybe from one of the other compounds where people are clearing weeds. They said some of their cows had been sick from insecticide spray. But there was just a chance it was rabies, too. 'You should go to the MRC and get shots,' they advised, 'Just to be sure.'

I wanted to take Patch to Abuko, to the clinic, but Ray said we must go to the MRC first. He was terrified I might have been infected by Snowball's bite. We left the two stiff white and black bodies in a cloth and asked someone to bury them for us. I didn't want to look at them again.

At the MRC the gateman said sorry, they were closed, the President was coming for a tour of the labs and wards. I snarled at him: 'Look, I've been bitten by a cat that might have had rabies. It died. Two experienced vets told me I need injections. You must let me in.' He let me in, afraid I would bite him, maybe.

The Gambian male nurse who did my first batch of jabs began chatting about the malaria problem, something I felt pretty involved in since my own unpleasant experience. 'I've been working here for seven years,' he said, 'And I've never known such a bad year.' I heard that over 200 adults had died of it, which is very unusual. Usually the children die; the adults get better.

Malaria is one of the three top kid-killers in the country. It is a difficult thing to talk about, because bad vibrations about it, when shown on TV, for instance, in the UK can scare people off coming here for holidays, which is a shame. They have to realise that their tidy doses of Malaprim or Paludrine, or, better still nowadays, Mefluquine, taken dutifully as prescribed, give them protection which is seldom available to Gambians, even if they could afford it . . . would you want to take a drug daily or weekly for your entire life?

I comfort myself with the knowledge that so many brilliant minds are working on the problem, here and in Europe and America, that one day the Third World will be free of this accursed mosquito-borne disease. I went back to worrying about Patch and grieving over Nyet Kunyul and Snowball. The MRC jabbed me on the fronts of my shoulders and the backs, and on my thighs and arms, and told me to come back again for more and then again for more. It is painless, not at all like the hideous shots to the stomach of yesteryear, but a nuisance all the same.

'We NEVER use insecticide,' I told Ray as we drove home. 'I know,' he said, for the MRC, while sticking their needles into me, said they didn't think the cat had rabies, but better be safe than sorry. 'I think someone poisoned them.' He muttered unworthy suspicions about N-, S—'s superstitious wife, which were quite unfounded, but all the same . . ?

We found Patch still lying under her yellow and green canopy and took her to Abuko. We described all the symptoms of the others, and they said it was probably a cat virus. They injected something into Patch and we went home. He was fine in a few days. We felt ashamed of our wicked thoughts about N—. It's the hot weather, I think, it takes small silly ideas and heats them up until they boil over.

Awa-dingding seemed not at all distressed at the loss of her two oldest sons. She seemed, in fact, to dislike all her children equally. But so long as any old feral toms stalked the bush like tigers at night, she was at risk of another pregnancy. So too was Spotty, her daughter, Snowball's sister. I should have arranged something with the people at Abuko when I was there, but my mind was on rictal grins, dead fur, dead babies, poison bait, and the spectre of rabies. Sometimes I'm an infuriatingly competent, practical, methodical person. Sometimes I just go to pieces. Dead cats get me that way. Maybe I'd be all right in a human war zone, calm and efficient and dry-eyed with all the hurt hidden inside.

By coincidence (oh, how I love these Gambian coincidences) Joe brought Yanna to see us. A Czechoslovakian, educated in England, she was setting up a little tourist lodge and art centre across the river he told us. Then he mentioned, casually, 'And she's a vet.' A vet! I clutched her arm, gave her a glass of wine, and introduced her to Awa-dingding and Spotty. The following week she came with her instruments and anaesthetic and we did two hysterectomies on the living-room table. I was her theatre nurse. I was very calm and efficient, even when we discovered several tiny babies inside each cat. I poured disinfectant on Yanna's hands and handed her forceps over and boiled water and felt like someone in a hospital soap opera. I am old enough to remember the imported American TV show, Dr Kildare, and the strains of its theme tune thrummed through my head all the time, and stopped me from feeling squeamish.

The cats recovered magnificently. Awa-dinging lost the hunted skinny persecuted look she'd had from birth, though she still didn't like her children. Spotty, minus any babies but with a milk supply already established, happily became wet-nurse to the three smaller kittens, until they were almost the same size as she.

I wrote a short story about two cats that died and a woman who changed into a predatory bird at night, with piercing eyes and trembling wings . . . no-one ever read it except Joe and Andrea, but it made me feel better. To write about bad things is cathartic.

But who would I show my stories to now? For Andrea came across with a letter from her children in the States: 'Mom, for Pete's sake, you have to come home.' After four years here, Andrea felt she ought to start behaving like a mother. 'I gotta go,' she drawled and then sat on her little stool and put her head in her hands and wept. 'But only for a couple of months, just to see they're OK,' she added, sitting up and wiping her face with a shoulder of her purple and black tie-dyed kaftan. Perhaps in the States, she might sell some of her work and come back with money for a year more of beans and sweet potatoes. Perhaps she would be able to persuade her children (all grown-up and going places) to come here and visit. She'd have to try to explain to them about Joe. She imagined their voices: 'You mean he's black? Gee, mom!' What would she wear? Would kaftans look OK on a New York sidewalk? The date of her departure loomed nearer and nearer and she cried often as she packed her African life into boxes and cases and Joe prepared to move back to his room in Kololi. Would she come back? We were dismayed at the thought that she might not. Then Joe asked her to marry him, and she said, 'Gee, yeah.' So we knew she would come back after all.

So many good-byes. A few months earlier we'd said good-bye to Tom and Joan for he had ended his contract with the hospital and was heading back to Scotland. Hugs and tears and silly jokes. The two most lovable souls we'd ever met, and they'd gone. Nadhia flew back to Paris. Caroline wound down her UN job to go to England and take a Master's degree. Brendan was back in Cork. Peter was in Mozambique now, his letters full of narrow escapes from landmines and negotiations with former terrorists. For so many foreigners, Gambia is merely a stopping-off place, a rung on a promotional ladder, a springboard to a job somewhere more significant in the world order. For me it had become the final destination.

Cats died and kittens were born. Fatma in the Gamtel office told me her baby had died the same day the 1993 census revealed that the population had capped a million. Our bananas wilted but blood-red peppers and dusky mauve aubergines flourished. Friends left but family came. Carol began as a librarian but became a proper teacher in the school in Bakau where over a dozen different nationalities study together. Cameron played with his best friend Ali and Ali's little sister Ami, chattering to them in Wollof. And Musa came back.

Musa, our very first, infuriating, lovable, scruffy, well-meaning watchman? Yes, that Musa. He looks smarter now, and I see him washing his clothes and draping them over the wanjho bushes to dry. He still scatters cigarette packets and old rags and empty cans around the watchman's hut, but when I grumble he picks them up. Then he throws them deftly over the wall, where they form animal, vegetable and mineral installations on the path leading to our gate. I once saw an installation in a trendy gallery in Glasgow, made of potatoes, bits of tree branches and old newspapers. I think Musa's look marginally better. His English is a little better; his appetite for gunpowder tea is undiminished. He sleeps less, though persuading him to weed the garden is a matter of negotiation and extra cigarettes. We squabble with him often, but he know our ways and we know his.

I went to Britain with Ray again, but I didn't like it much. Hospitals with names as famous and loved as St Bartholomews and Harefield were threatened with closure. People worked far harder for fewer benefits. Single parents were targetted. Two wee boys murdered a toddler. A gay serial killer was at large. The names of everything had changed and the institutions of my past had vanished, all in the space of a few years, without anyone there seeming to care. I came back here, to my cocoon, my hidey-hole, my retreat from that other life. I felt the sun and saw the smiles and I knew this was home.